For Richard,

from Dode

of Dundee

GREATEST GAMES
DUNDEE
UNITED

GREATEST GAMES
DUNDEE UNITED

MIKE WATSON

For Thomas, the next generation.

First published by Pitch Publishing, 2014

Pitch Publishing
A2 Yeoman Gate
Yeoman Way
Durrington
BN13 3QZ
www.pitchpublishing.co.uk

A CIP catalogue record is available for this book from the British Library.

ISBN 978-1-90962-635-5

Typesetting and origination by Pitch Publishing

Printed in Spain

Contents

Acknowledgements

JANE and PAUL CAMILLIN at Pitch Publishing made this project possible, for which I am most grateful. Paul also provided advice and support throughout, most importantly in the latter stages as location of images proved unexpectedly problematic.

Through Paul I worked with Gareth Davis, Derek Hammond, Eric McCowat and Duncan Olner, who were all very helpful in various ways.

Nobody is more knowledgeable about Dundee United than Peter Rundo, club historian and programme editor (now beginning his 32nd season in that job!). I am proud to say that Peter has been a close friend since we first met on the terraces at the Arklay Street end at Tannadice more than 50 years ago and his advice and assistance at various stages of this book have been invaluable.

Many other people have contributed in some way and I can only hope that my memory didn't fail me as I compiled this list of honour:

Derek Robertson and Keith Haggart at Dundee United.

Dave Bowman for the foreword.

All those Arabs who responded to the invitation to let me have their suggestions of great games.

Mark Tadman at Just Sport (Pro Club) Limited.

John Litster, editor and publisher of *Scottish Football Historian*, who enabled contact with club historians Robin Marwick (Albion Rovers), George Park (St Bernards) and David Beecroft (Edinburgh City).

Hugh Andrew at Birlinn and Bill Campbell at Mainstream for permission to use extracts from their publications.

Staff at the Local History Room in Dundee City Council's Central Library and the Mitchell Library in Glasgow for their assistance in tracing obscure reports and providing access to bound copies from their newspaper archives.

Ken Gall – now domiciled in London for more than 20 years but still an Arab – for his general advice and for much time spent proofreading. Of course, any inaccuracies remain my sole responsibility.

The photographs appear courtesy of Alamy Images, Colorsport, DC Thomson, Dundee United FC, Fotopress, Getty Images, Alan Richardson and Peter Rundo.

Finally, researching and writing any book requires copious amounts of time, a valuable commodity that becomes precious when used at the expense of immediate family. My wife Clare was enthusiastic when I first suggested the project and her support never wavered, even when the time required away from her and our three-year-old son, Thomas, became greater than had been anticipated. To them both go my love and thanks.

Mike Watson
August 2014

Introduction

WHAT constitutes a great game? How long is a piece of string? For some football fans a last-gasp winner – or even an equaliser – can turn what has up until then been an utterly forgettable performance by their team into a 'great' game, particularly if it involved an old rival. Of course, that's a rather narrow interpretation of what makes watching your team special, though there are many fans – and fair play to them – who adhere to the time-worn cliché 'if they win, then I'm entertained'.

When I first attempted to compile a list of the most notable games played by Dundee Hibernian and Dundee United through 105 years of the club's rich and varied history, certain occasions naturally jumped out: the five major trophy wins; the UEFA Cup Final, though it ultimately ended in anti-climax, was also an automatic choice. Victories over some of Europe's biggest clubs, too, self-nominated – but then what?

I decided to include under the heading of 'great', those occasions when a record score was achieved, or the most goals in a game happened, or when a player scored a record number of goals, or when a fightback was particularly remarkable (even when, on two occasions, it didn't avoid a defeat).

I didn't have great difficulty in reaching a total of 50 games that I felt merited inclusion but I did anticipate the inevitable reaction of many Arabs who would wonder why on earth a certain match had or hadn't been included.

There can be no such thing as a definitive list of the club's greatest games but I felt it might help if I involved fellow Arabs by inviting them to let me know what encounters – apart from the obvious ones – should be included.

The club's matchday magazine and weekly e-newsletter conveyed that invitation and I was thrilled by the response. There were not that many suggestions that I didn't have on the original list and, with very few exceptions, they have been included.

Any football fan relishes the opportunity to proclaim, when a particular match is brought up in discussion, 'I was there.' But this club is about much more than the present or the recent past. Its history, particularly the often faltering steps that it took to advance to where it is today, is of fundamental importance to an understanding of the club and what makes it so special to so many people.

There were occasions when Dundee Hibernian (1920s) and Dundee United (1930s) came perilously close to going out of existence. That would have left a void not just in the city of Dundee but in Scottish football, a void that United have filled with such distinction on so many occasions over the past 50 years, based particularly on the Herculean efforts of managers Jerry Kerr and Jim McLean.

I hope, for whatever personal reason, you will enjoy the moments and the memories recalled in this book – and in doing so will join me in keenly anticipating great Dundee United games to come.

Mike Watson
August 2014

Foreword by Dave Bowman

I WAS delighted to be asked to provide the foreword for *Dundee United Greatest Games* because the club has been a major part of my life. I spent 12 great years as a player at Tannadice, a period that saw many more highs than lows and left me with memories that I cherish to this day.

When Mike Watson first asked me to write this foreword I didn't need to think twice – because he told me I had played in six of them! No, seriously I'm very pleased to have my name associated with such a comprehensive showcase of the most memorable matches that the club has been involved in throughout its proud history.

You might think my personal great game for the club would be the 1994 Scottish Cup Final. That was a huge occasion in the club's history and I was so proud to be part of it but the game that sticks most in my mind came two years later.

We had suffered the shock of relegation in 1995 and everyone at the club knew that we just had to bounce straight back. As we prepared for the second leg of the play-off against Partick at Tannadice I remember saying to Maurice Malpas – who wasn't playing that night – 'You, me and a few others are coming to the end of our days with United; after all we've achieved we can't leave the club when it's in the First Division, we just can't.'

That was the determination I took with me on to the park that night and there was no way we were going to lose. I had hoped it might have been a bit more straightforward, but we got there in the end and I'll never forget the crowd and how much it meant to them.

There is an old saying that football is all about opinions and United supporters will want to have a copy of this book to see whether they agree with the choice of the club's greatest games. Probably, many will ask 'Why isn't this match or that match there?' but the nature of football is such that you could never get agreement on what should or shouldn't be included.

What Mike has done is to write about a wide range of matches covering 100 years so that, as well as games that people will actually remember, there are many that younger supporters will have been told about by their parents or grandparents over the years.

But there are also some matches so far back in time that they give a flavour of the history of Dundee United when the club was a very different club to the one it became under Jim McLean in the modern era.

So I hope you enjoy the book and that we all, as United supporters, will soon have more great games to add to a future version.

Dave Bowman played 429 times for United between 1986 and 1998 and also won six caps for Scotland. He was a member of the 1994 Scottish Cup-winning team and is now a youth coach with the club.

v Albion Rovers 6-1

Scottish League Second Division
Tannadice
19 December 1914
Attendance: 250

DUNDEE HIBERNIAN	ALBION ROVERS
Grieve	Harrigan
Chaplin	Trainer
Forbes	D. Ewing
Govan	Gray
Hughes	R. Ewing
MacDonald	Wallace
Low	Boylan
Cheyne	Ralston
Martin	Hendry
Linn	Denholm
Cavanagh	Greenlees
Manager: Pat Reilly	*(Club run by committee)*

IN normal circumstances, Dundee Hibernian manager Pat Reilly would have been looking to build on the most successful season in the club's five years in existence. They had finished 1913/14 fourth in the Second Division and Reilly might have had in mind a promotion challenge in the new campaign, perhaps even a tilt at the championship.

But there was nothing normal about the summer of 1914 and when Britain declared war on Germany on 4 August that event had for some time seemed inevitable.

It might have been thought that the football season, to begin 11 days later, would have been postponed but it kicked off as scheduled. Although newspapers optimistically suggested that the conflict would be over by Christmas, the first casualty lists were already beginning to appear as Dundee Hibs travelled to meet Dunfermline Athletic at East End Park on the opening day.

The decision of the football authorities to carry on like nothing had happened was widely condemned. There was considerable questioning of the appropriateness of men being paid to chase a ball while their fathers, brothers and cousins were putting their lives on the line in France. But the Liberal government, led by Herbert Asquith, was apparently of the belief that it would prove beneficial for the morale of the general public if professional football was allowed to continue.

However, it was made clear to the respective football associations that no one should be allowed to make their living from the game during the conflict. For that reason, the Scottish League decreed that 50 per cent was the minimum reduction in pay that should be applied at First Division clubs, where most of the players were full-time.

For Dundee Hibs players, who were all part-time, the cut was 20 per cent. To take account of wartime conditions and the need to attract crowds, the League also announced that admission to grounds would be reduced and at Tannadice it was halved, to 3d.

The wage reduction was not a concern for those players who joined the rush to sign up for a very different type of payment – the King's shilling. Hibs players Tom Boland and Fred Stoessel were among the early volunteers at the recruiting office in Dundee.

Whether a man decided to enlist or not depended on his own response to the situation, though in some instances it could be influenced by the moral pressure exerted upon him. As far as Scottish football was concerned, the pattern was uneven. Some of the bigger clubs, most notably Hearts and Queen's Park, saw virtually their entire first team squads enlist; in Hearts' case they met at Tynecastle and then walked to the recruiting office. At other clubs, especially Celtic and Rangers, players were more cautious.

Other Hibs players soon followed Boland and Stoessel's example and this led to the club's directors responding in a similar spirit of commitment to the cause. They announced that, to help the players' families while at the same time being seen to aid the war effort, for the duration of the war the board would pay the wages of their players in the military. Given the club's precarious financial situation at the time it was a remarkable gesture and the board went further, deciding that all servicemen in uniform would be admitted to Tannadice at half price.

As the season developed, it was clear the progressive loss of players to the forces made it impossible for the Hibs to maintain the momentum of the previous campaign and they didn't win any of their opening six matches. Arguably the team's most important asset did remain, though. With 18 goals from 22 matches, centre-forward Collie Martin had ended 1913/14 as the leading Second Division scorer and in the new campaign he actually improved on his prolific rate.

David Martin – the origin of 'Collie' isn't known – was born in Brechin in 1890. He had played against the Hibs for Brechin City in the Northern League before being spotted by Dundee. But when he failed to make the breakthrough at Dens Park, Hibs manager Pat Reilly stepped in to sign him in July 1913, thus enabling Martin to join what today remains a select band of players to have signed on at Tannadice direct from Dundee.

He was an immediate success, scoring regularly including five on the road to the club's first national final, the Qualifying Cup. That ultimately ended in disappointment but, on a personal level, he had the consolation of ending the season as the Second Division's top marksman. Martin again scored freely as season 1914/15 progressed and by mid-December he had 14 to his name from 16 appearances.

By then, Dundee Hibs were languishing in 11th place (out of 14) as they prepared to face Albion Rovers at Tannadice. Rovers sat two places above them in the table and had become something of a bogey team. Seven weeks earlier, when the teams met at Meadow Park in Coatbridge, the home side had won 3-0, a repeat of the scoreline in the second replay of that Scottish Qualifying Cup Final the previous December. The first league meeting of 1914/15 simply continued the trend set by the five matches between the two the previous season, none of which the Hibs had managed to win.

As they prepared to face Rovers at Tannadice, revenge might well have been a motivating factor used by Reilly in his pre-match talk to the players. However there was no logical reason for them to take the field with confidence and a win by the narrowest of margins would have been a more than welcome outcome.

There didn't appear to be much enthusiasm for the encounter among Hibs supporters because the following day's match report estimated the attendance at just 250 which, if accurate, was their lowest of the entire season. There was of course a war under way and it was just a few days before Christmas; after the turn of the year attendances did at least reach four figures.

As things would turn out those who chose to stay away were the losers because the game didn't just result in a resounding win, it saw a player score five goals in a match for the first time in Dundee Hibernian's five seasons as a league club.

With the war the main focus of newspapers, reporting of football was limited, particularly the Second Division. What information was given tended to make reference to little more than the names of the goalscorers and unfortunately that practice was not dispensed with even when an exceptional performance had taken place.

The first half at Tannadice was described as 'scrappy', due largely to a frost-bound pitch, but the men in green dominated it and took an early lead through Martin. He soon scored his second, which came as a result of a defensive blunder. In a Hibs attack, Stephen Trainer won the ball near the penalty spot but dithered and allowed Martin to dispossess him before firing past Duncan Harrigan.

With around half an hour played the score was 3-0 after the Hibs won a penalty. There was no doubt as to who should take the kick and Martin lashed the ball into the net. That was his third and it's interesting to read newspaper reports describing it as a 'hat-trick', because his goals came 'in succession'. At that time, a player who scored three times was not given that accolade if goals by a team-mate or an opponent were scored before the third was reached.

Isaac Hendry pulled a goal back for Albion Rovers shortly before half-time but no sooner had play resumed than Martin had the ball in the net again. This time he dribbled past three defenders before shooting strongly past Harrigan, who by now must have been heartily sick of the sight of the centre-forward.

And he was not finished. He was on hand when the hapless Harrigan dropped the ball from a cross and Martin had to do little more than touch it into the goal, stretching the lead to 5-1.

The match seemed to be winding down towards the final whistle when, with just a few minutes remaining, something strange happened – Dundee Hibs increased their tally to six and the goal wasn't scored by Martin. More confusion in the visitors' defence allowed James Cheyne to add his name to the scoresheet to complete a resounding victory, only the Hibs' fourth in 18 league games played that season.

The *Evening Telegraph* summarised proceedings in the quaint language of the period, 'The Tannadice Park team worked with an enthusiasm and vim which was quite refreshing and the dashing raids of Martin fairly upset the backs, who frequently were quite at a loss what to do.'

The representative of the *Coatbridge Express* was there primarily to report on his local team but he, too, was fulsome in his praise for Martin and the Hibs, writing, 'To be plain, the Hibs were absolute masters of the situation and Martin was quite rampageous. Encouraged by success, the hard ground had no terrors for them and they gave their opponents a trouncing which will not be forgotten for a long time. Needless to say the Rovers' return was rather sorry.'

The measure of Collie Martin's feat in scoring five times is that in the 105-year history of Dundee Hibernian and Dundee United only four players have equalled it while just one has exceeded it, with six.

Then what happened?

Martin maintained his prolific scoring for the rest of the season. In the remaining eight Second Division matches he hit a further 11, ending with the remarkable total of 30 from just 25 league appearances. He retained his crown as the division's leading scorer, which in itself was particularly noteworthy as at no stage of the season did the Hibs occupy a place in the top half of the table and the team managed to score only 48 league goals in total!

Martin scored a further eight times in other competitions that season, which turned out to be the only one in which the Second Division operated during the First World War. At the end of the campaign the clubs met and, having decided that travel was both too awkward and too costly, they formed into regional leagues, with Dundee Hibs playing in the Eastern League between 1915 and 1918.

Martin began 1915/16 where he had left off and after nine Eastern League matches he had 11 goals to his name – but the penalty he scored against Armadale on 16 October was to be his final goal for the club.

That month he became one of the three million men who volunteered for the British armed forces during the first two years of the war (conscription was introduced in 1916). He was the 12th Dundee Hibernian player to do so and like most of his team-mates he joined his local regiment, the Black Watch.

Martin was promoted to corporal, the rank he held when it was announced in March 1917 that he had been killed in action near the Belgian town of Ypres. He was 27.

In a letter to his family, his company sergeant-major said, 'The Germans tried to raid us and Collie was hit by a shell. He never spoke and died in a few minutes. When I saw him he had a smile on his face. He was a good soldier and greatly respected by everyone. He was a great favourite and Brechin today is the poorer for the loss of one of her gallant sons.'

Although every member of the team that played against Albion Rovers joined the forces at some stage during the war, thankfully Martin was the only one who lost his life. But for another of those men, the horrors of war nevertheless exacted a heavy price. Jock Low returned suffering from injuries sustained in a gas attack, serious enough to prevent him adding to the 72 Scottish League appearances he made for the club between 1911 and 1915.

v Broxburn United 2-2

Scottish League Second Division
Tannadice
18 April 1925
Attendance: 3,000

DUNDEE UNITED	BROXBURN UNITED
Bridgeford	McKinlay
Kay	Reid
Osborne	Whitecross
McRoberts	Baker
Richards	McBeth
Gilfeather	McIlvenny
Simpson	Hair
Oswald	Cheetham
Mackie	Graham
Bauld	Wardrope
Gilmour	Walker
Manager: Jimmy Brownlie	

THE very nature of professional football, wherever it is played, is such that the fortunes of most clubs fluctuate regularly, often quite dramatically. However, there are surely not many who can identify a period in their history that compares with the juxtaposition experienced by Dundee United from 1922 to 1925. Between those years the club (known as Dundee Hibernian until 1923) went from being weighed down by apparently insurmountable debts, with attendances in the low hundreds and no league in which to compete, to playing – and surviving – at the highest level in Scotland.

Although the First World War ended in 1918, the Second Division of the Scottish League was not re-instated until 1921. Those clubs excluded, among them Dundee Hibs, formed their own competition called the Central League and used that as a negotiating tool, not just to return to the Scottish League, but with the guarantee of automatic promotion to the First Division, something that had never previously existed.

But in order to produce two divisions of 20 clubs, initially three of the First Division's 22 clubs were to be relegated, with only the Second Division champions winning promotion. The last two clubs in the Second Division would drop out of the Scottish League altogether.

Sadly, after finishing second-bottom in 1922 Dundee Hibernian were one of those left out in the cold with no obvious alternative league in which to play. But fortune did smile on Tannadice when Celtic decided to withdraw from the Scottish Alliance (which comprised the reserve teams of First Division clubs) and offered to back the Hibs as their replacement. Such was the Glasgow club's influence that the Hibs were admitted, to the relief of their directors.

The board had been re-structured during the summer of 1923 and one early decision was momentous. In July it was agreed that the club colours of green and white should be changed to 'white jersey and black pants, with white-topped black stockings'. No reason was stated explicitly but it was all part of a plan to move away from the club's roots in Dundee's Irish community.

Dundee United's Greatest Games

In August Pat Reilly, the man primarily responsible for founding Dundee Hibernian, resigned as a director for 'business reasons'. He remained as manager but defeat followed defeat, crowds dwindled and interest in the club within the city and in the local press waned. New players were signed but to no positive effect. These were turbulent times at Tannadice and the board's decision to appoint a new manager in December led to the departure of Reilly. Peter O'Rourke was installed but, far from improving, the team's fortunes declined further and he also departed after just three months.

It would be impossible to overstate the importance of Reilly in terms of Dundee Hibernian, from the formation of the club, through winning a Scottish League place to the many occasions when he personally helped out financially. But what is perhaps most striking is that he was manager for a period covering 12 seasons and was in charge for 388 competitive matches, a figure since exceeded among Tannadice managers only by Jerry Kerr and Jim McLean.

Despite the club's plight on and off the field in 1923, the board had no intention of throwing in the towel. Instead the directors began canvassing for support with a view to returning to the Scottish League and they were successful with re-election at the League's AGM.

Since the decision the previous year to change the colours, the Irish presence had also been removed from the boardroom with the departure of Reilly and William Burke. The men now in control were unequivocal in their belief that, if the club was to have a future, it had to distance itself from any remaining association with Irishness – or Irish nationalism, which many people (wrongly) regarded as one and the same.

Dundee Hibernian had never been a vehicle for Irish nationalism and had never been a sectarian club, but perception often outranks fact and, to demonstrate that a new broom had swept through Tannadice, the board decided a change of name was required. In October 1923 the club became Dundee United.

Four months earlier, Jimmy Brownlie had been appointed player-manager. Then aged 38, he had spent his entire playing career at the top level with Third Lanark, winning 16 caps for Scotland. He was entering a quite different world at Tannadice, where for too long survival had been the benchmark of success. Initially he needed to recruit a squad good enough to compete in the Second Division and the supporters demonstrated their enthusiasm when – given the few hundred that had been the norm a few months earlier – an astonishing 10,000 saw the opening league match against Cowdenbeath.

In what was a landmark season for the club, only the first ten league matches were played as Dundee Hibernian. The arrival of Dundee United on 27 October was a rather inauspicious one, their first match ending in a 3-0 defeat at Dumbarton. But, considering the club's state on Brownlie's arrival, his first season was more than satisfactory with United ending a creditable ninth out of 20 in the Second Division.

Brownlie had not just instilled confidence in his players and the supporters, but the board too. That was shown by their decision to accept the manager's recommendation that, if the club was to make a serious attempt to reach the First Division, the players would need to be full-time.

Brownlie again re-shaped his squad, bringing in players with First Division experience and United came racing out of the blocks. By mid-October they were clear at the top of the table following a ten-match unbeaten run and, though that position was briefly relinquished, by the end of the year it had been regained.

But as the season's climax approached the players began to wobble and a defeat by Alloa Athletic, followed two weeks later by a totally unexpected reverse at the hands of mid-table Dunfermline at Tannadice, must have concerned some supporters.

However, the next two matches saw a return to winning ways and this set up a day to remember with the visit of East Stirlingshire on 11 April. A United victory would bring First Division football to Tannadice for the first time and a crowd of 7,000 shouted the team on. The players didn't disappoint them, a goal in each half from Willie Mackie and Dave Richards securing a 2-1 win and guaranteeing the second promotion place, at least.

Brownlie was lifted on to the shoulders of jubilant fans and seven days later they returned – well, around half of them did – hoping to witness the cake being iced with the win that would ensure the championship flag would fly at Tannadice the following season.

The visit of Broxburn United took place on what was the penultimate day of the league campaign. Only Clydebank, three points behind United, could prevent Brownlie's men being crowned champions. But should the two clubs finish level on points, Clydebank would take the championship with a superior goal average.

Broxburn – at the time one of four Second Division clubs from West Lothian – were awkward opponents. They were secure in the upper half of the table and United had worked hard to win a close contest 1-0 at Sports Park in December.

Having secured promotion to the top level for the first time, the United players were under considerably less pressure than the previous week and they began confidently. Leading scorers Willie Oswald and Bobby Bauld were the main threat and the Broxburn defence struggled to keep a tight hold on them. But United's domination grew and it was no surprise that they went ahead after 20 minutes when Bauld collected the ball on the edge of the area and rifled a shot past McKinlay.

They continued to dominate but there was no further scoring before the break and play in the second half became scrappy, perhaps because the United players felt all they needed to do was hold on to their lead to become champions. If so, Broxburn must have sensed the complacency because they began to come more into the game.

They hadn't looked like scoring, however, so it came as a shock to the system for United and their supporters on 75 minutes when the scores were levelled. The goal came as a result of a shocking blunder by United goalkeeper Frank Bridgeford, who let a weak effort from Broxburn winger Jimmy Walker slip through his hands – and then through his legs. Ironically, Walker had played 23 times for United the previous season, on loan from Dundee.

Normally a placid man, Brownlie was seen on the touchline urging his players to regain the initiative, something they did fairly quickly though without threatening to regain the lead. Then, with just five minutes remaining, Broxburn struck again – or, to be more accurate, Bridgeford struck again.

The man who had been an ever-present throughout the season must have been eager to make up for his earlier mistake but he compounded it when centre-forward David Graham broke from midfield and sent in a less-than-threatening looping cross towards the far post. To the horror of the Tannadice faithful, Bridgeford misjudged its flight completely, allowing the ball to fly over his head and in off the post.

Clearly stung, United attacked from the re-start and immediately got back on level terms. Willie Mackie received the ball in the penalty area with his back to goal, then swung round and sent an unstoppable shot past McKinlay. Either team could have won during a frantic last few minutes but there was no further scoring.

As there was no telephone line at Tannadice, the only means of receiving the results of other matches on a Saturday was to go to a telegraph office. So the crowd would have dispersed unaware as to whether United had achieved their objective of securing the

Second Division championship and many would not have known until they bought their newspaper on Sunday morning.

But word would surely have spread from those who couldn't wait and had headed straight for a telegraph office in the city centre. There they would have learned that Clydebank had only drawn their match with Bo'ness, meaning United remained three ahead with just one match to play and were therefore confirmed as champions.

That it was their first major honour was a notable achievement, but just three years after it looked like there was no future at all for the club it was astonishing and Brownlie was rightly given the credit. It was the most dramatic turnaround in the fortunes of the club building a reputation as Dundee United and it must have given supporters cause to pinch themselves.

Then what happened?

The United board spent a considerable £2,830 on purchasing the land on which Tannadice stood and planned ground improvements, including the construction of a 3,000-seat grandstand. The latter ultimately didn't arrive but money was spent on bringing the ground and the playing squad up to the necessary standard for the debut at the top level and, defying most predictions, Brownlie succeeded in keeping Dundee United in the First Division the following season.

v Nithsdale Wanderers
14-0

Scottish Cup First Round. Tannadice
17 January 1931. Attendance: 800

DUNDEE UNITED	NITHSDALE WANDERERS
W. McCallum	Smith
Taylor	Hamilton
Penson	Murray
Milne	Welsh
Gardiner	James Frew
Bruce Harley	Cree
D. McCallum	Black
Bain	Ballantyne
Williamson	Adamson
Kay	Cunningham
Cameron	John Frew
Manager: Jimmy Brownlie	*(Club run by committee)*

THE year 1931 was characterised by several events of note, some naturally of greater importance than others. The economic collapse known as the Great Depression had taken hold and unemployment in Scotland had risen to more than 20 per cent. Largely as a result, the government led by Prime Minister Ramsay MacDonald resigned and was replaced by one drawn from all political parties.

The Highway Code was issued for the first time and the Abbey Road studios – where in the 1960s The Beatles would record most of their albums – was opened.

In football the year saw the tragic death (following an injury sustained during an Old Firm match at Ibrox) of Celtic goalkeeper John Thomson; it was also the year future Scotland manager Ally MacLeod was born.

And Dundee United recorded the biggest win in the club's history.

As 1931 dawned, Jimmy Brownlie was in his eighth season as manager at Tannadice. Since arriving in the summer of 1923 he had led United to the Second Division championship in 1925 and 1929, keeping the club in Division One for two seasons on the first occasion but unable to prevent them tumbling straight back down the second time around. The contrast in income for clubs dropping out of the top division was stark and relegation after one season was a severe financial blow for United. Although the board were confident that the club would be the best-supported in the Second Division, they budgeted on an average attendance of 4,000 to balance the books. But they also decided the full-time status that Brownlie had convinced them to introduce in 1924 could no longer be afforded.

The hard economic times were hitting football clubs hard and the realities had to be addressed. Even where attendances had been maintained, they produced lower gate receipts because, with record numbers of people out of work, most clubs operated an unemployed gate where admission was at half the normal price. With that, plus the loss of fixtures against Dundee and the bigger clubs, Brownlie was told to remove some of the higher earners from his squad and replace them without paying transfer fees.

Brownlie had to make do with free transfer players, supplemented by some promising youngsters from the junior grade. He did, however, win the argument that at least the retained players should remain full-time and these included five who had been regulars the previous season. They provided the backbone of the new side and one of them, beginning his fourth season at Tannadice, was full-back Bill Taylor whom Brownlie made captain.

When the momentum of a promising start to the campaign faded, Brownlie strengthened the side in October with the loan signing of Celtic winger Denis McCallum. United's fortunes improved, though there was a setback following goalkeeper John McHugh's move to Portsmouth in November. Chairman William Hutchison explained this as the inevitable reaction to the club losing money on a weekly basis.

However, with his team third in the Second Division, Brownlie must have been relatively satisfied with their progress at the halfway stage of 1930/31. Home attendances were also holding up reasonably well; the Black and Whites were the best-supported club in the division and, over the season as a whole, their average would also exceed that of three clubs in the First Division.

But the McHugh transfer was a gamble because, without a reserve team, the club didn't have another goalkeeper on the books and had to resort to trialists. Eventually one of them, Bill McCallum, was signed in time for the Ne'er Day derby visit of St Johnstone.

That match attracted the season's largest crowd, and ended in a draw that enabled United to retain their place in the promotion push. As ever, players and supporters alike were able to anticipate the welcome distraction provided by the Scottish Cup.

Normally a home draw against a non-league club is seen as little more than a formality. But this was not Nithsdale Wanderers' first Scottish Cup visit to Tannadice. Eight years earlier the club from the Dumfriesshire town of Sanquhar had travelled north and beaten Dundee Hibernian 1-0. It should be said, though, that that was not regarded as too much of an upset because the Hibs were then themselves a non-league club, spending that season in the Scottish Alliance.

At the time, Nithsdale Wanderers were emerging as a decent team and were included in the Third Division of the Scottish League when it was introduced later that year.

It was remarkable that Nithsdale was able to sustain a semi-professional club at all. Sanquhar, with a population of less than 3,000, was really a village rather than a town and a remote one at that, situated in the hills between Ayr and Dumfries. But Wanderers had been in existence since 1897 and first visited Dundee in 1903 when they lost a Scottish Cup tie 7-1 at Dens Park.

Wanderers more than justified their status as a Scottish League club, to the extent that in their second season they won the Third Division championship. They then ended the following season in a secure mid-table position in the Second Division. That was as good as it got for them, though, and the next season (1926/27) they finished bottom – as did United in the First Division – so the clubs never met in the Scottish League.

The Scottish League had by then abandoned the Third Division so Nithsdale joined the South of Scotland League. That was where they were four years later when for the second time the Scottish Cup draw sent them to Tannadice. However, by then they had been forced by financial troubles to adopt amateur status.

Whereas Wanderers had drawn a crowd of 8,000 when they played Dundee Hibernian in 1923, it seems that Tannadice fans were now distinctly underwhelmed at the prospect of watching their team face an amateur club. The match with St Johnstone had attracted 10,000 and the week following the cup tie 8,000 would see another derby, this time against Forfar Athletic. Yet not even 1,000 people bothered to turn up for the visit of Nithsdale.

At the same time, Dundee were playing Highland League club Fraserburgh at Dens Park but that was hardly one to entice the fans either. Those absent from Tannadice would turn out to be the losers.

Despite the gap between the clubs, United manager Jimmy Brownlie refused to underestimate Wanderers. Jack Qusklay, then United's trainer, recalled that the players believed there was little need to train in the week prior to the tie, 'They felt they could take things easy, claiming they would reach double figures. But I would have none of it and got Mr Brownlie to gather them together and insist that they approach the match like a league game. He told them that the non-league club could not be taken for granted. The players did as they were told, but I felt more than a wee bit embarrassed when the game turned into a stroll for them!'

It didn't take long for the gulf between the two sides to become obvious. Barely five minutes were on the clock when United's leading scorer Jacky Kay took advantage of confusion in the Nithsdale defence to hit the opening goal. Defensive confusion would prove to be a largely permanent feature of the visitors' afternoon and the goals began to rattle past their luckless goalkeeper Bill Smith.

He probably wished he could have remained as anonymous as his surname, but he had no such luck. By half-time centre-forward Tim Williamson had not only registered a hat-trick, he had gone one better and, with Jock Bain and Bruce Harley also scoring, United led 7-0 at the break.

Clearly the players (possibly as a means of making a statement to Brownlie and Qusklay) had no intention of showing their opponents any compassion because the second half was very much a carbon copy of the first. Bain completed his hat-trick, right-winger Denis McCallum helped himself to a double and left-winger Jimmy Cameron got one. Appropriately, perhaps, having started the deluge Kay also finished it although, as a proven goalscorer at the top level, he must have been disappointed not to have come closer to Williamson's total.

Having scored four in the first half, Williamson was on course to establish himself as the club's record scorer in a single match but he managed just one more in the second. That still made him only the second player to register a 'nap hand' for the club – and just three others have achieved it since.

The *Courier* reporter's comment that 'Nithsdale were a plucky enough lot but for the most part seemed to be bewildered' summed up a day that the few fans who witnessed it would not easily forget.

The *Sunday Post* struck a similar note, 'When the result appears in the football annuals many years hence, all that are left of the eight hundred will be able to say proudly to the grandchildren…"Yes, I saw Nithsdale Wanderers at Tannadice in 1931."'

As a footnote, it's worth reporting that United's record score was not even the highest of the day because Partick Thistle beat Royal Albert 16-0! Also that afternoon, Ayr United beat Clackmannan 11-2, while Dundee could only beat Fraserburgh 10-1.

Then what happened?

The low crowd must have disappointed the board but they would have consoled themselves as any deficit on that tie would be more than compensated for in the next round when the visitors were Celtic. There was newspaper speculation that a new Tannadice ground record would be set.

But the day of the match brought anti-climax for fans and directors. A snowstorm caused a postponement and when it was played the following Wednesday, the afternoon kick-off restricted the attendance to 13,000. The club took a financial hit as a result but for Brownlie there was some satisfaction.

United were the better team in the first half and merited their 2-1 lead, though Celtic proved too strong after the break and scored twice more. But United had given them a tougher contest than any of the three First Division clubs Celtic subsequently overcame to win the trophy.

That enabled Brownlie and his men to concentrate on the league, which they did to good effect. At the end of the season they took the second promotion place in the Second Division by three points from Dunfermline Athletic.

v Edinburgh City 9-6

4

Scottish League Second Division
Tannadice
28 November 1934
Attendance: 2,000

DUNDEE UNITED	EDINBURGH CITY
Robertson	Arbuthnott
Yorke	McFarlane
MacRitchie	Hunt
Corbett	Hope
Masson	Ferguson
Kay	Johnstone
Ross	Westwater
Gardiner	Buchanan
Milne	Williamson
Smith	Wilson
King	McMeekin
Manager: Jimmy Brownlie	*(Club run by committee)*

IN the 21st century a 4-4 draw is regarded as a freak outcome in football and usually, rather than highlight that eight goals have been scored and those watching have been served up some real entertainment, media coverage wil focus on the defensive errors that led to the score. Which is quite depressing really.

Given that the main aim of football is to score goals, occasions when a game produces a larger-than-normal amount ought to be celebrated. When all's said and done, every goal profits from a mistake somewhere in its build-up.

A match producing eight goals in the 1930s, though, would scarcely have raised an eyebrow. During that decade Dundee United won promotion once and finished in the top half of the Second Division table on three other occasions – which is one means of conveying that they were in no sense one of the leading sides in the lower league throughout that period.

Despite that, in the 30s the Black and Whites scored more than 80 league goals four times, and on two of those occasions hit more than 100. Even in 1933/34, when United finished second-bottom in the Second Division, the team scored 81 goals while conceding eight more. That meant each game involving United that season produced an average of almost five goals.

Even in defeat, rarely could Tannadice fans have headed home feeling short-changed in terms of goalmouth action.

It would not be an exaggeration to say that in that era most clubs were regularly involved in high-scoring games that would have modern day fans regarding a calculator as a matchday necessity.

To illustrate the point, during the 1930s Dundee United played league matches that ten times saw eight goals scored (in total); nine and ten were each scored on six occasions, 11 goals twice and fans witnessed 12 and 13 goals once each. And, in what remains a club record, in November 1934 a match at Tannadice ended with no less than 15 having been scored.

Dundee United's Greatest Games

Dundee United 9 Edinburgh City 6 reads more like the result of a rugby match; it works out at a rate of a goal every six minutes.

Edinburgh City were founded in 1928. The club aimed to become the capital's equivalent of Queen's Park, maintaining amateur status and with their players predominantly drawn from those in middle-class occupations. The club even mirrored the Glasgow club by adopting black and white as their colours, although not the hooped version worn by Queen's Park.

City achieved the notable feat of being admitted to the Scottish League in 1931 – after just three years in existence and having given no indication that they had either the standard of players or the necessary support to sustain a place in the Second Division.

However, in 1931 the Great Depression was at its height and unemployment stood at record levels. Based in Scotland's industrial heartland, Clydebank was hard hit and the town's football club was unable to overcome financial difficulties, forcing it to drop out of the Second Division and subsequently disband in July.

The Scottish League was not exactly bowled over in the rush to fill the vacant place, the only applicants being Edinburgh City and Nithsdale Wanderers. Although City had not been in existence long enough to have attracted a significant support, presumably being based in a city of 300,000 (despite it already having four Scottish League clubs) counted for more than having a home in the rural south-west. So the club formed in 1928 was duly elected ahead of Nithsdale, founded in 1897, who had spent four years as a Scottish League club in the 1920s.

There is no other way of describing Edinburgh City's membership of the Scottish League from 1931–39 than as spectacularly unsuccessful. If that sounds like an exaggeration, consider this: the club finished bottom of the Second Division in six of those eight seasons and in seven of them conceded more than 110 goals.

As City travelled to Dundee in November 1934 they may well have recalled their previous visit to Tannadice, exactly a year earlier. It ended in a 9-3 defeat by United and the City players probably told one another that, whatever happened, they could only improve on it this time round. Cold comfort on a cold day it may have been on the return journey but, strictly speaking, as events transpired they were right.

The match was played on a wintry Wednesday afternoon and hardly merited taking time off work for those fortunate enough to be in a position to contemplate doing so. Those factors combined to restrict the attendance to less than 2,000, little more than a third of that season's Tannadice average. It was played in midweek because the United directors feared an even smaller turnout had it been played, as scheduled, the following Saturday.

It was unusual for the city's two clubs to be allocated league games at home on the same day, though in 1934 that wasn't seen as a problem in terms of policing because, other than for cup ties and local derbies, it was not common for fans to travel in numbers.

On this occasion it was certainly understandable for the United board to anticipate that their Second Division match with Edinburgh City wouldn't compete with the visit of another club from the capital 200 yards up the road, so they brought it forward to avoid clashing with the First Division meeting of Dundee and Hibernian.

That suggests there must have been a trend at the time for a significant number of fans to watch matches at both city grounds, irrespective of which club was their preferred one.

Despite it being the lowest attendance of the season at Tannadice, those who did make the effort to be there were the select few because they were treated to a spectacle none of them would forget.

In the days before floodlights midweek games caused problems for the smaller clubs, whose players were almost always part-time. Fortunately, most of the United squad lived locally, allowing them to require only half a day away from their jobs for home matches and right-back Willie Fleming was the only man unable to get time off from his employers.

Edinburgh City had finished bottom of the Second Division in the preceding three seasons and they had not demonstrated any improvement during the first months of 1934/35, so when half of their normal team was unavailable for the visit to Tannadice it meant that an already weak side was weakened further.

Imagine, then, the shock when, with just half an hour played, the visitors had stormed into a 4-1 lead. City didn't take long to find their rhythm and Williamson fired them ahead after just four minutes. United fought back and were on top when, against the run of play, McMeekin made it 2-0 on 22 minutes. When Alex King pulled one back for the Black and Whites two minutes later it seemed United had finally got into gear. Not so, because two more goals inside a minute, from Buchanan and Wilson, saw United three down with only a third of the match played.

That was the signal for manager Jimmy Brownlie to make a significant tactical switch. Bobby Yorke's natural position was as an attacking left-half, although Brownlie had played him in the problem position of centre-forward for the previous five games. That had paid off with Yorke scoring five times during that spell, but with the first appearance of new teenage signing Arthur Milne at centre-forward, Yorke was handed the job of filling in at right-back in place of the absent Fleming.

With his team staring defeat in the face, Brownlie reached the conclusion that Yorke's talents were wasted in defence and pushed him forward, though not into the forward line; he changed positions with right-half Dave Corbett. With Yorke providing extra drive from midfield United stepped up a gear and in a remarkable eight-minute spell George Ross, Arthur Milne and Jimmy Smith all found the net to make the half-time score 4-4.

Brownlie no doubt told his players they had broken the resistance of the amateurs and urged them to take control, because after the break United attacked relentlessly. Despite their efforts, with 58 minutes played the score was unchanged. Five minutes later, United were leading 7-4.

Nineteen-year-old Milne scored twice in a minute to complete his hat-trick – all with his head – and in the 63rd minute George Ross got his second. A Williamson penalty for City made it 7-5, after which both sides appear to have taken a breather, although Smith missed a penalty for United.

Then, for the fourth time in the match, two goals came inside two minutes, with Milne – in the process creating a club record for a debutant – scoring his fourth, quickly followed by another from King. The scoreline of 9-6 was completed in the final minute when Williamson struck again for Edinburgh City and you have to spare a thought for him – he hit a hat-trick and his team scored six away from home, yet still ended up losing by a margin of three goals.

That was the first occasion that a Dundee Hibs or Dundee United team had won a match in which they had trailed by three goals. In the 80 years since, such a turnaround has been achieved just once more, in 1958.

Despite the number of high-scoring games in that era, for a match to feature 15 goals, involve a team recovering from three down to win by three and for three goals to be scored in five minutes made it extraordinary.

The *Courier*'s reporter highlighted the almost surreal occasion very effectively, 'As for amusement, the very nature of some of the goals and the rapidity of the scoring kept the audience in the best of humour, after the homesters had drawn level before the interval. It was serious drama in its first phase. It was a pantomime in its second.'

Then what happened?

Apart from wonderment at the avalanche of goals, newspapers the following day were full of praise for the breathtaking arrival of Arthur Milne. Happily for United supporters, that four-goal haul was not just beginner's luck but was the sign of things to come. Over the next three years he would score 77 times in just 73 league matches.

The nine goals United scored that day couldn't be characterised as random because just two weeks later the clubs met again, this time at Marine Gardens, Portobello, where United won 8-2. The following week they beat Brechin City 9-2 at Tannadice and Brownlie's team ended the season with 105 goals scored, the highest in the Second Division, although they finished fourth.

Edinburgh City re-joined the Scottish League after the Second World War but after three more years of struggle they resigned and joined the junior grade. They ceased playing in 1955 but remained as a social club. In 1986 the football team re-emerged and City now play in the Scottish Lowland League.

v Queen's Park 6-3

5

Scottish Cup Second Round
Tannadice
9 February 1935
Attendance: 21,623

DUNDEE UNITED	QUEEN'S PARK
Robertson	Johnstone
Fleming	Campbell
MacRitchie	Dickson
Corbett	Gardiner
Masson	Lyon
Yorke	Stewart
G. Ross	Crawford
Gardiner	Kyle
Milne	Dodds
Smith	Bremner
King	Martin
Manager: Jimmy Brownlie	*(Club run by committee)*

WHEN Dundee United knocked Queen's Park out of the Scottish Cup in 1935 it was regarded as a truly remarkable result. What was hardly less remarkable was that United were even in existence that day.

At the end of 1931/32 the club finished second-bottom and returned to the Second Division just a year after winning promotion. Not only that, they had a goal difference of -78, having conceded 118 times, both figures creating unwanted club records. Thankfully, they remain all-time lows 82 years later, as does the season as a whole.

It had been Willie Reid's first campaign as manager and the directors decided against replacing him in the hope that United could live up to the 'yo-yo' tag they had earned following three promotions and three relegations in seven years.

They did not, rarely featuring in the top half of the table and ending 1932/33 13th; almost three decades would pass before United returned to play at the top level of Scottish football.

These were grim economic times and two clubs who started 1932/33 in the Second Division, Armadale and Bo'ness, were unable to complete the season, overcome by their financial plight.

Unemployment was reaching record levels and the city of Dundee was suffering the consequences. With the Dundee United Football Company Ltd declaring a loss of £3,300 on the past year, no one associated with the club could assert with confidence for how much longer Scottish League football would continue at Tannadice.

When the directors informed the players in the summer of 1933 that no bonuses would be paid until the end of the season – and even then only if United finished in the top three – real fears were expressed that the club, founded in 1909, might not complete its first quarter-century.

The Black and Whites won only two of their first 11 league games and the patience of the supporters was stretched beyond breaking point. Crowds diminished until they were numbered in hundreds rather than thousands, and when bottom club Edinburgh

City visited on 18 November 1933 newspaper reports the following day estimated those attending at just 200. It wouldn't have been too difficult for the writer to produce a precise figure by conducting a head-count, but that remains a record low for a first-team match at Tannadice.

That was the extreme, but crowds were averaging less than 2,000 and this led chairman Ernest Robertson to send out this stark warning at the beginning of 1934, 'Unless support improves or the club can carry on through the first round of the cup, it is doubtful if it will be able to fulfil the remaining fixtures.'

Scottish Cup defeat at Alloa extinguished any hopes of a reprieve and, faced with crippling debts of £18,000, a meeting of shareholders held in February accepted that the club was insolvent. Days later, a letter was delivered to the Scottish League's offices in Glasgow stating that Dundee United could not fulfil their eight remaining Second Division fixtures and were therefore resigning from the league.

That seemed to have sounded the death knell yet within a week two city businessmen came forward with the necessary cash to enable the club to limp through to the end of the season. If that represented a huge stroke of good fortune, so too did the fact that the Scottish League management committee had not met since United's letter of resignation arrived. It was possible for the letter to be withdrawn, as if it had never existed.

The new men in charge brought legendary manager Jimmy Brownlie back to Tannadice for a third time and United finished the season second from bottom. That meant having to seek re-election at the Scottish League AGM, though there cannot have been a single Tannadice fan who cared a jot about that – at least the club was still alive.

That Dundee United meant something in Scottish football was demonstrated by the fact that they were easily re-elected, allowing Brownlie to plan for a bright new dawn.

No one aware of Brownlie's record in his first stint as manager from 1923–31 should have been surprised that the new season compared to the previous one was like night and day. The point is adequately illustrated by the first two home league games of 1934/35 each attracting crowds of 7,000 – more than three times the 1933/34 average.

Brownlie had breathed new life into the team, who sat fifth in the Second Division as the Scottish Cup began. A confident 6-2 first-round win at Highland League Fraserburgh earned United a home draw with Queen's Park, then an established mid-table club in the First Division. Although the Queen's players were amateurs, they were of a considerably higher calibre than Brownlie's men and few people even expected United to earn a replay.

Arthur Milne had established himself as the star player for the Black and Whites, which was remarkable because he had made his United debut less than three months earlier. But he didn't so much announce as trumpet his arrival by scoring four times in that match, a feat he soon repeated. Having just turned 20 the little centre-forward still had much to learn but he had already established a productive relationship with his inside-right, Bobby Gardiner.

With the economic depression a major factor in the reduction in attendances, most clubs provided an unemployed gate where admission was half price. Despite the revival following Brownlie's return United operated one and for the Queen's Park cup tie that must have contributed to the huge crowd of 21,623, in a season when the league average was 4,500.

Queen's Park almost took the lead in the first minute when a long-range Bremner effort hit the bar, but it was United who did most of the early attacking with Gardiner and Milne going close.

Although it should not have been a surprise, it was against the run of play when Queen's Park took the lead after 20 minutes, Dodds deflecting a shot past United goalkeeper Peter Robertson. It didn't take the Black and Whites long to get back on terms, though. Just three minutes later a George Ross shot was handled by a Queen's Park defender and Jimmy Smith took the penalty. Johnstone saved it at full stretch, but the ever-alert Milne netted the rebound.

The tie had now clicked into top gear and both sides had chances to take the lead before United did so with 32 minutes played. Slick footwork by Gardiner ended with a pass to Milne, who put Smith in to score. But the amateurs soon forced their way back and six minutes before half-time Dodds headed in a Crawford cross for the equaliser.

The pace of the match had been so frenetic that it seemed everyone – the crowd as well as the players – welcomed the break but when play resumed the ebb and flow of the first half soon picked up again. Willie Fleming came to United's rescue when he cleared the ball off the line with Robertson beaten, then Gardiner had the ball in the net, only to see it ruled out for an infringement in the build-up.

But midway through the second half United did regain the lead when Milne converted a cross from the left by Ross. That was the forward's second and eight minutes later he made it a hat-trick when he beat four Queen's defenders before scoring a quite brilliant goal. The *Sunday Mail* described it as 'a goal in a thousand. The little man dodged and diddled his way through the Queen's defence, sent them the wrong way, and scored'.

Tannadice was now seething with excitement and two minutes later the crowd must have been in danger of losing all self-control as Milne made it five for United and four for himself when he was quickest to react to a lob from Gardiner.

Now reeling, Queen's Park were unable to stem the flow of what was almost incessant United attacking. Soon Gardiner was sent tumbling in the box as he seemed set to score another. Alex King made no mistake from the spot, meaning United had scored three goals in four minutes and four in 11 minutes. Incredibly, the underdogs now led their illustrious visitors 6-2.

Right at the death Queen's Park centre-forward Dodds completed what must have been one of the least celebrated hat-tricks ever, for a final score of 6-3 to the Second Division battlers. Gardiner and Milne (both under 5ft 6in) were the names on the lips of every United supporter as they were dubbed the 'Mighty Midgets'.

The *Sunday Post* described a fantastic occasion which would live long in the memory of all those who were there, 'It made old men young and young men younger as they shouted themselves hoarse in that dynamic second half. The full-throated roar, which never seemed to die away for an instant, might have been heard at Hampden. The wave of enthusiasm started just after half-time when Milne gave United the lead. It surged its way through the packed ground, found its way among the home players and the amateurs were helpless against the tide'. Just reading that leaves you excited.

United were the only one of six lower-league clubs facing First Division opposition that day to win and it's perhaps difficult to appreciate fully the impact of that result now, given the status of the two clubs almost 80 years later. Try imagining Queen's Park beating United 6-3 in the 2014/15 Scottish Cup and you might be close.

Then what happened?

Despite the hardship of the time, United took three train-loads of supporters to Edinburgh for the third-round tie against a Hearts side challenging for the First Division title. By half-time a sensation was on the cards with the Black and Whites two ahead, but the Tynecastle side levelled the tie and the clubs met again four days later at Tannadice.

Hearts were called heartless when they refused to agree to an unemployed gate for the replay and were met by a noisy demonstration when the team and officials arrived at Tay Bridge station.

It proved to be another tremendous cup tie, United coming from behind to take the lead with just eight minutes remaining, only for the Maroons to equalise immediately. Extra time on a muddy pitch proved too demanding for part-time limbs and Hearts scored twice more but United's players were heroes to a man, a fact that was recognised by the board.

Centre-half Bill Masson later recalled that one of the directors came into the dressing room and gave each player £10, a very substantial bonus for part-timers who were paid only around £2 a week.

Having never fallen below sixth in the Second Division since the beginning of December, and boosted by those Scottish Cup exploits, United eventually finished fourth, which represented an astounding turnaround in their fortunes within a year.

v East Stirlingshire 12-1

6

Scottish League Second Division
Tannadice
13 April 1936
Attendance: 400

DUNDEE UNITED	**EAST STIRLING**
Morrison	Newman
Collington	Scobbie
Murray	Bulloch
Skelligan	Corrance
Watson	Muir
Anderson	Kemp
Hutchison	Hart
Gardiner	Brown
A. Milne	Meechan
Ross	McPhail
Kay	Blair
Manager: Jimmy Brownlie	*(Club run by board of directors)*

A GLANCE at the Second Division table for 1935/36 shows Dundee United in seventh, 15 points adrift of the promotion places. On the face of it this would appear to have been a nondescript season, all too common at Tannadice during the 1930s. But a closer look reveals that Jimmy Brownlie's team scored 108 league goals, which remains the highest for any season in the club's 105 years.

The final game of 1935/36 saw the establishment of another club record that still stands: when United beat East Stirling 12-1 at Tannadice it marked the biggest league win recorded by the club. But even that isn't the end of the story of what was actually an exceptional season because, in a quite phenomenal rush of goals, 42 of that season's total of 108 came in the final six games.

Having seen their club dramatically pulled back from the brink of extinction in February 1934, United supporters must have been relieved six months later simply to see a new season get under way at Tannadice. Had it been suggested to them that it would end with the club in fourth place, derision would probably have been the most common reaction.

Yet that's precisely what happened with the charismatic and battle-hardened Jimmy Brownlie defying the odds in his second spell as manager, despite having no resources for bringing in players. The fans also responded magnificently to the efforts of Brownlie and his team. Despite unemployment in Dundee reaching 20 per cent in the mid-1930s, attendances at Tannadice during the 1934/35 season doubled to an average of more than 4,500, the highest in the Second Division.

Most of the players whose efforts had returned some self-respect to the club were given the opportunity of building on their success the following season. But in June 1935 Brownlie made a signing he knew would be hugely popular with United supporters when he secured the return of Duncan Hutchison.

Hutchison had first joined Dundee United in 1927, with Brownlie having to pay no more than a signing-on fee for him. He was a sensation, scoring regularly and in an exciting fashion that the crowds loved. In two seasons, the man given the nickname 'Hurricane Hutch' by United fans – because of his all-action style – scored 64 times in 73 Second Division matches in black and white.

The second campaign ended with United as Second Division champions, but their leading marksman was destined to play a mere three matches in the First Division. When Liverpool made an approach in March 1929 the United board made it clear they would not be averse to a serious offer, but Hutchison himself stated that he was happy to stay at Tannadice.

With United now back at the top level and the club apparently more financially secure than at any time, the immediate threat of Hutchison's departure appeared to have receded. So when the announcement came in August that he would be leaving to join Newcastle United, Tannadice fans were stunned – and angered.

The fact that the fee of £4,000 was more than three times the previous record transfer received by the club cut no ice whatsoever and public protests took place outside Tannadice. The fans went as far as to organise a boycott of the following Saturday's derby match at Dens Park, resulting in a crowd around 5,000 below the norm for recent clashes.

As United had won one, drawn one and lost one of the First Division games Hutchison had played (he scored three times) it was by no means certain that they would have been able to sustain their place at the top level even if he had remained. Without him, it came as no great surprise that they never rose above the bottom two places from the midway point of the season and made a swift return to the Second Division.

But Hurricane Hutch had entered Dundee United folklore and he would never be forgotten by those supporters fortunate enough to have seen him grace the jersey. Six years later he retained that iconic status and there was great anticipation of what was described as his 'homecoming'.

Hutchison was then aged 31, but he remained more than capable of finding the net regularly during that season. He was, however, overshadowed by Arthur Milne, a young man who was recalling images of Hurricane Hutch the first time around, scoring at a rate of more than a goal every game.

It must have been hugely disappointing, then, both for Brownlie and for Tannadice fans that, despite the prolific partnership which Hutchison and Milne established, at no stage in season 1935/36 did United mount a meaningful promotion challenge.

By the beginning of March the campaign was to all intents and purposes over, but it was to have a sting in its tail with that torrent of goals. In an almost surreal sequence, the club's final six fixtures saw United score no less than 42 times in what is a record for consecutive league matches at senior level in Scotland.

The run began with a 6-3 win at Edinburgh City on 7 March and the following week Cowdenbeath were trounced 6-1 in the first of three consecutive games at Tannadice, a result repeated when Stenhousemuir were the next visitors. Doubtless Leith Athletic arrived determined to avoid a third six-goal drubbing; if so they managed it on one level, though that would have been scant consolation because they were hammered 8-2.

A week later, in what should have been the final match of the league season, United made the short journey to Forfar and were given a much sterner test, eventually requiring a late penalty to win 4-3.

Where such a prolific burst of scoring had arrived from was inexplicable. At a time when mid-table clubs normally wound down towards the season's end, Brownlie's men had scored 30 goals in those five matches; yet in the previous 28 they had registered slightly more than twice that number, 66.

United still had one more fixture because the visit of East Stirling had been postponed earlier in the season. However, it seems United supporters had largely signed off for the summer, regarding the season as being done and dusted. The final match took place on a Monday evening and, admittedly, there was little at stake in terms of league placings, with United lying seventh, one place above East Stirling – though a win for the Falkirk club would see them change places. When the sides had met at Firs Park in December United won 3-2, which suggested the league table did not lie and there was very little between them.

But with their team having struck such a rich vein of form and having rattled in the goals at an unprecedented rate, it might have been thought that Tannadice fans would have welcomed one last hurrah – not least because were United able to score four times they would register 100 league goals in a season for the second time in the club's history.

It seems surprising, then, that an estimated 400 turned up for what would prove an historic occasion, a figure less than ten per cent of that season's average for league matches.

It is difficult to record such a non-contest other than in numbers, though perhaps the most notable fact about the match is the most unlikely one – East Stirling took the lead.

That happened after just six minutes when United goalkeeper Bob Morrison failed to cut out a cross, leaving Rab Hart the simple task of touching the ball home. It took only a further four minutes for United to equalise and then the floodgates opened.

* 10 minutes: East Stirling centre-half John Muir dithered as a cross came in, leaving Duncan Hutchison with little more than a tap-in.
* 22 minutes: from a free kick 25 yards out, left-half Doug Anderson lifted the ball over the defensive wall and into the top corner.
* 30 minutes: left-back Walter Bulloch sliced a clearance and Hutchison was again on hand to capitalise.
* 35 minutes: United reached their century of league goals for the season as Jacky Kay beat two men before crossing and George Ross volleyed into the net.
* 38 minutes: Kay was again the provider of an inviting cross and this time Bobby Gardiner controlled the ball before leaving East Stirling's trialist goalkeeper without a prayer.

The half-time score was 5-1 and none had been netted by Arthur Milne. Any hopes the visitors might have had that he was having an off-night or that United would ease up after the break proved groundless.

* 50 minutes: there was more than a hint of farce about a scenario where the East Stirling goalkeeper gathered the ball, apparently under the impression that Milne had been ruled offside. He released the ball in readiness for a free kick but, having heard no whistle, Milne thumped it into the net – and the goal stood.
* 67 minutes: this was the longest gap between goals, but it began amazing sequences of three goals in four minutes, four in five and five in nine. The first was another defensive blunder by the hapless Muir, presenting Milne with a gift the youngster gratefully accepted.
* 69 minutes: Muir then left the field to have treatment and in his absence United scored three more. Ross weaved his way through what passed for the East Stirling defence before finding Milne, who duly completed his hat-trick.
* 71 minutes: this time Milne was the provider, crossing for Kay to rise and head in number nine.

* 72 minutes: straight from the re-start United reached double figures with what was described as the best goal of the game. Hutchison picked the ball up in midfield and beat several men before shooting powerfully into the net from just outside the penalty box for his own hat-trick.
* 76 minutes: the unfortunate Muir had by now returned, though on the wing – which may have been tactical. Regardless, Ross claimed his second after another mazy run, with the punch-drunk East Stirling defenders probably having given up the ghost.
* 89 minutes: surprisingly, the final 14 minutes produced just one more goal, when Gardiner raced down the left wing before crossing, the ball being met by Kay with a great diving header to complete the dozen.

The *Courier*'s report highlighted East Stirling's catastrophic defending as the major factor in the rout, 'There was a fatal hesitancy and long before the finish there must have been sympathy for the junior keeper who was on trial for East Stirling. He suffered from lack of protection. He seemed to become distressed and general dejection was obvious in the ranks of the visitors as United kept piling them on with almost unbelievable simplicity. An accountant would have found it difficult to keep touch with the scoring.'

The trialist goalkeeper must have been hugely relieved that he was able to remain anonymous.

Then what happened?

Milne's hat-trick meant that he finished the season with 32 goals, the highest since Hutchison in 1928/29. Hutch's three that momentous day gave him a total of 14, one less than Gardiner.

Over the 1935/36 league season, although United netted 108 goals they also conceded 81, which meant that the club's matches produced a grand total of 189 – an average of nearly six per game.

Watching United was never less than good value and attendances at Tannadice reflected that, showing another increase that went against the trend during extremely tough economic times. Which merely makes the dismal figure for the visit of East Stirling all the more perplexing.

Though the season had ended on a high with that scoring spree, as was common at the time several of those who had been regulars were handed free transfers. Surprisingly, one was fan-favourite Kay, scorer of a double in what turned out to be the last of his 250 games for the club. He had been at Tannadice since 1927, during which time he clocked up 91 goals in black and white.

When the clubs next met at Tannadice a mere six months later the Second Division match produced ten goals, though with quite a difference – East Stirling won 6-4.

The next time Dundee United would score four or more goals in five consecutive competitive games was more than 77 years later – in November and December 2013.

v Hearts 3-1

Scottish Cup First Round
Tannadice
22 January 1938
Attendance: 15,482

DUNDEE UNITED	HEARTS
Nicolson	Waugh
Collington	Anderson
Grieve	McClure
Skelligan	Robson
Watson	Dykes
Yorke	Miller
Duncan Hutchison	Briscoe
Clarkson	Walker
Rumbles	Biggs
Robertson	Black
Adamson	Warren
Manager: George Greig	*Manager:* Frank Moss

D URING the 1920s and 30s Dundee United built a reputation as Scottish Cup giant killers. When United were a Second Division club, Dundee were beaten 1-0 in a replay in 1929 and Queen's Park were hammered 6-3 in 1935, both at Tannadice.

However, even allowing for hope springing eternal in the minds of football fans, when the first-round draw was made in 1938 it produced a tie that appeared – even to most United supporters – to be a real mismatch because Hearts were flying high, engaged in a neck-and-neck contest with Celtic for the First Division championship.

By contrast, United were floundering in the lower reaches of the Second Division and might have gone out of existence two years earlier. Only the intervention of city councillor and local businessman George Greig had kept the Tannadice ship afloat, paying off the club's debts in the summer of 1936.

After telling the board and manager Jimmy Brownlie that their services were no longer required, Greig proceeded to run the club on his own, giving himself the unprecedented title of manager-director. To general bemusement, it soon emerged that not only was he taking on the management of the club, Greig would also manage the team. Aged 65, he had no recent experience of football, though he had played semi-professionally in England 40 years earlier. He was in no way qualified to take over from Brownlie but, although fitness and tactics were the responsibility of trainer Johnny Hart, Greig insisted on picking the team.

Unsurprisingly, the remainder of 1936/37 was eminently forgettable. The fans' favourite, leading marksman Arthur Milne, departed in March and United finished fifth from bottom.

The next season followed the same pattern of United bumping along in the lower reaches of the table with attendances at Tannadice averaging less than 2,000. Then from out of the gloom there appeared the kind of occasion that uplifts the soul and helps explain why football is such an enduring obsession for so many people.

The Scottish Cup then carried with it an allure that meant many people who were not regular attendees at matches went out of their way to be there. The city of Dundee reacted with enthusiasm to the tie with Hearts. It would have required eight of that season's Second Division matches at Tannadice to equal the cup-tie attendance of 15,542 and United's gate-receipt share, £827, would have been most welcome to Greig, providing a very healthy boost to club finances.

In passing, it's worth noting that the attendance was one of only three of that day's 32 ties to reach five figures and the other two were in Glasgow, each involving two First Division clubs.

In the days long before the Tannadice terracing – or rather the discarded railway sleepers that then constituted terracing – offered any cover, those present must have been oblivious to the cold but they were rewarded by being a part of an occasion they would never forget.

Perhaps the Hearts players – who included the legendary Scotland inside-forward Tommy Walker – underestimated their opponents. They could have been forgiven for doing so but it was soon evident that United's part-time players were highly motivated and refused to adopt the role of underdogs.

They played at a level and with an intensity far in excess of anything they had previously produced that season, though when winger Tommy Adamson converted a cross from Duncan Hutchison to put United ahead after 20 minutes it must have seemed no more than a minor irritant to the men in maroon.

Their mood may have changed, though, when centre-forward Willie Rumbles made the score 2-0 four minutes before half-time. Despite being a good six inches smaller than Hearts centre-half Jimmy Dykes, Rumbles won the ball from a cross into the penalty area and then rattled a shot into the net as Tannadice erupted again.

If not before, the Hearts players now realised they were in a real cup tie. The door marked 'exit' was staring them in the face and doubtless their half-time talk involved some soul-searching as well as harsh words from manager Frank Moss.

Predictably, the First Division team emerged for the second half in determined mood and Arthur Biggs and Andy Black came close to reducing the deficit. But the United players – who had no manager to give them a pat on the back or exhort even more effort – dug in to repel those raids before pushing forward themselves and sensationally scoring a third in the 49th minute.

The tenacious Rumbles was again involved, robustly challenging goalkeeper Willie Waugh, who was unable to collect the ball. As it ran loose, Rumbles stabbed it in the direction of inside-left Bert Robertson who piloted it into the unguarded net for 3-0.

Tannadice was now a cauldron of excitement although it was quickly cooled when, within 60 seconds of the re-start, Jimmy Briscoe pulled a goal back to signal a possible Hearts revival. Many United supporters must have been unable to prevent their minds drifting back three years to the clubs' last Scottish Cup meeting at Tannadice, when the men from the capital had come from behind to beat United 4-2 in extra time. The possibility of history repeating itself loomed large.

The visitors mounted a series of attacks but were able to make little impression on the United defence, with Dave Collington and Willie Watson leading by example and George Nicolson safe in his handling. Yet, despite being unable to assert their authority, the Maroons were offered a glorious opportunity to reduce the deficit to a single goal when they were awarded a penalty after 70 minutes.

There must have been groans from the United support who probably deemed it inevitable that it would happen because Hearts' penalty-taker was their star player Walker, usually reliable from the spot.

The inside-forward was also the man entrusted with Scotland's penalties, one of which he famously scored in the 1-1 draw with England at Wembley in 1936. He would also score the only goal when Scotland returned to Wembley and defeated the Auld Enemy three months after the cup tie, but he was not a hero at Tannadice.

In one of the great contrasts that football often produces, United keeper Nicolson was only 19 and had been playing junior football with Kirrie Thistle when the season began. He was signed in September 1937 to cover an emergency when regular stopper Dave Watson was suspended and played so well that he retained his place. It is difficult to imagine, though, that he wasn't a little anxious at the prospect of going one-on-one with one of the biggest names in Scottish football.

Anxious maybe, but gallus without a doubt because Nicolson belied his lack of years and experience, delaying the kick being taken by pacing up and down and back and forward. After Wembley, you would have thought it unlikely that a noisy Tannadice or some basic gamesmanship would have fazed Walker but, for whatever reason, he sent the ball at least a yard wide of Nicolson's left-hand post and the roar that followed could hardly have been exceeded had United scored a fourth goal.

At that point, the Hearts players must have concluded that it wasn't to be their day. Roared on by the crowd, the 34-year-old legend Duncan Hutchison drew on his experience by constantly calling for the ball to be played either to himself on the right wing or to Tommy Adamson on the left where it could be kept out of danger, thus relieving some of the pressure on the home defenders, most of whom were almost out on their feet during the final ten minutes.

It seemed sheer willpower was the driving force in those final moments but the weary United men were heroes to a man as they did what was needed to ensure there was no further scoring. An astounding victory against all the odds was marked in classic style by a jubilant pitch invasion at the final whistle.

Given the size of the crowd and the scale of their achievement, Greig was not exactly generous in the £2 per man bonus paid to the United players – the same as was paid for winning a league match. The players, who with the exception of Hutchison were all part-time, then received a basic wage of £2.

The result was a major upset and one to savour for everyone associated with Dundee United. They had defeated a Hearts team including five players who played for Scotland that season, plus four expensive signings from English clubs. And the team was managed by the former Arsenal and England goalkeeper Frank Moss, who had assembled a squad of players at Tynecastle that newspapers reported to be worth £50,000.

Moss was responsible for introducing to Scotland the diamond formation that proved so successful in his playing days when Arsenal won three consecutive league championships. At Tynecastle he built it around his star player, calling it the 'Walker Plan', which was almost a daily topic on the football pages of Scottish newspapers that season.

The system had been working quite effectively for Moss in the league, but it was noticeable at Tannadice that he had no plan B when it patently wasn't working. The *Courier*'s reporter made no effort to hide his contempt for Hearts, commenting, 'Pitted against eleven working chaps out to win a bonus if it were physically possible, they [Hearts] showed less skill than juniors, less method than juveniles and less adaptability than schoolboys. We saw nothing of the Walker Plan or any other plan.'

The two centre-forwards, both Englishmen, provided a fascinating contrast which in microcosm captured the gulf between the two clubs in terms of status and resources.

Dundee United's Greatest Games

United's Willie Rumbles was a carpenter who came to Scotland looking for work and found it in the Dundee shipyards. Having played non-league football in the north of England he offered his services to United, but they declined even to offer him a trial. After spending three months with Brechin City he was eventually signed on the recommendation of United trainer Willie Cameron and made his debut just the week before the Hearts cup tie. After scoring seven times in seven appearances, he suddenly announced to the club that he was emigrating to Australia and was never seen again.

Arthur Biggs had spent four seasons with Arsenal when manager Moss paid the then sizeable fee of £2,500 to bring him to Tynecastle. He only stayed for a year and it's safe to assume the chastening experience of that visit to Tannadice did not rate among the highlights of his career.

Then what happened?

By any standards, United's triumph was outstanding but it didn't disturb the natural order of things as both clubs immediately returned to their respective levels.

The Black and Whites lost heavily in the next round to eventual Scottish Cup winners East Fife and won only one of the remaining 12 Second Division matches after the Hearts tie. Their second consecutive fifth-bottom finish – allied to the club's still-dire financial situation – led to the entire playing staff receiving free transfers at the end of the season.

Meanwhile, the Edinburgh club put the Tannadice humiliation behind them and made a real fight of it in the First Division, finishing runners-up, just three points behind Celtic.

v St Bernards 7-1

8

North Eastern League Supplementary Cup
Tannadice
15 November 1941
Attendance: 5,000

DUNDEE UNITED	ST BERNARDS
Brownlee	Matthews
Robertson	C. Philip
Fordyce	Mackie
Reid	Dingwall
Simpson	Wood
Adamson	James Duffy
Ross	W. Wilkie
Watson	Logie
Juliussen	J. Wilkie
Duncan	Dougan
Cook	John Duffy
Manager: Jimmy Allan	*(Club run by committee)*

ALTHOUGH the name St Bernards will be unknown to most of today's football followers, they were one of the earliest professional clubs in Scotland, having been founded in 1878. Based in the Stockbridge/Canonmills district of north Edinburgh, the club had been continuous members of the Scottish League since 1893 and two years after that won the Scottish Cup. As recently as 1938 St Bernards had reached the semi-final of that competition when their left-back and captain was a certain Jerry Kerr.

The stature enjoyed by St Bernards at the turn of the 20th century can be gauged by Dundee FC inviting them to play in the match which inaugurated Dens Park in August 1899.

The Saints' first visit to Tannadice came 11 years later when they met Dundee Hibs in the Second Division. Over the years they consistently proved awkward opposition in Scottish League games; when the competition was suspended on the outbreak of war in September 1939 the clubs had met a total of 36 times, with Hibs/United winning just 12.

The Scottish League decided not to resume the First and Second Divisions and instead introduced east and west divisions to reduce travel. United and St Bernards were in what was called the Regional League East, but that lasted only for the 1939/40 season. The League then left clubs to make their own arrangements and United closed down for a year. They resumed in 1941 as members of the North Eastern League and again St Bernards were among their opponents.

With only eight clubs in the league it was split into two competitions, one covering each half of the season. In between, added interest was provided by the North Eastern League Supplementary Cup and it was in the first leg of the first round of that trophy that St Bernards visited Tannadice on 15 November 1941.

When the clubs had met in a league match there just five weeks earlier honours were shared in a 2-2 draw, with both United goals being scored by Bert Juliussen.

Had it not been for the war, Juliussen would not have been at Tannadice that day; he wouldn't have been in Scotland at all. Born in Northumberland in 1920, he joined Huddersfield Town as an apprentice though he had not made an appearance for them by the time war was declared in 1939. In part that was due to the fact that the man in possession of the centre-forward jersey was Willie MacFadyen, a Scotland international who would become United's manager in 1945.

The war caused the contracts of all professional players to be cancelled, though some remained with their former clubs while awaiting their call-up papers, which told them where to report for service with the forces.

Juliussen was drafted into the army and, like several other footballers, became a PE instructor. Throughout the conflict he was based in Perth with the Black Watch, meaning he was well placed to turn out for local clubs in Fife and Tayside. But with Dundee and St Johnstone having thrown in the towel for the duration of the war and the leagues having been regionalised United became an attractive option. It was in August 1941 that manager Jimmy Allan offered him a trial in a friendly.

Juliussen scored and Allan immediately signed the centre-forward, no doubt hoping he could continue to find the net in competitive matches. Simply to report that he could would be an understatement because the man United fans immediately warmed to – and soon nicknamed 'Julie' – scored in his first nine appearances in the North Eastern League. He registered 14 goals in those matches, including a hat-trick and three doubles.

The level of fitness essential to his army job and his daily exposure to training doubtless gave Juliussen an edge over most opponents because, with full-time football banned during the war, other players had to train whenever and wherever they could, often alone. That said, Julie was clearly a natural goalscorer as his exceptional exploits over many years demonstrated.

The draw in the league meeting against St Bernards would lead you to believe that the fans who turned up at Tannadice that November day were anticipating a close encounter. Except that in those uncertain times the vagaries of war meant fans paying at the turnstiles really had no idea what to expect because they got very little prior indication about who would be playing for either side.

That was because, although players signed seasonal contracts with clubs throughout the war, they could not always guarantee that their commanding officers would release them to play. That was always dependent on the requirements of the wartime economy and the demands of forces training. And at a time when communication between clubs and players was difficult, managers often didn't know whether a player would be available for a game until he walked into the dressing room.

Several players who turned out for United between 1939 and 1945 were servicemen who had been professionals before the war. Although United's status didn't enable the club to attract the top names of the day, the type of player not usually seen at Tannadice proved an attraction. Norwegian internationals Boye Karlsen and John Sveinsson were popular with the fans and other prominent names included Scotland internationals Willie Cook and Jimmy Simpson. Both the last-named were in the United side that faced St Bernards.

Simpson was making a return to Tannadice, where he had spent two seasons from 1925–27. A schoolboy international, he made his United debut at 16 on the day they played their first match in the First Division. He was a regular throughout that and the following season but after United's relegation Rangers paid a large fee for him. Simpson won many honours with the Ibrox club and played 14 times for Scotland, all but one as captain. Despite the variety of United's wartime guests, the bulk of those who donned the black and white during that period were local players, several having either played for the club before hostilities began or continuing to do so after they came to an end. One of those was goalkeeper Charlie Brownlee, who made more appearances for the club during the conflict than any other player (101) – and one of those was the match against St Bernards.

There was necessarily a large turnover of players, not just between seasons but within seasons. Between 1941 and 1945 United typically fielded between 50 and 60 players a campaign, including trialists. That goes some way to explaining the wide variation in results, often in consecutive matches, many of which were high-scoring.

For example, in the first four months of 1941/42 United scored five goals on two occasions, but two other times conceded five. Keeping the ball out was obviously more of a problem because the team had also suffered 7-2 and 9-3 defeats, the latter at Tannadice to Raith Rovers seven days before St Bernards arrived in the Supplementary Cup.

After conceding nine goals, the return of a player of the calibre of Simpson in United's defence was a boost, as was the debut of experienced full-back Willie Fordyce who had been signed from Arbroath.

St Bernards also had a player of note in their ranks, though in the case of Jimmy Logie he had yet to make his name. As happened to so many professionals, the career of the inside-forward had to be put on hold during the war but after it he became a regular with Arsenal, winning two league championships and an FA Cup medal, as well as playing for Scotland.

In the cup tie United initially found themselves on the back foot as St Bernards made most of the early running, though Brownlee was never troubled.

United then began to dominate play and opened the scoring in the 23rd minute, inside-forward George Watson netting from the penalty spot after Juliussen had been fouled. Nine minutes later Juliussen opened his own account and, taking advantage of an injury to centre-half James Wood, added two more in four minutes immediately before half-time.

Despite having secured his hat-trick and his team holding a 4-0 lead the Englishman showed no sign of easing off after the break, although it wasn't until the 68th minute that he found the net again.

In terms of play the second half was actually fairly even, and it seemed that United's moves came to nothing unless the ball reached Juliussen. Whenever it did, the men in black and white looked like scoring and goal number six came in the 77th minute, with the deadly centre-forward again the marksman.

After that the game began to peter out, although John Wilkie did manage to register a goal for St Bernards on 83 minutes after United failed to clear a corner.

That could have offered scant consolation to the Edinburgh club, but it appears it had the effect of stirring Juliussen back into action, because just two minutes later he completed his double hat-trick with a ferocious shot that James Matthews got his hand to but couldn't keep out.

The Yorkshireman became the only player in the history of Dundee Hibernian/ United to score six goals in one match.

Yet it could easily have been seven. It is interesting to ponder whether the penalty which Juliussen himself won would have been entrusted to him at almost any other point of the match than when it occurred – with the score at 0-0. It surely would have been given to him by the time the centre-forward had bagged his second, though his individual brilliance that day means he still retains a unique scoring record in the club's 106th year.

Then what happened?

In the second leg, played a week later at the Royal Gymnasium ground in Edinburgh, the clubs played out a 3-3 draw with one goal scored by Juliussen. That gave United a 10-4 win on aggregate and manager Allan then led the team to victory over East Fife (4-3 on aggregate) which secured a meeting with Aberdeen in the final. A 4-1 first leg win at Tannadice seemed to have put United in a strong position but Aberdeen turned things round at Pittodrie, winning 6-2 to take the trophy.

Juliussen continued his outstanding form for the remainder of the season, ultimately scoring 38 times in 26 appearances in all competitions. His availability was more limited in the following three campaigns but when he left Tannadice at the end of the war he had averaged well over a goal a game with 89 from 76. No other player has managed a better average for the club – and no other player has scored six times in a match.

St Bernards closed down at the end of that season, intending to re-emerge after the war. But, after being forced to sell their ground, the club was wound up in 1944 and, sadly, never played again.

v Celtic 4-3

9

Scottish Cup First Round
Tannadice
22 January 1949
Attendance: 25,000

DUNDEE UNITED	CELTIC
Edmiston	Miller
Berrie	Boden
Jardine	Mallan
Ogilvie	Evans
Ross	McPhail
Grant	McAuley
Quinn	Weir
Dickson	Johnstone
McKay	Gallacher
Mitchell	Tully
Cruickshank	Paton
Manager: Willie MacFadyen	*Manager:* Jimmy McGrory

DURING the 1920s and 30s Dundee United built a reputation as a club often capable of punching above its weight – and league status – in the Scottish Cup, with unexpected defeats of First Division clubs Dundee, Queen's Park and Hearts.

There were also occasions when the Black and Whites came extremely close to getting the better of clubs from a higher level. In 1928, after a 3-3 draw at Dens Park, Dundee scored the only goal of the replay. At Tannadice, United led Celtic 2-1 at half-time in 1931 but the Glasgow club scored twice after the break. Two years later United were again ahead at half-time, this time against St Johnstone – who finished that season fifth in the First Division – but the final score was 4-3 to the visitors.

Perhaps the closest occasion came in 1935. United led 2-0 at half-time at Tynecastle, only for Hearts to level. The Black and Whites also led 2-1 in the replay with just eight minutes remaining but again the Maroons equalised and in extra time their full-time status told as they scored twice more.

Without a doubt the most famous of all Scottish Cup ties played at Tannadice – before or since – was against Celtic in 1949. It produced an iconic match in the history of Dundee United, not to mention one of the all-time great Scottish Cup upsets.

The period after the Second World War saw unprecedented attendances at Scottish football grounds. After six years of real hardship and suffering in many forms, people relished the release from fear and uncertainty, in the knowledge that finally life was getting better. The economic boom that followed the conflict meant people had money in their pockets and more of it was spent on leisure activities such as holidays, the cinema and football.

When the Dundee United board appointed Willie MacFadyen as manager in 1945 the hope had been that the former Scotland international would lead the club into the top division and establish it there.

That didn't happen but, although the buck as ever stopped with the manager, questions ought to have been asked of the directors as to why, despite having greater resources than almost all other B Division clubs (between 1946 and 1952 United were never less than the third-best-supported club in the division) MacFadyen was denied the funds to buy the players needed to win promotion.

Despite that, United supporters remained commendably loyal and were rewarded with some fine football which produced plenty of goals. The main reason for that was a dynamic centre-forward named Peter McKay. Despite standing just 5ft 5in tall he terrorised post-war B Division defences, becoming United's all-time record scorer with 199 goals in just 237 appearances in the three main competitions.

McKay was the leading light in a forward line that Tannadice fans dubbed the 'Famous Five' – after the more widely known Hibernian unit of the same era. In addition to McKay, the Tannadice version consisted of Frank Quinn, George Grant, Andy Dunsmore and George Cruickshank, and in league matches alone between 1948 and 1954 they collectively made 676 appearances and scored 303 goals. All but Dunsmore played in the team that humbled Celtic in 1949.

When the draw for the first round of the Scottish Cup was made that year United lay tenth in the 16-club B Division. A year earlier MacFadyen's men had gone some way to continuing the club's cup reputation when they travelled to Firhill Park and took Partick Thistle, who finished third in the A Division that season, to extra time before going down 4-3. But Celtic were an altogether different proposition, not least because of their fine Scottish Cup tradition.

They had won the trophy 15 times and only once in the 20th century had they been knocked out by a club from a lower division.

The tie had to be all-ticket, with a limit of 25,000. Prices were increased to 1/6d for the ground and 3/6d for the stand, which produced receipts of £1,940. To put that in context, takings at the following week's league visit of Alloa Athletic were £437. Tannadice probably housed an unofficial record attendance for the cup tie because at one stage a gate in Sandeman Street was burst open and others without a ticket were seen scaling the walls and the fence at the Arklay Street end.

Whether they were there legitimately or not, no one inside Tannadice that day would forget a pulsating match containing just about every ingredient involved in making cup football the compelling spectacle it is.

That is not simply because part-time United took the scalp of mighty Celtic. Thankfully, giant-killing has always been an essential feature of cup football, but it's often characterised by 'the wee team' scoring the only goal. To register two or even three is unusual, but for the underdogs to have the ball in the net seven times is unheard of. Adding to the uniqueness of that day is the fact that three of those United strikes were actually ruled out by the referee.

The early-afternoon rain had abated by kick-off but it left a heavy pitch which, it was assumed, would favour the greater fitness levels of Celtic's full-time players. Nonetheless, any thoughts of pacing themselves were alien to the United team led by captain Bobby Ross and they immediately placed the emphasis on attack.

That approach seemed to have paid off after 15 minutes when leading scorer Peter McKay won the ball in a challenge with Celtic goalkeeper Willie Miller and prodded the ball into the net. But the celebrations were cut short when the referee awarded a free kick for McKay's challenge.

The little centre-forward was demonstrating his usual terrier-like style and a lead for United was not long delayed. After 21 minutes left-winger George Cruickshank drew Miller out of his goal and shot for the unguarded net. The only way full-back Alex Boden could keep the ball out was by diving full-length to push it around the post and from the resultant penalty McKay opened the scoring.

With Celtic now on the back foot United drove forward at every opportunity and they created further chances before eventually doubling their lead on 29 minutes. Frank Quinn raced clear of his marker down the right then fired over a cross that Jimmy Dickson controlled before spinning and lashing the ball into the net.

Tannadice was now a cauldron, but it was only to be expected that Celtic would assert themselves and two minutes later they did just that. From a Boden free kick the ball broke to Charlie Tully in the penalty box and he found the net through a crowd of players.

Back came United, with George Grant now the driving force from midfield. That was the area where United got the better of Celtic with Grant and Duncan Ogilvie not only beginning moves by feeding their own forwards with passes but also limiting the service in the opposite direction by their opponents.

Just before half-time United seemed to have restored their two-goal advantage when George Mitchell pounced on a loose ball in the Celtic box and shot past Miller – only for the referee to rule that McKay was offside.

Though they could have become disheartened by having two of their four 'goals' disallowed, United showed no signs of it. Celtic manager Jimmy McGrory appeared to have instilled a sense of what was expected into his men because they re-emerged more determined and dominated for the first time in the match. Eighteen-year-old United goalkeeper Alec Edmiston kept them at bay with some breathtaking saves, betraying no sign of playing in only his third senior game.

However he couldn't hold out indefinitely and Celtic found an equaliser ten minutes into the second half. Tully met a Pat McAuley free kick in the box and fed Jackie Gallacher, who slotted past Edmiston.

At that point many United fans probably feared the worst; that the underdogs had had their brief moment of glory and the visitors would assume control of the tie. Perhaps, but there was no evidence that the men in black and white entertained such thoughts as they again sought to take the game to Celtic.

Seven minutes later McKay played the ball to Cruickshank down the left and as the winger raced clear the linesman's flag was raised. But the referee waved play-on and when the cross came in it was met by Dickson who guided it into the net. The ref awarded the goal but, after being surrounded by Celtic players, he consulted the linesman and then changed his mind. Now it was the turn of the United players to protest but in this case to no avail.

The *Glasgow Herald*, not a newspaper known for being overly critical of Scotland's big two clubs, said of the incident, 'It looked as good a goal as has ever been scored at Tannadice. The referee, well up with play, was obviously in no doubt whatever about its validity. The manner in which he was prevailed upon, or dragooned, by the entire Celtic team into consulting a linesman and changing his decision provided an undignified spectacle.'

Unbelievably, in just over an hour's play United had had the ball in the Celtic net five times – yet the score stood at 2-2. Play raged from end to end with the crowd in a ferment and Edmiston protected the United goal fearlessly. But his heroics were if anything eclipsed by the exploits of his forwards as the game entered its decisive phase, with three goals arriving within a five-minute spell.

Despite the fact that the wet pitch was now badly cut up, United continued to play a passing game and an intricate exchange on 75 minutes had the Celtic rearguard bewildered. Dickson won the ball and passed to Cruickshank, who sent it on for McKay to complete the move by firing a shot low into the net.

Back came Celtic and they were to profit from the only mistake that Edmiston made. He fumbled a John Paton corner, leaving Gallacher with a simple tap-in for 3-3. At that stage, with 11 minutes remaining and both sides having given their all, you might have thought they would have settled for a replay. Not those men in black and white, though, because straight from the re-start they regained the lead.

Again a slick move was the key and eventually the ball reached Dickson just inside the penalty box. He let fly with such force that Miller could do no more than palm the ball away from the goal to what he thought was safety. He was mistaken, because the inrushing Cruickshank caught it on the volley and the ball raged into the net for the game's outstanding goal.

This time there were no protests from the Celtic players – and there was no comeback either. Their spirit had been broken by what must have seemed to the well-paid aristocrats from Glasgow as the unbreakable will of the United players.

Ten minutes remained when the score went to 4-3 but Celtic rarely threatened to peg United back again and the exultant Tannadice crowd carried their team through those last few minutes. When the final whistle sounded, hundreds rushed on to the pitch to carry them again – this time shoulder-high in triumph.

In common with everyone else fortunate enough to be at Tannadice that day, Bob Miller of the *People's Journal* was left breathless. He described it as, 'One game I'll remember as long as I can talk football. Never have I seen such scenes of jubilation as on the Tannadice slopes that day.'

Then what happened?

Unfortunately, the euphoria couldn't be carried forward to the next round and as frequently happens following a major upset, the players' superhuman efforts could not be replicated.

A visit to Dumbarton didn't appear too daunting a prospect and when it ended even at 1-1 United's players and supporters must have felt confident of the job being completed in the replay.

However, in an outcome that encapsulated the unpredictability of cup football, United's brief spell in the limelight ended in a 3-1 defeat.

10

v St Johnstone 4-3

Scottish League Second Division
Muirton Park
6 September 1958
Attendance: 3,700

DUNDEE UNITED	ST JOHNSTONE
Lucas	Taylor
Young	Brown
Rae	Hawthorne
Stewart	Ewen
Gibson	McKim
Douglas	Docherty
Hunter	Anderson
J. Wallace	Ward
C. Wallace	McInnes
Sturrock	Carr
Martin	Pattison
Manager: Tommy Gray	*Manager:* Bobby Brown

I N the 105 years following formation in 1909, Dundee Hibs/United have played almost 4,000 matches in the major competitions. In only two of them did they recover from a three-goal deficit to record a victory. One was against Edinburgh City in 1934 with the other coming 24 years later against St Johnstone.

To a major extent, the 1950s was the decade that passed Dundee United by. Leaving aside those affected by wars, it was the only one in which Tannadice saw no top-division football and it also produced a number of records, almost all of which those who hold the club close to their hearts will want to forget.

In the period following the Second World War many clubs across Scotland recorded the highest attendances in their history and United were one of them. Previously, only once had the average for a league season at Tannadice exceeded 8,000 – and that was in the first season as a First Division club, 1925/26. Yet averages in excess of 8,000 were recorded in each of the six seasons from 1946, a period in which United were never less than the third best-supported club in the division and in 1947/48 were the best-supported – despite, bizarrely, finishing second-bottom.

That serves to highlight the almost unswerving loyalty of the fans who regularly turned up at Tannadice to cheer on the Black and Whites. Although United gave them much to shout about by scoring regularly the players also gave the fans much to shout at because goals were shipped at the other end just as often – and frequently more often.

With a club-best finish of seventh (out of 16) in what was then called the B Division, the fans must have been hoping that, with the resources provided by those healthy gates, the 1950s would be a happier and more successful era. Sadly these hopes would be dashed.

Of the nine seasons that fell entirely within the decade, only the first two saw United mount a promotion challenge. In 1950/51 Willie MacFadyen's team were second from the end of December until their penultimate match, yet finished fourth. The following season United moved second with three matches remaining but collected just one more point and again finished fourth.

45

That was as good as it got in the 1950s and during 1953/54 United sank to one of the lowest points in their history. A record Scottish League defeat was suffered when Third Lanark won 9-1 at Cathkin Park in September, though it stood for only four months. In January, MacFadyen took United to Fir Park, the scene of many personal glories for the man who was Motherwell's top scorer when they became champions of Scotland in 1931/32. He cannot have enjoyed his return because United were hammered 12-1 in what, thankfully, still stands as the club's heaviest defeat.

Devastating as those results were, United's season was perilously close to having a catastrophic end as they came within a hair's breadth of dropping out of the Scottish League.

As the season progressed United found themselves in serious trouble at the foot of B Division and they were staring relegation in the face. C Division comprised the reserve teams of many A Division clubs but it was also where United's reserves played. It was completed by some of the smaller clubs that had been in the Second Division prior to the war but had been denied full membership of the Scottish League.

In order to ensure their own safety, United had to reach third from bottom in B Division but even that proved beyond them. The team caused considerable nail-biting to manager, directors and supporters alike by finishing level on points at the bottom with Dumbarton – but with a marginally superior goal average. The club avoided the ignominy of falling into C Division only because Rangers' reserves won the west section of that division and were ineligible to take up the promotion place.

United had survived, but only by the slimmest of margins – and despite, rather than because of, their own efforts.

MacFadyen resigned later that year and the next five seasons saw the club go through four managers, which perhaps helps explain why the best finish United achieved during that period was mid-table. But the bad news from the 1950s doesn't end there because the worst run in the club's history took place in February and March 1957, when seven goals were conceded in each of three consecutive matches.

When you consider also that heavy defeats in 1957/58 and 1958/59 included 6-0 at Cowdenbeath, 8-1 at Clyde, 8-2 at Berwick Rangers and 7-1 by Alloa Athletic at Tannadice, it will be appreciated that being a United supporter during the 1950s required nerves of steel, unlimited patience and a short memory.

So it's good to be able to record that one of the most remarkable matches in the club's entire history also took place during that decade.

By the start of 1958/59 Tommy Gray had been manager at Tannadice for almost 18 months. As a cost-saving measure he had been appointed on a part-time basis, a move that was never likely to provide the basis for United to reach the First Division. They finished ninth out of 19 in the Second Division in Gray's only full season in charge and the Black and Whites started the new campaign sluggishly, finishing bottom of their section in the League Cup.

The only wins that they did manage to record in the competition were against St Johnstone, so when they returned to Muirton Park for a league match United should have been reasonably confident of further success.

Despite the fact that summer was not yet officially over, conditions were atrocious. Thunder and lightning greeted the players and the rain was relentless. It seemed that the Perth side adapted better and they seized the initiative, putting the United defence under pressure. United's attempts to use the offside trap were suspect and it seemed only a matter of time before Saints seized the lead.

In the 26th minute Jimmy Anderson took possession and moved infield before unleashing what appeared to be a speculative shot from 30 yards. But United goalkeeper Bill Lucas was caught flat-footed and the ball struck the underside of the bar on its way into the net. That at least had the advantage of shaking the Tannadice men out of their lethargy and Tommy Martin's shot was the first time Bill Taylor had been tested in the Saints' goal.

St Johnstone continued to dictate the play and they increased their lead on 33 minutes, though the goal was a gift. A shot from Joe Carr would almost certainly have been held by Lucas in dry conditions but the ball's soap-like quality allowed it to slip out of his hands and squirm over the line.

United were now giving a fair impression of a groggy fighter making maximum use of the ropes as twice within a minute shots were deflected past the post with their defence little more than spectators.

It was no surprise when four minutes before half-time the lead became 3-0, the result of a well-worked move by St Johnstone with every one of their forwards touching the ball before Frank Pattison found the net via a post. And it could have been worse because in the next minute Lucas produced a superb point-blank save from Jim Ward.

It would be interesting to have had an insight into Gray's dressing-room call-to-arms at half-time. Though it might have been prudent to put the emphasis on not conceding again, the concept of damage limitation didn't exist at the time and neither did substitutes. So the manager can only have reminded his men that they had already beaten the men from Perth twice within the past month and that an early goal in the second half was essential.

Even so, Gray could not possibly have imagined that, within just two and a half minutes of the re-start, his team would have reduced the deficit by two-thirds. The weather hadn't improved but United's hopes brightened in the 47th minute when inside-forward Jimmy Wallace, a close-season signing from Aberdeen who had failed to find the net in his first eight games in black and white, scored from 12 yards.

St Johnstone may have been caught cold but even that couldn't explain what happened next. From the kick-off, rather than pressing forward, the home side sent the ball back to defender Billy Hawthorne. For reasons known only to himself he decided to chip it back to his goalkeeper but Taylor somehow contrived to allow the ball to slip out of his grasp, over his head and into the net.

It was a stunning change in the game's dynamic and doubtless the United players were as surprised as anyone at the turn of events. The clouds darkened and, this also being in the days before clubs in the Second Division had floodlights, there seemed a possibility at one point that the referee might call an end to proceedings. But he allowed the players to soldier on and in a complete reversal of the flow of the first half United went on the offensive with Saints struggling to contain them.

The treacherous surface was the cause of mistakes by both sides, though when another goal came it was due to United's Dave Sturrock having escaped the Saints defence as he rose unchallenged to head home a Clive Wallace cross after 64 minutes.

That forced the home team to re-assert themselves and the match was then more evenly balanced, with both sides having opportunities to add to their tally. But when it seemed a point each would be just reward for their combined efforts in serving up a memorable match that defied the conditions, there came one last twist.

Again it was the result of an error, this time a slip in the 85th minute by St Johnstone's Gus McKim.

Clive Wallace was again the provider, sending in a cross that the centre-half would have cleared had he not lost his footing, allowing Jimmy Wallace to complete an astonishing turnaround by scoring his second and United's fourth.

In some respects the events of that afternoon were the result of part-time players being asked to perform in what was rarely less than a thunderstorm, but as the old adage has it, the conditions were the same for both sides and United's players deserve huge credit for their never-say-die spirit and refusing to accept that the three-goal deficit represented a lost cause.

Despite being soaked to the skin, at least the United supporters would have gone home happy.

Then what happened?

Gray didn't last much longer as manager. The following month he was replaced, on a full-time basis, by Andy McCall, though he himself resigned at the end of the season, having been unable to prevent the club finishing third-bottom of the Second Division. For Dundee United, the only way was up.

v Berwick Rangers 1-0

Scottish League Second Division
Tannadice
30 April 1960
Attendance: 16,900

DUNDEE UNITED	BERWICK RANGERS
Brown	Boyd
Graham	Wood
MacFadyen	Campbell
Neilson	McLeod
Yeats	Rugg
Fraser	Gemmell
Norris	Foulis
Irvine	Purves
Campbell	Craig
Gillespie	McManus
Ormond	Whitelaw
Manager: Jerry Kerr	*Manager:* Danny McLennan

WHEN he was appointed manager of Dundee United in June 1959, Jerry Kerr knew the Second Division inside out having led Alloa Athletic for four years. United had not finished third from bottom by accident and he would have been well aware that the playing staff required radical surgery.

He quickly began assessing them and deciding on those he believed could make a contribution. The remainder were shown the door and Kerr was given every encouragement by the board to bring in fresh faces.

The low level of achievement by United throughout the 1950s was reflected in attendances at Tannadice. The league average for 1949/50 was 8,867; nine seasons later it was just 2,961, the club's lowest since 1937/38. The players were part-time and it seemed the supporters were too.

A manager arriving at a club with such a recent record would not have anticipated much, if any, ability to flourish a chequebook in the transfer market, so Kerr must have been as surprised as he was delighted to discover that considerable funds had been placed at his disposal.

The reason for this was Taypools, an organisation formed in 1956 and run for – but not by – Dundee United with the sole aim of raising money for the club. It was an immediate success and by 1959 made donations of around £10,000 a year. Amounts of that magnitude not only offset annual losses on the club's balance sheet, but allowed for sufficient funds to improve Tannadice (the Shed was built in 1957) and the playing squad.

Kerr resisted the temptation to spend hurriedly. He did bring in six players during the close-season but none cost a significant fee. The team for United's first match of the season had five players making their debuts yet only four of that 11 would play on the final day, in a team that contained two other players brought in by Kerr for a combined £5,000.

Dennis Gillespie had been one of his leading players at Alloa and in August the new United manager paid £3,000 to bring him to Tannadice. As the season approached its climax, he paid Albion Rovers £2,000 for Tommy Campbell and though those may not appear 'big' signings, in relative terms they were. It should be noted that United had first paid £1,000 for a player as recently as 1957.

One of the players Kerr inherited on his arrival was Ron Yeats. A Scotland schoolboy international, Yeats was signed in 1957 and two years later the centre-half had made himself an indispensable part of the team. Kerr had been suitably impressed with Yeats's performances against Alloa and was now concerned that the player had been called up for his National Service and was based in Hampshire. Following a meeting with his commanding officer, permission was received for Yeats to be released for United's Saturday games.

The season had a successful start with the Black and Whites comfortably winning their League Cup section. During that period Kerr had introduced two players who would form a partnership over the next five years that produced more than 150 goals. Jim Irvine, a young inside-forward from junior football, arrived shortly before Gillespie.

The pair lost no time in developing an understanding – within a fortnight they were the main architects of an 8-1 demolition of Queen's Park at Hampden when Irvine scored four, one more than Gillespie.

Unfortunately such form was not often in evidence during the first three months. When October ended with four winless matches, leaving United ninth, Kerr decided action was needed. He brought in wing-half Tommy Neilson from East Fife, making him club captain. That proved to be the turning point of the season but, even though their form improved dramatically, the manager added more firepower to the attack in December when Dave Whytock was signed from Brechin City. Whytock scored a debut hat-trick in a 6-0 demolition of East Fife – the team's sixth consecutive win, a sequence that carried them into third place.

The long journey to Stranraer in January provided an indication of Kerr's meticulous approach and the directors' determination to maintain United's promotion drive. Faced with a 175-mile coach ride at a time when even dual carriageways were rare, an overnight stop broke the five-hour trip and ensured the players were not travel-weary. The benefit was evident in United's 3-0 victory.

But the five matches that followed produced just one win, which prompted the manager to return to the transfer market; almost like a jigsaw, Kerr was piecing together a team capable of challenging for promotion.

Two Scottish Cup ties against First Division Partick Thistle had provided United with significant additional revenue which the directors made available to Kerr. Gibby Ormond, a left-winger and former Scottish League international, was bought from Airdrie and he quickly made his mark, scoring in a debut defeat of Albion Rovers. One of the men in the opposition ranks that day, centre-forward Tommy Campbell, joined Ormond at United a few days later. Everything Kerr touched seemed to be turning to gold because Campbell became the second player during the season to score a hat-trick on his first appearance. More importantly, it came in a 5-1 defeat of Hamilton Accies, one of United's main rivals in the promotion chase.

That lifted the Tannadice men into second place with six games remaining, though four were away. After two wins and a defeat in the first three, United remained second but faced visits to Queen of the South and Falkirk, both of whom still regarded themselves as promotion contenders.

Despite seeing his team lose a 4-3 lead in the dying minutes, Kerr was satisfied with a draw at Dumfries and the following week it was United's turn to strike at the death. With five minutes remaining Falkirk had scored the only goal and United's hopes of stepping up were under real threat. Then, in a drama-packed finale, Campbell won a penalty which Jimmy Briggs coolly converted. Unwilling to settle for a point, United pressed relentlessly and had their reward when Irvine scored a crucial winner in the final minute.

Now only a Tannadice clash with mid-table Berwick Rangers stood between United and the First Division. St Johnstone were already champions while United and Hamilton had 48 points, though Kerr's men effectively had an extra point in their favour because their superior goal average was unlikely to be bridged. Queen of the South, only a point behind, were still in the chase but the task facing the United players was unambiguous – win and the prize was theirs.

The final day of April was the final day of the league season but it didn't seem like spring as rain swept across the city. Not that the weather could dampen the enthusiasm and the expectation – rather than mere hope – of the near-17,000 who packed Tannadice. The contrast with 12 months earlier, when only 2,200 were there to witness the 2-1 loss to Brechin City which confirmed Dundee United's status as Scotland's third-worst league club, could hardly have been greater.

Those fans were the real die-hards among United's support and they must have found the journey travelled within just a year hugely satisfying. That they were able to do so was testament to the vision and leadership of Kerr.

As if to offer inspiration, one man in attendance was Jimmy Brownlie, the manager who had guided United to three promotions a generation earlier. The rain had relented by kick-off and the manner in which the men in black and white responded to the urging of the crowd suggested butterflies were not a problem.

The plan was clearly to seek an early goal and eight minutes had been played when the breakthrough came. Bobby Norris outpaced the Berwick defence down the right and played the ball into the penalty area as Campbell was arriving. Despite being challenged by John Rugg, Campbell, with his back to goal, trapped the ball then spun through 180 degrees before delivering a shot from 12 yards that gave goalkeeper Matt Boyd no chance.

A massive roar split the air above Tannadice – United were on their way, but the match had a long way to run.

Berwick served notice that they were not there simply to make up the numbers by coming close to equalising after 20 minutes. It was a frenetic passage of play that first saw United goalkeeper Alec Brown manage to push out a shot from Craig. The ball broke to Gemmell but, with Brown not yet back on his feet, the Berwick wing-half completely missed his kick. As Gemmell tried again to get his shot away Brown dived fearlessly to claim the ball but sustained a head knock that required treatment.

United raised their game and the Berwick goal was peppered with shots in what was thrill-a-minute stuff. With 90 per cent of the play Kerr's men should have been out of sight, but slack finishing and some determined defending prevented any further scoring.

The rain returned for the second half but the pattern was unchanged. The crowd were desperate for a second goal and the United players tried all they knew to oblige. Gillespie was denied when his shot hit Rugg and was deflected wide, then Yeats came close when he got his head to a corner. Berwick remained a threat, however, especially their 18-year-old striker Willie Purvis, who twice shaved the post as United's players and supporters held their breath.

Inside the final ten minutes the tension must have been unbearable. Captain Tommy Neilson did his best to settle things with a 30-yard shot that was headed over the bar with

Boyd beaten. That led to United's 13th corner of the second half and 20th overall, but still the score remained 1-0.

With the yelling and whistling from the crowd leaving the referee in no doubt as to what he should do, the man with the whistle refused to sound it, despite a signal from the linesman that the match had run its course.

Finally it was all over and agony turned to ecstasy as a mighty roar was immediately followed by a pitch invasion from thousands of black-and-white-clad fans scarcely able to take in Dundee United returning to Scottish football's top table after an absence of 28 years.

The players were mobbed and carried shoulder-high as the celebrations began. Not until Kerr had addressed them over the loudspeaker would the crowd disperse on a historic day that no one present would forget.

On the day one goal had proved enough. That it was scored by Campbell – his ninth in just seven appearances since Kerr brought him to Tannadice – provided firm evidence that he was the final piece in the promotion jigsaw.

Then what happened?

Inevitably, the media were exercised by the question of whether or not United could survive in the First Division. Kerr had no doubts, stating, 'I have faith in the boys who have taken us up. They are a young side, average age only 22. They will get the chance to establish themselves. But that doesn't mean I will not be looking for reinforcements. Even Real Madrid are never satisfied!'

He was as good as his word. Only seven of the team that clinched promotion proved able – in Kerr's judgement – for the First Division and the new faces he added enabled United to achieve a comfortable mid-table finish the following season.

United fans, whose support on that final day had been magnificent both in quantity and quality, rallied to the cause with a club-record seasonal average of over 11,800.

As an aside, the 16,900 crowd at Tannadice for the Berwick match was the highest in senior football in Scotland, on a day when Rangers and Celtic were both at home. Bizarrely, though, it was comfortably exceeded by the 27,000 that attended the Scottish Junior Cup semi-final between Ardeer Thistle and Greenock at Partick Thistle's ground.

v Celtic 4-5

Scottish League First Division
Tannadice
13 January 1962
Attendance: 14,476

DUNDEE UNITED	CELTIC
Brown	Haffey
Gordon	MacKay
Briggs	Kennedy
Neilson	Crerand
Smith	McNeill
Fraser	Price
Carlyle	Chalmers
Brodie	Divers
Mochan	Hughes
Irvine	Jackson
Gillespie	Carroll
Manager: Jerry Kerr	*Manager:* Jimmy McGrory

NONE of the players in the victory over Berwick Rangers that secured Dundee United's return to the First Division in 1960 were born when the club last played at that level. That gap of 28 years was a major factor in Jerry Kerr's determination that such a hard-won prize would not be easily relinquished.

In his first season in charge Kerr had assembled a young squad, most of whom he was confident would continue to improve in the First Division. So additions in preparation for the challenges ahead were minimal, with the manager having convinced the board that the main outlay should be in the form of improving the performance of his existing players rather than spending on wholesale changes to the squad.

That improved performance would, Kerr argued, most likely be achieved if the players were full-time.

United had not been a full-time club since their relegation in 1932 and Kerr saw it as essential that he was able to work daily with the players to maximise their chances of establishing the club at the top level.

The two main additions to the promotion-winning squad added experience that would prove crucial. During the summer Kerr signed 36-year-old goalkeeper Lando Ugolini, who had played for many years at the top level in England with Middlesbrough. Then in November, as United hit a difficult patch, he brought in left-winger Neil Mochan, who had for a time been a club-mate of Ugolini on Teesside. The former Scotland international had won every domestic honour with Celtic and, even at 33, he still had much to offer United.

As the season got under way Kerr had promised, 'We will give all that we have to stay up,' and set a target of 18 points for the halfway stage. That was reached with two games to spare and United spent the bulk of the campaign in a comfortable mid-table position, gaining notable victories over Aberdeen, Hearts and Hibs. Those three all ended the season above the Black and Whites, who came ninth, and in the 18-club First Division United had done much more than survive.

That was more than almost any supporter had dared hope for but there was one aspect of the season that meant everyone wore a grin as wide as the Tay at its conclusion. The 3-1 defeat of Dundee at Tannadice in September had been much celebrated, though no one could have known at the time it would prove the deciding factor in United finishing above their city rivals in the league for the first time. Just a point separated them in the final table, with United in the top half and Dundee not.

When Kerr was placed in charge at Tannadice in 1959 United had just finished 37th out of 39 clubs in the Scottish League. Two years later they were ninth, which was by any standards a terrific achievement.

Centre-half Ron Yeats had grown in stature during 1960/61, becoming a rock at the heart of the defence, and the board had rebuffed various approaches for him. But when Liverpool offered £30,000 in July it couldn't be refused; at the time the record fee received by the club was just £8,000.

Kerr believed he had a promising replacement for Yeats in Doug Smith and his judgement was not misplaced – the number five jersey would become Smith's personal property for the next 15 years. More generally, the manager felt confident the playing squad could achieve his primary aim for the second season in the First Division – consolidation.

Again, he would be proved correct as, like the one before, United spent the majority of the campaign in mid-table. Given that the club had never previously managed more than two consecutive seasons in the First Division, such anonymity – threatening neither end of the league – was regarded as more than acceptable by supporters.

By January, Kerr's men sat tenth, the slot they would also occupy at the season's end. As that would suggest, their form had been inconsistent – best illustrated when a 4-0 defeat of Hibs was immediately followed by a 7-2 drubbing at Third Lanark. A first win over one of the Old Firm since the return to the top level was anticipated by the Tannadice faithful, who had been disappointed in November when a thrilling encounter with Rangers ended in a 3-2 defeat.

Seven weeks later it was Celtic's turn to visit Tannadice and, having held the Glasgow club to a draw a year before, there were realistic hopes that this time United could go a step further. It would be the match of the season.

In part, those realistic hopes were rooted in the fact that the Celtic side was hardly a vintage one by their own standards. The past eight seasons had produced just two Scottish League Cup successes and had also seen uncharacteristically low league finishes of sixth and ninth. That said, the Glasgow club were fourth when they arrived at Tannadice and would end the season one rung higher.

The form of neither side could have led any supporter that winter's day to anticipate what unfolded in a torrid first half for United. A display of defensive dithering by Kerr's team allowed Celtic to score three times in an eight-minute spell and it seemed they had ended the game as a contest with just half an hour played having built a 4-1 lead.

After 13 minutes Mike Jackson received the ball just outside the penalty area and, as the United defence backed off, he advanced before hitting a rising shot past Alec Brown to open the scoring. Before United or their fans had had time to gather their thoughts, the lead was doubled. Just 60 seconds later John Hughes bustled his way into the box past half-hearted challenges and had almost reached the byline when he turned to shoot, beating Brown from an acute angle.

Captain Tommy Neilson tried gamely to raise his colleagues and urge them on but on 21 minutes the tale of woe continued. Brown came out of his goal intent on gathering a corner from Bobby Carroll but completely missed the ball, leaving Jackson with the simple task of heading into the unguarded net.

It was a disastrous spell but to their credit United's heads didn't stay down and only two minutes later Jim Irvine was on the spot to score from close range. That was a boost for the young inside-forward, who had been the club's leading scorer in the league for the past two seasons. But that was only his third in the current campaign having just returned after two months out injured.

United now rallied and the supporters must have hoped their team might make further inroads into Celtic's lead before half-time. However their wishes were dashed on the half-hour mark when a bizarre goal restored the visitors' advantage. Doug Smith had been enjoying an excellent first season as a United regular but he handed Celtic their fourth goal. Attempting to hook clear a high ball into the box he succeeded only in slamming it against the onrushing Hughes and it rebounded into the net.

The dazed United players must have been rather relieved that no further damage was sustained before half-time. The break enabled Kerr to make some changes, basically re-shuffling his forward line, with only winger Wattie Carlyle retaining his position. That suggested the manager did not accept his team's cause was beyond some hope, but before the new formation had time to settle yet more misfortune came. Pat Crerand let fly with a speculative shot from 20 yards and the ball took a deflection off a United defender, leaving Brown wrong-footed as it ended up in the net.

Even with 44 minutes remaining, at 5-1 surely that was that? It would appear the never-say-die United players didn't think so. They probably felt – rightly – the score in no way reflected the balance of play and set about trying to reduce the deficit. But when nothing had changed by the mid-point of the half some United fans decided to call it a day and began to head for the exits. They would soon regret their lack of faith.

In the 67th minute former Celt Neil Mochan split the visitors' defence with a pass that bore all the hallmarks of his great experience. Irvine darted in one-on-one with goalkeeper Frank Haffey and sent the ball past him for 5-2. Six minutes later Mochan was again involved as his chipped pass into the danger area was headed down by Wattie Carlyle to Irvine, who shot home to complete his hat-trick and make it 5-3.

Now there were murmurs of 'just maybe' around Tannadice, hope fired by the sight of an anxious Celtic management bringing the injured – and clearly in pain – Hughes back on to the pitch. In the days before substitutes, players unable to carry on in normal circumstances were often returned to the fray, even if they constituted no more than nuisance value. But it smacked of desperation with the Celts still two goals ahead. Not for long, though.

As the match entered its final ten minutes Carlyle, whose fast raiding wing play increasingly had the Celtic defence on the back foot, took a pass from Neilson, held off Jim Kennedy and did brilliantly to squeeze a shot past Haffey at the near post. It was 5-4 with nine minutes plus injury time to go.

United now threw everything at Celtic in search of an equaliser, something that not long before had appeared impossible. Twice they came agonisingly close and each time that man Carlyle was at the heart of it.

In the 89th minute he cut inside on the edge of the box and let fly with a shot that was headed for the net until Haffey, at full stretch, tipped the ball over the bar. That brought a howl of dismay from United fans but it was nothing compared to the uproar that followed with seconds remaining when the winger clashed with Billy McNeill in the box and the resultant penalty claims were ignored by the referee.

That was the last play of what had been a pulsating match. United's blistering final half-hour could not have been more of a contrast with their blundering first 30 minutes, with Celtic just managing to hold on – a scenario nobody could have foreseen a minute into the second half.

Then what happened?

United didn't have to wait too much longer for their first Old Firm win since promotion. It came two months later when Carlyle scored the only goal of the match at Ibrox.

Irvine's hat-trick kick-started his season and he went on to finish with 14 goals, three less than top-scorer Carlyle. Unbelievably, 52 years later Irvine remains the only Dundee United player to have scored a treble against either Celtic or Rangers.

v Dundee 5-0

Scottish League First Division
Dens Park
11 September 1965
Attendance: 15,058

DUNDEE UNITED	DUNDEE
Mackay	Donaldson
Millar	Hamilton
Briggs	Cox
Neilson	Houston
Smith	Easton
Wing	Stuart
Rooney	Bertelsen
Munro	Cousin
Dossing	Cameron
Gillespie	McLean
Persson	Cooke
Manager: Jerry Kerr	*Manager:* Bobby Ancell

ASK any Arab what match he or she most keenly anticipates and, almost without exception, you'll receive the answer 'the derby'.

The term is derived from the horse race of that name, first run in 1780, which became a major event 100 years later and attracted huge numbers to Epsom each June.

By that time, football was becoming popular and by the end of the 19th century some matches were attracting sizeable crowds. The biggest – apart from cup finals – usually occurred when clubs from the same city or local area played each other and for that reason the term 'derby match' developed.

The Dundee version of the derby first took place when Dundee and Dundee Hibernian met in a friendly at Dens Park in March 1915. The Dark Blues won 4-0, understandable given their status as one of Scotland's top clubs at the time, while the Hibs, whose players were all part-time, had been in existence for less than six years.

But a tradition of competitiveness began to build right from the start. The *Saturday Evening Post* reported, 'The rivalry between the teams is shown by the number of stoppages for fouls ... shortly before the close Low and Cargill got to grips and the referee promptly ordered them to the pavilion.'

The first derby in one of the major competitions didn't happen until ten years later, by which time the Hibs had become Dundee United and, led by the charismatic and inspirational Jimmy Brownlie, had won promotion to the First Division for the first time.

A goal-less draw was watched by 18,000 at Dens and the crowds that packed either ground whenever the two met in league or cup matches demonstrated the keen rivalry among supporters of both clubs and the excitement their fixtures generated within the city. The record was set in 1951 when 38,000 saw the teams fight out a thrilling 2-2 draw in the Scottish Cup at Dens.

That rivalry, though intense, has always been devoid of the hatred that can characterise derby clashes in some other cities. The relationship between United and Dundee fans is such that they often congregate in the same pubs before and after derby matches, irrespective of the outcome.

For many years, Dundee enjoyed a clear advantage in terms of results. Prior to 1960, when United became an established club at the top level for the first time, there had been only 22 derbies in the three major competitions (Scottish League, Scottish Cup and Scottish League Cup). Dundee had won 12, United just four.

Five years later, as the 1965/66 season got under way, there had been 18 more, in the three competitions and the Summer Cup (which took place only in 1964 and 1965, but had first-class status). For Arabs, the change in fortune was dramatic as their club won ten of them, twice as many as Dundee.

Further, their love affair with Dens Park was beginning to flower because United had left with full points on their last three league visits 'across the road'.

During the previous campaign, United manager Jerry Kerr had responded to his team's lacklustre early form in time-honoured fashion by introducing new faces to the squad. But this time the arrivals were quite different because they came from Scandinavia. Greenock Morton had begun to introduce players from that part of Europe early in 1964 but that was thought to be a fad never to catch on. However, when Kerr went to see Dunfermline play the Swedish club Örgryte in an Inter-Cities Fairs Cup tie he was struck by the skilful wing play of Orjan Persson.

Within weeks, Persson was a United player and he made his debut alongside Finn Dossing, a Dane, against Hearts in December 1964. The following week Dossing's compatriot Mogens Berg swelled the contingent to three and in January Persson's club-mate – and fellow international – Lennart Wing arrived to complete a quartet regarded as exotic, such was the monochrome nature of Scottish football at the time.

The new signings inspired a dramatic turnaround in fortunes. Before their arrival United lay third-bottom of the First Division, yet ended the season comfortably in mid-table. Dossing, Persson and Wing were in the United team at Dens Park in September 1965, though Berg was absent. He would miss the entire season due to a serious back injury.

It was only three years since Dundee had been crowned champions of Scotland, but just three of the players from that momentous season were in the home team that day. They had their own Dane in Carl Bertelsen but the latest newcomer was actually making his debut in dark blue. Earlier that week, manager Bobby Ancell had paid Clyde £12,000 for a 28-year-old inside-forward by the name of Jim McLean.

No matter their age, every Arab is aware of the match now known only as the Dens Park 'Massacre of '65'. It's as fondly recalled – at least by those who were there – as any of the club's trophy wins or European triumphs and it remains the subject of a song that is sung with great gusto wherever fans gather.

It is a given in football that the form book goes out of the window in a derby – which was just as well as United had lost their previous four matches of the new season. One saw Dundee win 3-1 at Tannadice in a League Cup tie just ten days earlier.

But it was soon apparent that United hadn't arrived at Dens Park with an inferiority complex. Kerr made a bold tactical decision when he handed Francie Munro the task of policing Dundee's record signing and playmaker Charlie Cooke. What made the decision bold was the fact that Munro was not yet 18, although he had played more than 40 first-team games.

United made a whirlwind start with play concentrated in the Dundee half and efforts from Persson and Dossing both went close. Soon after, despite his special role, Munro found the time and space to beat Dundee centre-half Jim Easton, only to send his shot wide.

That demonstrated the way the wind was blowing and the breakthrough by United was not to be long delayed. In the 14th minute they were awarded a free kick after Easton had blocked Persson. Wing floated the ball into the box where Persson got his head to it. The ball wasn't cleared by the Dundee defence and Dossing was the quickest to react, stooping to nod it into the net.

Thereafter, to some extent United took their foot off the gas, though they continued to dominate. All the home side could muster in the first half were shots from Bertelsen, McLean and future United striker Kenny Cameron. United goalkeeper Donald Mackay – a future Dundee manager – dealt with them all confidently.

The second half was only ten minutes old when the Terrors increased their lead – and it was a cracker. A Benny Rooney corner was met by Wing and the left-half directed the ball towards Dossing. With his back to goal, the Dane showed why he was such an effective striker by controlling it before spinning round and firing past the helpless Ally Donaldson in the Dundee goal.

United were now in complete command, moving the ball to the wings at every opportunity and stretching an increasingly bedraggled Dundee defence. Persson was particularly effective, giving Dundee's Scotland full-back Alex Hamilton a torrid time, and the Swede was instrumental in the third goal. His shot was headed off the line by Dundee captain Bobby Cox, but it went only as far as Munro, who controlled the ball before squaring it for Dennis Gillespie to complete the job at 3-0 after just over an hour.

Arabs were now in full voice, urging their heroes to rub salt into the home side's wounds. That's what the Terrors tried their utmost to do while Dundee struggled to make any impression and became increasingly dispirited.

Yet, for all United's domination, with only three minutes remaining the scoreline was unchanged. Dossing had been relentless in pursuit of his hat-trick and twice Donaldson was hurt diving at the feet of the United predator. Dark Blues fans hadn't liked that and they were even more glum when Dossing's persistence was finally rewarded, ironically with one of his softest attempts of that or any other day. A low effort shouldn't have troubled Donaldson but he was left embarrassed as he fumbled the ball, allowing it to trickle over the line as he desperately scrambled back.

Dundee's players – and those supporters who had remained – were now willing the final whistle to blow but their torture wasn't complete. It seemed that the defenders in dark blue had no legal means of stopping the rampant Persson and when Cox brought his tormentor down in the final minute a penalty was the only outcome. Wing stepped forward to score emphatically and complete the rout.

The papers the following day were fulsome in their praise of an outstanding team performance by United, with Dossing and Persson first among equals. The *Sunday Post* began its report, 'Just crackers! United the fizzy, fiery, sparkling kind – Dundee wide open at both ends!' It also commented, 'It was no day to judge how Jim McLean will fit into the attack'. For jaunty Jim, the only way was up.

Then what happened?

The following week Kerr's men again scored five in a derby, this time against St Johnstone at Tannadice. That raised United to fifth and it proved to be no flash in the pan as that was where they ended the season. For good measure, they completed the derby double with a 2-1 win at Tannadice in January and stood four places above their rivals in the final table.

Dundee United's Greatest Games

The season produced some exhilarating performances with the Scandinavians central to the exciting attacking play. Their contingent had become five-strong when Norwegian winger Finn Seemann joined in October and supporters saw their team score freely, with five on a further two occasions as well as seven once.

Dossing was on fire during the season, claiming 25 of the 79 league goals scored. Both those figures have been bettered only once in the half-century since – on an individual level by Kenny Cameron with 27 in 1968/69 and by United's championship-winning squad of 1982/83, which scored 90.

That Kerr had built United into an established First Division club was confirmed by coming fifth in 1965/66. It was the highest finish United had achieved and earned a place in European competition for the first time.

Despite that, many Arabs still regard the season as being most memorable for that derby victory at Dens Park. After all, it's been immortalised in song!

The Dens Park Massacre of '65

Get down on your knees and pray
It's the anniversary
Of the Dens Park massacre of '65 ('65!)
It's the day we won't forget
And the Dundee will regret
It's the day we gave them 1-2-3-4-5!

It was the 11th of September
A day we all remember
Finn Dossing in the centre he scored three
Lennart Wing fae the spot
And Gillespie wi' a shot
A shot that 'keeper Ally didna see!

(Then repeat first verse)

It was certainly a day not to forget.

v **Barcelona** 2-1

Inter-Cities Fairs Cup Second Round First Leg
Camp Nou
28 October 1966
Attendance: 22,459

DUNDEE UNITED	**BARCELONA**
Davie	Sadurní
Millar	Benítez
Briggs	Gallego
Neilson	Eladio
Smith	Fusté
Wing	Pereda
Seemann	Torres
Hainey	Muller
Mitchell	Zaldúa
Gillespie	Filosia
Persson	Rife
Manager: Jerry Kerr	*Coach:* Roque Olsen

WHEN Jerry Kerr was appointed manager at Tannadice in the summer of 1959, Dundee United had just finished third-bottom of the Second Division and hadn't managed a serious promotion push in seven years. There could hardly have been a starker contrast seven years later when Kerr would become the first man to lead a British club to victory in Spain in European competition.

The Inter-Cities Fairs Cup was introduced in 1955 with the main aim of promoting international trade fairs. Initially, it was open only to clubs from cities that hosted such fairs and where these clubs finished in their national league was of no relevance. As an example, Hibernian participated in three consecutive competitions from 1960/61, despite never having finished above seventh in the league in any of the preceding seasons.

The Fairs Cup was not run by UEFA, which led to the anomalous – some would say ridiculous – situation where some clubs participated in two European competitions in the same season. The most prominent occurrence came in 1960/61, when Barcelona reached the quarter-finals of the Fairs Cup and the final of the European Cup. In 1971 the Fairs Cup finally came under the auspices of UEFA, who unsurprisingly re-named it the UEFA Cup.

From 1963 the SFA decreed that participation by Scottish clubs in the Fairs Cup should be on the basis of league position and three years later United, having finished fifth in 1965/66, qualified for the first time.

Just to be competing in Europe represented a real achievement. After all, this was a club that had been part-time during the almost three decades that it languished in the lower reaches of Scottish football, re-appearing at the top level in 1960.

Having had to adopt the role of bystanders as Dundee enjoyed two seasons of European competition, Arabs were on a high as they prepared for their club to seize the limelight at their neighbours' expense.

Naturally, there was a great sense of anticipation among United's devoted followers as the first-round draw was made. However, it turned to anti-climax with the news that they had received a bye! The feeling was that that was not at all a lucky break as the European newcomers would have benefitted from acclimatising to foreign competition against one of the smaller clubs, before being handed a more demanding opponent.

When the second round draw was made it paired Kerr's team with not just a demanding opponent, but the most demanding opponent possible. Barcelona were the holders of the trophy, the third time the Catalans had lifted the Fairs Cup. Barcelona had won the 1965/66 competition just two weeks before they were drawn to meet United, the final having been held over from the previous season as Barcelona had four players in the Spanish squad for the World Cup finals in England.

Then, as now, the Catalans were one of the giants of world football and the prospect of them gracing Tannadice was one that had everyone associated with United salivating. It is doubtful that more than a handful hoped for anything more than the team giving a good account of themselves; where they existed, thoughts of progressing were hardly touched by realism.

The Camp Nou (Catalan for 'new field') was then only nine years old and was one of the most impressive stadiums in existence. Its magnitude and grandeur no doubt took the players' breath away as they sampled the pitch on arrival. They would also have been aware that the last British club to play there in the Fairs Cup had been Chelsea who were hammered 5-0 less than six months previously.

That said, while a sense of awe may have gripped them as they took the field for the match, it quickly became evident Kerr's men had not allowed that to translate into an inferiority complex.

Barcelona began a possession game from the start, hoping to frustrate United before building up to what they no doubt assumed would be the inevitable goals and subsequent victory. Their problem was that Jimmy Briggs and his team-mates weren't having any of it.

Demonstrating that they weren't just there for the adventure, there was urgency in their movement, bite in their tackling, intelligence in their positioning and precision in their passing. Kerr had departed from the traditional 2-3-5 formation of the time to adopt 4-3-3, which seemed to flummox the Catalans but certainly worked for the Terrors.

United were building in confidence while Barca didn't seem to know what to make of their upstart visitors. Goalkeeper Sandy Davie had had to deal with just a single shot, one that came at him through a ruck of players, when the men in white shirts boldly worked the ball to the other end of the pitch. The build-up ended with Billy Hainey bursting through the home defence and placing the ball out of the reach of Sadurni in goal to put United ahead after only 13 minutes.

The Camp Nou was less than a third full but the couple of hundred Arabs who had made the trip were responsible for the only audible response to an improbable scoreline. That began to change as the first half wore on as the Barca fans became increasingly frustrated at their highly-paid players' inability – despite the predictable onslaught – to break down a resolute United side which continued to seek opportunities to increase their lead.

Ever chasing, ever challenging, using short passing to break out of defence and covering effectively, it seemed United's players had been at this European lark for years. There were certainly more signs of confidence than apprehension from them as the second half got under way, although Barcelona had dispensed with the silky approach and were now engaging in a more physical style. But despite getting rather less than they expected from the Yugoslav referee, United remained unruffled and probed whenever possible.

Then Hainey again broke into the penalty area where he was brought down crudely by Torres – so crudely that the referee couldn't fail to award a penalty.

That certainly stoked up some angry noise from the home fans but, pushing it out of his mind, Norwegian winger Finn Seemann slammed the ball into the net. The celebrations were quickly cut short as the ref ordered the kick to be re-taken, claiming that Orjan Persson had strayed into the area. The United players and fans couldn't believe it and must have feared a conspiracy, but one man who remained totally focussed was Seemann.

Having placed the first kick to Sadurni's right, he now feigned to the left then sent the ball into precisely the same spot as the goalkeeper lurched in the opposite direction.

United had entered dreamland but there was no time to let minds wander because a third of the match remained. Perplexed, Barcelona now became slightly desperate but, although Davie was kept busy, there were few scary moments. Josep Fuste did manage to beat the United goalkeeper near the end and that may have provided Barcelona with some hope for the second leg but it didn't appease their now irate, whistling fans.

The victory was astounding – and all the more so when it is remembered that Finn Dossing, the Dane whose goals had propelled United to their best finish of fifth and with it European qualification, had missed the game through injury.

The result undoubtedly ranked as a huge upset but only if it was viewed in isolation. Those who actually watched the game acknowledged that the triumph, though hard-earned, was fully deserved in terms of the manner in which Kerr's men were organised, took the game to their opponents, built a two-goal lead and then successfully defended it for more than a third of the 90 minutes.

Even now, it still ranks as one of the club's finest moments. It was also an occasion that brought Dundee United to the attention of football fans across the continent.

The *Courier* wrote, 'A victory grown out of courage supreme, sharp and sure football, teamwork of the highest football order. A victory that will most certainly get very special placing in the record book at Tannadice. It was certainly a famous evening.'

Then what happened?

Despite that first leg, as holders of the trophy and with a long-established European pedigree, Barcelona were still expected by most pundits – and not just in Spain – to overcome the deficit at Tannadice and reach the next round.

Comments attributed to some of the Barca players suggested that was their mindset but perhaps they had not been fed the information that Dundee in November is somewhat less balmy than Barcelona in October. Allied to that factor was the presence of a capacity all-ticket crowd of 28,000, hugging the touchlines in a manner quite unlike the Camp Nou. That attendance created a Tannadice record, one that will stand in perpetuity now that the stadium is all-seated.

The Catalans were never allowed to get into their stride and indeed were forced on the defensive as United went in search of a goal that would extend their lead. It took just 17 minutes, when Ian Mitchell took a Persson pass and beat Sadurni as he advanced from his goal. The nerves of players and crowd alike were suitably soothed, although Barcelona pressed forward and came close a couple of times. But just before half-time Dennis Gillespie had the ball in the net, only for the effort to be dubiously ruled out when the referee ruled that Persson had strayed into an offside position.

United would not be denied for much longer, though, and the second half was only three minutes old when a sensational goal finally ended Barcelona's resistance. Hainey –

scorer of the first in the Camp Nou – picked the ball up near the touchline and with the Barcelona players expecting a cross instead sent a shot towards goal from 30 yards. The wind assisted its progress as it raced past the despairing stretch of Sadurni and into the net.

There cannot surely have been a louder roar at Tannadice, before or since, than the one that greeted that quite exceptional piece of skill.

That gave United a barely comprehensible 4-1 aggregate lead, yet it could have been more because the Terrors suffered a second offside decision after a Seemann header had hit the net.

In the circumstances, the United players didn't protest too vociferously and were able then to see out the remaining 20 minutes against what was little more than token resistance from the holders.

For United to have emerged victorious over the two legs would have been remarkable, but to do so by a three-goal margin after winning both games was an outcome that would have been dismissed as risible had it appeared in a novel.

But happen it did and it is a source of some disappointment that due credit was not given to Kerr. The manager – using a bold and at the time unfashionable 4-3-3 system – was the architect of victories that have been equalled, though not surpassed, by any other United team on European fields. It is certainly arguable that the defeats of Barcelona in 1966 are the most notable of all, given the club's complete lack of experience on the European stage.

United would have feared no club in the next round but would have preferred one of less stature than Juventus. Despite a defiant performance in the Stadio Comunale a 3-0 first-leg loss was too much to overcome, though Arabs did have the consolation of adding another scalp when the long-delayed appearance of Dossing in Europe saw him return and score the only goal at Tannadice in front of another capacity crowd.

As a sad footnote to those Barcelona matches, Julio César Benítez, the full-back who played in both legs, died 18 months later at the age of 27 from gastroenteritis contracted after eating poisonous shellfish. His funeral was attended by 150,000 at the Camp Nou and the Uruguayan was buried in a cemetery near the stadium.

v Celtic 3-2

Scottish League First Division
Celtic Park
3 May 1967
Attendance: 40,741

DUNDEE UNITED	CELTIC
Davie	Simpson
Millar	Craig
Briggs	Gemmell
Neilson	Murdoch
Smith	McNeill
Moore	Clark
Berg	Johnstone
Graham	Gallagher
Hainey	Wallace
Gillespie	Lennox
Persson	Hughes
Manager: Jerry Kerr	*Manager:* Jock Stein

THE 1966/67 season would have been a landmark one in the history of Dundee United had they achieved nothing more notable than appearing in Europe for the first time. But the team led by Jerry Kerr did rather more than that. For this was a season in which new heights were scaled in a campaign of vivid contrasts, perfectly illustrated by the final two league games, both in Glasgow, within a period of four days.

Apart from a month-long tour of southern Africa in the close-season of 1963, United had never played a match outside of the UK. No other European country had been visited so, with a first taste of European competition beckoning, Kerr arranged an end-of-season trip to Iceland and Denmark.

Coming at the conclusion of the most successful campaign in the club's history, this might have been seen as a reward for the players. To some extent it was, but Kerr was determined to look forwards rather than back and wanted some acclimatisation, giving the squad a feel for travel and training and playing in different conditions as well, no doubt, as seeking the benefits of further bonding by the group over the two weeks.

The visit provided valuable preparation with all five of the games won quite comfortably, albeit against part-time opposition. The final opponents were Viborg, a match which saw Finn Dossing return to face the club he had left to join United.

Given the signing of Billy Hainey from Partick Thistle in March, it was understandable that the only summer addition to the squad was inside-forward Jackie Graham from Morton.

On the opening day of 1966/67 Hainey would write himself into the record books – twice. For the first time, substitutes were allowed in competitive matches, though only to replace a player unable to continue through injury. Hainey became United's first when he replaced Dennis Gillespie in the League Cup against Dundee at Tannadice. He also became the first United substitute to score with the second goal in a 2-0 win.

However, they won only once more in their section and failed to qualify, finishing second. The First Division campaign also began less successfully than Kerr would have hoped, with only three of seven matches being won prior to the Fairs Cup visit to Barcelona. Within that sequence, though, another club record was established.

The first half against Ayr United at Somerset Park was unremarkable, ending without a goal for either side. But the second was explosive as the visiting United scored seven times without reply, Dossing, Persson and Mitchell all hitting doubles in what remains the club's biggest away win in the top flight.

Not even the euphoria of the double defeat of Barcelona and the prospect of taking on Juventus in the next round could ignite United's league form. By Hogmanay, as the team prepared for the visit of Celtic, only four of 15 matches had been won and ten weeks had passed since the last victory at Tannadice, explaining why United sat disappointingly in 11th in the 18-club First Division.

By contrast, champions Celtic were on course to retain their title and had also reached the quarter-finals of the European Cup. Such was their form, they were unbeaten in their last 46 matches in all competitions, stretching back more than a year.

The match appeared to be going to form in the first half when Bobby Lennox gave Celtic an early lead. Dossing equalised ten minutes later but, straight from the re-start, Willie Wallace restored the Glasgow club's advantage.

After the break United proceeded to tear up the script, raising their game to a level not seen since the Barcelona tie, and when Dennis Gillespie equalised for a second time they didn't sit back and await a response from Celtic.

Kerr urged his men to stay on the attack and just two minutes later they were ahead. Perhaps finding themselves in unfamiliar territory on the back foot, the Celtic defence were unable to cope with the direct running of Dossing and Hainey, though it was Ian Mitchell who supplied what proved to be the *coup de grâce*, ending Celtic's unbeaten run and earning United a deserved victory – their fourth over the Glasgow club at Tannadice since returning to the top level in 1960.

Predictably, that gave United a lift and they won three of the next four league matches before the Scottish Cup began at the end of January. That was a competition in which Arabs were desperate to taste success and a large number travelled to Tynecastle, where Hearts were comprehensively beaten 3-0 in the third round.

Although Falkirk and Dunfermline proved more stubborn opponents at Tannadice in the next two rounds, both were seen off with a single goal and that opened the door to what was only the club's second appearance in the semi-finals.

With Aberdeen the opponents and Dens Park the venue, hopes of a first final were high, particularly after Jackie Graham's goal in the league match at Pittodrie the week before had given United a morale-boosting win.

The 41,500 spectators crammed in saw United maintain their record of no opposition player scoring against them in the cup that season. Sadly, that wasn't enough to prevent a huge anti-climax because a Tommy Millar own goal after only three minutes proved the only one of the game. The defeat came as a real body blow and effectively ended the season for Kerr and his team. Six league fixtures remained and, no less than for the supporters, to the players it must have seemed that they were to be endured rather than enjoyed.

But to their great credit they raised their spirits and the first four produced two wins and two draws. The next involved the small matter of a visit to Celtic Park. For United, only pride was at stake, but their hosts had rather more to play for: a single point was required to rubber-stamp their retention of the championship.

Fired by that sense of anticipation, a crowd well in excess of Celtic Park's average for the season was there on that Wednesday evening in May. It is possible, too, that more than a few were anxious for revenge – the Tannadice defeat was the only one Celtic had suffered in the league all season.

Although 1966/67 had already been a notable one for United, with that double defeat of Barcelona, a home win over Juventus and a Scottish Cup semi-final, for Celtic it was to be their stellar season.

By the end of April the Scottish League Cup, the Scottish Cup and the Glasgow Cup were on display in the Parkhead boardroom, with the retention of their league title a formality. They had also become the first British club to reach the European Cup Final with their opponents decided in a play-off that was taking place while Celtic faced United.

Jock Stein made only two changes from the team that had beaten Aberdeen to win the Scottish Cup five days earlier, while United had been forced to field a weakened side. Not only were the team's two leading scorers, Mitchell and Dossing, missing through injury, left-half Lennart Wing had returned to Sweden after being granted an early release from his contract to return to his job as a fireman in Gothenburg.

His replacement was Jim Moore, the reserve centre-half who was asked to play out of position in what was his first first-team appearance of the season.

United were initially content to contain Celtic and they succeeded for the first quarter of the match. Indeed, there had been no clear-cut chances created at either end before Celtic took the lead on 24 minutes. Tracking back in defence, Gillespie put in a rash tackle on Bobby Lennox, allowing Tommy Gemmell to score from the penalty spot.

Although Orjan Persson (twice) and Gillespie forced goalkeeper Ronnie Simpson to make saves, United didn't create many opportunities, though that changed soon after the break.

The second half was ten minutes old when Gillespie split the Celtic defence with a precision pass, sending Hainey through. He neatly rounded Simpson then slotted the ball home from a narrow angle.

Celtic upped their game in search of a second goal but when it came it was due more to United's efforts rather than their own. A high ball into the box was shielded – or so he thought – by Doug Smith as Sandy Davie came to collect but the United men were too casual, allowing Willie Wallace to stick out a foot and send the ball trickling into the net. That came after 63 minutes and two minutes later only a brilliant reflex save by Davie prevented Wallace scoring again as Celtic dominated.

United's resistance might well have been broken but only five minutes after they had conceded the scores were level again. Mogens Berg fed Jackie Graham and the inside-forward brought out a save from Simpson as impressive as Davie's at the other end. From the resulting corner by Persson, Gillespie rose highest to bullet a header into the net.

The action was now in complete contrast to the rather limp first half and if Celtic's players and fans were taken aback at a second equaliser they were genuinely stunned by what followed three minutes later as United took the lead.

This time it was the Celtic defence's turn to offer a gift because Gemmell sliced a through ball which he had more than enough time to clear. It ran to Graham who seemed to have overrun it as he approached the byline but, with the Celtic defence expecting a cut-back, he shot beyond Simpson with Jim Craig able only to help the ball into the net.

There were still 19 minutes remaining but the only time United's lead was threatened came when Davie was again required to dive full-length to turn a Lennox shot round the post. The men in white then held on to record the club's first win at Celtic Park and a truly remarkable league double over what many Celtic supporters regard as the best team in their club's long and success-filled history.

Dundee United's Greatest Games

For the second time that season Kerr's United got the better of Stein's Celtic – and each time they did it the hard way, coming from behind twice. The effect was to deny Celtic their aim of completing a league season undefeated – something they have yet to achieve.

Then what happened?

Illustrating the vagaries of football, and just how inconsistent United were during that season, three days after that remarkable Parkhead triumph the team returned to Glasgow for their final game.

They may have taken place just four miles apart but the two matches were literally worlds apart. Instead of a 40,000-plus crowd, just 1,109 were at Firhill; instead of playing above themselves United turned into serious underperformers; and instead of a glorious win the outcome was a dismal 3-0 defeat.

Three weeks later in Lisbon, a Celtic team containing nine of the players who tasted defeat to United brought great honour to their club and to Scotland by beating Inter Milan to win the European Cup.

Those remarkable wins against Barcelona and Celtic brought United attention from far and wide and were at least partially responsible for an invitation to represent Dallas Tornado in the North American Soccer League that summer. In one of the many attempts to establish 'soccer' in the US, British and Irish clubs crossed the Atlantic and adopted the persona of the host clubs for a six-week period from the end of May.

As United prepared to depart, so did the first of the Scandinavians. Wing – voted supporters' player of the year – had returned to Sweden while his fellow countryman Persson defiantly called time on his Tannadice days, though not his career in Scotland, as he eventually joined Rangers.

In addition, Dossing's Midas touch was on the wane. Although the Dane did score 16 times in all competitions, Mitchell was the season's leading marksman with 22.

v Hearts 5-6

Scottish Cup Fourth Round
Tannadice
17 February 1968
Attendance: 9,021

DUNDEE UNITED	HEARTS
Mackay	Garland
T. Millar (Wood)	Sneddon
Cameron	Mann
Neilson	E. Thomson
Smith	A. Thomson
Gillespie	Miller
Seemann	Ford
Hainey	Townsend (Fleming)
Mitchell	Moller
Rolland	Irvine
Wilson	Traynor
Manager: Jerry Kerr	*Manager:* John Harvey

THE 1967 close-season saw the departure of Orjan Persson, the Swedish winger moving to Rangers in exchange for left-half Wilson Wood and former Scotland left-winger Davie Wilson. With Tommy Millar's brother, Jimmy, also arriving from Rangers (in a separate deal) that meant there were now three former Ibrox players in Jerry Kerr's squad. United's woeful record in the Scottish League Cup continued when they finished third in their section. That meant that in 22 attempts since the competition began in 1946, United had qualified on only three occasions. This time there were extenuating circumstances as the section also contained Aberdeen, Celtic and Rangers.

But the league campaign was to prove equally undistinguished; by the time the Scottish Cup began at the end of January the men in white had won only five of their 19 matches in the First Division and consequently lay ninth.

The Scottish Cup proved a welcome distraction and the draw was kind – United's third-round opponents at Tannadice were St Mirren, of the Second Division. The match got off to a bad start when full-back Jimmy Briggs suffered the agony of a broken leg after just three minutes. That blow, though not as heavy as it would have been two years earlier before substitutes were introduced, required some adjustment by Kerr as replacing a left-back with a right-half (Wilson Wood) wasn't ideal.

To their credit, it didn't take too long for the team to find their rhythm. When Ian Mitchell gave them the lead after 17 minutes things seemed to be going to plan but St Mirren refused to lie down and equalised before half-time. Two goals early in the second half from Andy Rolland and Ian Scott ensured United's passage to the fourth round, though it was less comfortable than it should have been.

That cleared the way for Hearts to return to Tannadice for a Scottish Cup tie for the first time since that momentous United win in 1938. But 30 years on there was a major difference because now the teams met as equals.

The Edinburgh club had enjoyed what remains the most successful period in their history between the mid-1950s and the mid-60s. They were league champions twice and runners-up on four occasions, as well as winning the Scottish Cup once and the Scottish League Cup four times.

Hearts were now a club in transition, however, and had finished below United in the First Division in the previous two seasons. Nor were their prospects improving: as they prepared for the cup tie they were 13th in the table, one rung above United.

Tannadice Street was a busy place on 17 February 1968. Both city clubs had been drawn at home in the fourth round, a situation that today would lead to one of the ties being re-arranged. That would be done on police instructions and in retrospect it's bewildering that the then chief constable didn't feel the need to insist on the same thing, because not only were United's visitors a club that carried a sizeable travelling support, Dundee were facing Rangers at Dens Park.

The only concession made was that the United–Hearts tie had its kick-off brought forward an hour to 2pm. Just over 9,000 were at Tannadice while the crowd at Dens was 33,000. The prospect today of allowing more than 40,000 supporters of four different clubs the opportunity of coming into contact in the city centre or on the way to and from the stadiums would cause palpitations among the authorities, both football and law enforcement. Further, in the 21st century violent confrontations between football fans in Scotland (with one obvious exception) are almost unheard of. That was not the case in the late 1960s.

Nevertheless, there was no trouble at either match or elsewhere in the city so those who sanctioned the two matches going ahead in the same street on the same day would claim to have been justified in their faith in human nature.

Hearts contained a face familiar to Tannadice fans. Inside-forward Jim Irvine had been a firm favourite in his five years with United, helping them to win promotion to the First Division in 1960 and scoring 75 times in 157 games. In 1964 he was transferred to Middlesbrough for £25,000 and three years later Hearts paid £10,000 less to bring him back to Scotland.

It was a wintry day and there had been snow better on which necessitated a pitch inspection. The hard surface made conditions tricky, not least for defenders whose inability to turn quickly would play a pivotal role.

Hearts seemed to adapt easier, which resulted in them securing an early lead. Only three minutes were on the clock when Rene Moller skipped past the attempted tackles of United defenders before crossing for Donald Ford to stab the ball past Donald Mackay.

United were struggling, literally, to find their feet and might have been further behind when Hearts had what seemed like a strong penalty claim rejected. But on 17 minutes the Maroons did double their lead. This time Moller was the marksman as he got the better of a one-on-one confrontation with Mackay and United's supporters must have feared their cause was already a lost one.

Any such notions would have lasted no more than 60 seconds because that was all that it took for the men in white to open their account. It came from a Hearts defensive blunder when captain Eddie Thomson was short with a pass to goalkeeper Kenny Garland, allowing winger Davie Wilson to reach the ball first and sweep it into the net.

Although the goal came into the 'gift' category, it had the effect of raising the United players and six minutes later the scores were level. Wilson had been testing Hearts on both wings and it was from one of his runs on the right that his cross wasn't cleared. The ball found its way to Andy Rolland, who drove home the equaliser.

That came at the mid-point of the half and with half an hour played United seized the lead. Mitchell and Dennis Gillespie were looking dangerous every time they got the ball and the Hearts defence, constantly in retreat, had begun to set an offside trap to catch them out. That is always a risky strategy and it led to Mitchell breaking free; as the men in maroon awaited a whistle that never came, the young striker went on to beat Garland.

Mitchell did appear to be in an offside position when he took possession and this led to protests from Hearts' players plus some of the visiting supporters throwing beer cans on to the pitch. Police issued warnings at that point and when there was a repeat they entered the terracing and escorted several maroon-clad fans to the exits.

A second wave of protest followed another United goal – their fourth in an amazing 18-minute spell. Again the Hearts players claimed offside, though this time without justification. Andy Rolland broke clear just inside the Hearts half and ran 40 yards before testing Garland. His shot was blocked but the ball ran to Mitchell, who scored. That made it 4-2 and, with only 36 minutes played, the crowd had been treated to a goal every six minutes.

No doubt every supporter reckoned they had had enough excitement for one half, but there was more to come. United had been dominant for some time but, fatally, took their foot off the gas. The ball emerged from a ruck of players after a free kick and Thomson redeemed himself for his earlier blunder by shooting strongly past Mackay for Hearts' third in the 43rd minute.

Even that wasn't the final significant action of the first period because full-back Millar was stretchered off after sustaining what proved to be a leg fracture, the same fate suffered by Jimmy Briggs in the previous round.

The second half couldn't have matched that crazy sequence of events but it made a spirited attempt to do so. Only two minutes after the re-start this rollercoaster of a tie took another twist when Finn Seemann was brought down and United had a penalty. The Norwegian took it himself but, though well struck, Garland dived to save brilliantly and the score remained 4-3. Not for long though, because from a corner after 54 minutes a hooked shot by Moller flew into the net for 4-4.

With the game now well-established in the 'you-couldn't-make-it-up' category, four minutes later United regained the lead. Billy Hainey received the ball 20 yards out and, with the Hearts defenders retreating in anticipation of a pass, the inside-forward lashed a shot low into the net beyond Garland.

What then followed was very odd – because the next 17 minutes was the longest period in the entire match without a goal being scored. That ended in the 75th minute when a shot by winger Tommy Traynor, who would join United two years later, was handled on the line by Jim Cameron and George Miller achieved what Seemann could not, scoring from the spot to even the match again.

With 15 minutes remaining it would have been impossible to persuade a single soul present in Tannadice that 5-5 would be the final score – and so it transpired, with one last flourish that was, to say the least, ironic.

Dennis Gillespie and Jim Irvine had formed United's strike force for five years from 1959 and the pair were to combine for the goal that would prove to be the winner of this extraordinary cup tie. The trouble was, they were no longer team-mates.

The match was in its 86th minute when a Hearts attack broke down, leaving United with a throw-in. Gillespie picked the ball up and, under no pressure, sent the throw across the edge of the penalty area. But it was to no white shirt and the ball was easily intercepted by Irvine, who drifted into the penalty area where he was not meaningfully challenged by a United defender before he dispatched a shot past Mackay and into the net.

Dundee United's Greatest Games

This time there was to be no comeback by Kerr's men, who trooped disconsolately off at the final whistle, drawing no consolation whatsoever from the thought that they had been participants in one of the most remarkable ties in the history of the Scottish Cup. Supporters of both clubs drew breath at the end, something they had been unable to do throughout.

For Kerr it wasn't a match he would remember with much affection, 'It may have been a wonderful game – but there was nothing for us at the finish. But we have no real excuses; we should never have allowed Hearts to fight back after leading 4-2.' The manager was angered and mystified as to why Seemann had taken the penalty because it had been agreed before the match that Gillespie would be entrusted with the task. The fact that a successful kick would have restored United's two-goal advantage simply added to his ire.

Then what happened?

Hearts used the Tannadice win as a springboard to the Scottish Cup Final, though they were second best to an excellent Dunfermline side.

United's league form improved marginally. They gained a measure of revenge with victory over Hearts when the sides met again at Tannadice a month later, when the score was a rather more mundane 2-1. Kerr's team ended the season one place above the Maroons, though that meant little since the Edinburgh club were 12th.

In fact, 1967/68 saw the lowest finish by United since promotion eight years earlier and it also marked the departure of the last three Scandinavians. Mogens Berg, Finn Dossing and Seemann made only a total of 37 league appearances between them during the season, at the end of which Berg was freed, while DWS Amsterdam paid £25,000 for Seemann.

In December, Dossing's contract had run its three years and, having again suffered a protracted absence due to injury, he decided to return home to Denmark. He departed a hero in the eyes of all Arabs, to whom he was – and remains – the Mighty Finn.

Little wonder, considering his prolific scoring rate of 76 goals in 115 appearances in the major competitions. Only Arthur Milne and Peter McKay have ever had a higher goals-per-game ratio with United, though in Dossing's case they were scored in the First Division.

So the curtain came down on the Scandinavian era at Tannadice. It lasted little more than three years but contained much excitement and some exceptional performances. Gone the five may have been; forgotten they most certainly were not.

v Hearts 4-2

17

Scottish Cup Semi-Final Replay
Hampden Park
9 April 1974
Attendance: 12,860

DUNDEE UNITED	HEARTS
Davie	Cruickshank
Gardner	Sneddon
Kopel	Clunie
Copland	Jefferies
D. Smith	Anderson
W. Smith	Brown
Payne	Aird (Gibson)
Knox	Busby
Gray	Ford
Fleming	Stevenson
Traynor	Prentice
Manager: Jim McLean	*Manager:* Bobby Seith

THE 1971/72 season was the 12th that United had spent in the First Division after their return to the top level following an absence of 28 years. Having led the club to promotion in 1960 in his first season in charge, manager Jerry Kerr had then consolidated to the extent that United had become a well-established member of the top division while qualifying for Europe three times through league placings.

By any definition, not least taking into account the previous failed attempts to gain a foothold in the First Division, that constituted genuine progress. But one aspect of the enhanced status demonstrably lacking was success in the two domestic cup competitions. During those 11 years United had not merely failed to reach a cup final; Arabs had seen their team contest just two Scottish Cup semi-finals and a single Scottish League Cup semi-final.

In 1967 Kerr's team was unfortunate to lose an extremely close-fought Scottish Cup semi-final with Aberdeen to an own goal, but rather than that providing a platform to build a cup pedigree the four subsequent seasons saw United produce the dismal return of just one quarter-final from eight attempts. It would be wrong to suggest that the continuing lack of cup success was the reason that the board decided Kerr should be edged sideways to become general manager in November 1971. However, it might well have been a factor, suggesting a feeling that after 12 years the man who brought United into the modern era may have taken them as far as he could.

There is a limit to how much any one man can achieve for a football club. In the eyes of the supporters, though, there was some dismay that the man who had dragged United out of the shadow of their greatest rivals for the first time, should be treated in such a manner. Kerr, at the time the longest-serving manager in British senior football, had earned his iconic standing at least in part by enabling United to shed the image of the city's poor relations. So when Kerr's replacement was announced the realisation that they had a former Dundee player and current coach as the new manager, initially at least, left many supporters feeling distinctly underwhelmed.

Of course, Jim McLean quickly won them over. Having signed 17 new players in his first six months in charge (significantly, nine of them were on schoolboy forms) his influence and its effectiveness soon became apparent.

As his second full season as manager was drawing to a close the first signs of the success that he would later bring to Tannadice were beginning to appear. This took the form of a style of football based on the Dutch and the West Germans, then leading the way in developing new ideas.

McLean had gone to study their methods at first hand and described what he learnt from them, 'They wanted to make passes. They wanted to keep the ball on the ground. And they wanted to play possession football. They had a whole approach to the game which gelled with the ideas I was beginning to formulate for myself.'

But those early signs also involved what would prove a key factor in McLean's ultimate successes – the emergence of high-quality, homegrown talent. In those days, promising youngsters still at school were signed by clubs on schoolboy forms, which came to be known as S-forms. The first of United's S-form players to emerge was Graeme Payne, and both he and Andy Gray made their debuts at 17 in August 1973. They appeared regularly throughout the season and in December were joined by a third 17-year old, Dave Narey, in the United team that came back from 3-1 down to earn a draw with champions Celtic in Glasgow.

The Tangerines were on course for an eighth-place finish (out of 18) in the First Division but for Arabs the priority had increasingly become the Scottish Cup, a competition in which the extent of the club's achievement remained those semi-finals in 1963 and 1967.

The early rounds had seen Second Division Airdrie beaten 4-1 at Tannadice, followed by another home tie, this time against a fellow First Division side, Morton. That was most notable for the fact that it was the first match played by United on a Sunday.

Until then the SFA had always prohibited Sunday football but political events forced them to relent. A mineworkers' strike during the winter of 1973–74 led the government to introduce a three-day working week to conserve electricity supplies, with factories and offices instructed to open either from Monday to Wednesday or Thursday to Saturday. Consequently, far fewer people were free on Saturdays to go to football matches, which led the SFA to allow Sundays to be used as an alternative, though all matches had to have early kick-offs because there was also a ban on using floodlights.

The Morton tie was settled in United's favour by a goal from Brian Rankin, his only one for the club, and the quarter-final brought a visit to East End Park, Dunfermline. Until the match was in its dying embers it seemed that was where United's interest would end, continuing the familiar Scottish Cup pattern, because as it entered injury time the home side held a 1-0 lead. Then a last-gasp header from winger Tommy Traynor earned a replay, sending the travelling Arabs home happy – and more than a little relieved.

Captain Doug Smith and his men capitalised fully on their narrow escape, winning 4-0 at Tannadice and thus setting up the club's third Scottish Cup semi-final. The venue was Hampden Park and the opponents were Hearts.

Although there was little to choose between the clubs – both league meetings that season were drawn – the bookmakers made Hearts narrow favourites, apparently because it was the capital club's centenary year and it was felt that would provide additional motivation. Random that may have been, but they nevertheless seemed to merit that judgement when Alan Anderson gave them a first-half lead. The Maroons' subsequent pressure might have seen them increase their advantage but United held firm and then went in search of an equaliser.

However, it didn't appear to be on the cards until salvation came in the shape of Paddy Gardner. Neither the occasion nor the venue was anything new for him, because he had been a member of the Dunfermline team that won the Scottish Cup in 1968, beating Hearts in the final. On his return to the hallowed turf six years on, the midfielder received the ball from a free kick and scored with a thunderous 30-yard drive.

That proved sufficient for United to fight another day and McLean was convinced the first match had produced a performance from the Tangerines that could only be improved upon. When the teams returned to Hampden three days later, a dramatic replay was played out in front of a disappointing crowd of less than 13,000, reflecting the low attendances that were prevalent in Scottish football during the mid-1970s. In that season, despite the increasing optimism that McLean was generating at Tannadice, United had their lowest average home league attendance since their return to the top level, just 5,315.

In the replay the Edinburgh side again gained the ascendancy and when Donald Ford headed them into the lead after 23 minutes it was no more than they deserved. United then lived dangerously and Sandy Davie in goal had to look sharp on more than one occasion to prevent further damage. The second half was a quite different story, however.

Whatever McLean's half-time talk involved, it was certainly effective because the Tangerines returned to the fray a rejuvenated team. They had been threatening the Hearts goal for some time when the equaliser came, though it was from the penalty spot. George Fleming was brought down by Jim Jefferies in the 57th minute and Smith performed his customary efficient job.

Just two minutes later, the still-celebrating Arabs went wild as Graeme Payne embarked on a slalom run through the Hearts defence that ended with the little winger firing past goalkeeper Jim Cruickshank. The 18-year-old Dundonian demonstrated not just composure but a keen sense of occasion as he registered his first senior goal.

That put United ahead for the first time in the tie, but half an hour remained and that seemed an interminable amount of time for the players to defend their lead. In fact, on McLean's orders, they had no intention of doing anything other than seeking to build on it and they created opportunities to do just that.

But none were taken and Hearts made it clear that they had by no means given up the ghost. They, too, attacked at every opportunity in what was now a pulsating tie and it was they who scored next. Substitute Willie Gibson had been on the pitch for eight minutes without having touched the ball but when he did he sent it decisively past Davie for the equaliser.

At 2-2 and with 12 minutes remaining some in the crowd may have wondered whether the teams might now try to run down the clock in the hope of extra time, which would have left more scope to recover from losing a goal. Such considerations wouldn't have lasted long, though, because the very next minute saw the game again turn United's way.

Paddy Gardner launched a cross deep into the Maroons' penalty area and few watching – least of all, it seemed, the Hearts defence – anticipated a shot from that range and angle. But Andy Gray, already mature beyond his years, met the ball on the volley and sent an audacious shot flashing into the net before Cruickshank could move. There was a delayed reaction as Arabs could scarcely believe what they had seen, then the night air was rent asunder in a huge roar as everyone in tangerine celebrated wildly.

The Hearts players, having worked hard to secure an equaliser, seemed shattered to find themselves behind again so soon and never recovered. Archie Knox was on hand to score a fourth in the 86th minute as United sealed the match and made sure it was a case of third time lucky to reach the club's first Scottish Cup Final.

Then what happened?

The following month, the tangerine army went on their first march in support of their club in a Hampden final. That most of them travelled more in hope than expectation was a sign not of defeatism, but of realism. Given that Jock Stein's Celtic had just secured their ninth league championship in a row, while McLean's project was still in its early stages, it was important that United's players gave a good account of themselves on their return to the national stadium. They certainly did, although the outcome was a 3-0 victory for Celtic.

Though naturally disappointed, McLean was not too downhearted, regarding the experience as being of value in providing his players – and the supporters – with a greater understanding of what was required to reach a position where winning trophies could become a reality.

Though not exactly just around the corner, that day would not be long delayed. Victory in a Hampden final, however, was something else; that would be delayed a further 20 years.

v Rangers 3-0

Scottish Premier Division
Tannadice
9 December 1978
Attendance: 15,247

DUNDEE UNITED	RANGERS
McAlpine	McCloy
Stewart	Forsyth
Stark	Dawson
Fleming	Jardine
Hegarty	Jackson
Narey	A. MacDonald
Payne (Addison)	McLean
Holt	Russell (Watson)
Dodds	Johnstone
Kirkwood	Smith
Sturrock	Cooper (Parlane)
Manager: Jim McLean	*Manager:* John Greig

I N seven years as Dundee United manager, Jim McLean had made real progress in shaping the club into one that would have the ability to challenge for the major domestic honours. Certainly there was satisfaction among Arabs in 1974 at seeing their club reach a Scottish Cup Final for the first time, though less satisfaction at the 3-0 defeat by Celtic at Hampden.

But that final was widely seen as a step forward and, after finishing the following season in fourth place – the best then achieved by the club – hopes were high for the first campaign of the new Premier Division.

That is not the way things developed, though, as the season turned out to be a chastening experience when it came down to a last-day escape from relegation – and only on goal difference.

McLean breathed a sigh of relief, then set about ensuring that there would be no repeat. The following two seasons saw the Tangerines improve markedly, claiming fourth place again, then third for the first time.

Despite elevating United to the status of Scotland's third-best club and reaching another Scottish Cup semi-final, the manager remained disappointed in May 1978, 'Our failure to mount a challenge to the "big guns" cast a shadow over Tannadice. Having started off in a buoyant mood, our failure to clinch a League Cup semi-final place… started a temporary downward trend.

'Then came the real reason for most of the disappointment, when our front men stopped finding the net. We have once again asked youngsters to do a man's job in the firing line and, at Premier level, it's just not on.'

More positively, he ventured the opinion that the club's future had never been more secure. Of nearly 50 players on the staff only seven were aged over 24.

Seven of the men who stood firm against Rangers in May 1976 to secure the point that maintained United's place in the Premier Division had left by the time 78/79 started. McLean's influence was seen by the emergence of a crop of fine young players through the youth system – Davie Dodds, Dave Narey and Graeme Payne were now regulars, while John Holt and Billy Kirkwood had played often enough in the previous season to serve notice that they, too, would soon become permanent fixtures. Ray Stewart had broken into the team towards the end of the season and, though only 18, he would be a regular from the start of the new campaign.

Additionally, the only signing of real significance that McLean had made was now the rock on which the team was being built. Paul Hegarty cost £27,500 – then the highest fee the club had paid – when signed as a striker from Hamilton Accies in 1974. But the manager felt his abilities were better suited to defence, where Hegarty built a partnership with Narey that would last for many years.

That third-place finish in 1977/78 meant United were beginning to make people sit up and take notice, but if they were to be regarded as serious challengers they had to be capable of competing with the Old Firm. McLean was aware that 'competing' meant being able to beat the Glasgow clubs on more than the odd occasion, but that was a challenge his players had yet to demonstrate they could meet.

The 1978/79 season began slowly with no victories in the first four league games, despite three of them being at Tannadice. But the next three were all won as United built some momentum and a point at Ibrox followed by a 1-0 victory over Celtic at Tannadice propelled them into second place. Then, after defeating Partick Thistle at the end of October, United took over top spot, a position they had retained six weeks later when the time came for the season's second league meeting with Rangers.

In the Premier Division's first three seasons United had faced the Old Firm a total of 24 times – and had won just three of them. Even worse, in Rangers' six visits to Tannadice during that period not only had United been unable to claim a win, they hadn't scored a single goal. It seemed the men in tangerine were struck by stage fright whenever Celtic or Rangers appeared on the scene.

Before 1978/79 got under way McLean had left his players in no doubt as to his determination that the dismal sequence must improve and already Celtic had been defeated. But, as the reigning champions, Rangers were still regarded by the bookmakers as favourites for this Tannadice clash.

United came roaring out of the blocks, refusing to give Rangers an opportunity to settle. Peter McCloy was forced to dive at the feet of Billy Kirkwood in the first minute but just two minutes later the big goalkeeper was beaten for the first time. Payne floated a free kick into the penalty box, where Dodds rose above the static Rangers defence to bullet a header into the top corner.

McLean had been saying for some time that his players were a match for any team, but they needed to find the confidence and self-belief to prove it. As United took control in an attempt to build on their lead, it seemed that barrier was finally being pushed aside. That said, luck also played its part because Bobby Russell should have equalised but instead hit the bar, then Derek Johnstone saw his shot from the rebound brilliantly blocked by Hamish McAlpine.

George Fleming – a huge favourite with Arabs – was running the game from midfield, his experience also bringing out the best in youngsters Payne and John Holt as United remained in control. So it was fitting that, when the lead was doubled after 20 minutes, it came from a move that was both started and finished by the tireless Fleming.

He created the opening with a clever reverse header to Paul Sturrock which wrong-footed the Rangers defence and 'Luggy' raced clear before sending over a cross which was side-footed past McCloy by the onrushing Fleming. It was a tremendous goal, worthy of a team aspiring to be champions, exhibiting the inventiveness, pace and clinical finishing that United were increasingly demonstrating.

Rangers were rattled, but hit back and full-back Ray Stewart had to look sharp to head a Johnstone header off the line. United remained in the ascendancy, though, and neither their players nor supporters wanted to hear the half-time whistle, fearful lest it stalled their team's momentum.

They needn't have worried because the men in tangerine picked up where they had left off and were not at all disappointed to note that Russell, Rangers' most dangerous player, failed to re-appear for the second half. Although the Ibrox men pressed, the United defence, in which Narey and Hegarty were enhancing their already growing reputation as a formidable force, held firm.

As the match entered its final ten minutes a further goal seemed more likely to come from the home side and that eventually proved the case. The United support had been in full voice all afternoon and wanted to see icing applied to the cake before the points were secured beyond doubt, though when the opportunity arose it did initially cause some tension among Arabs.

That was because the Terrors were awarded a penalty in the 82nd minute – so why the tension? Amazingly, United players had failed to score with 17 of the last 27 penalties the team had been awarded.

There had already been four misses that season and it seemed players were reluctant to take one given the additional pressure brought by that poor record. Narey stepped forward and took responsibility on this occasion. He had never before taken a penalty for United but his confidence may have stemmed from the fact that the previous month he had become the first United player to win a full cap for Scotland. Cool as could be, Narey clipped the ball home without any fuss, amid wild scenes of celebration in the Shed.

Now United's title aspirations had to be taken seriously. Rangers don't often lose anywhere by three goals and, surprising as it may seem, in more than three decades since then they have not lost again by that margin at Tannadice. That day was a watershed for McLean's team, not just the win but the manner of it instilling in them the belief that they need no longer enter the Old Firm arena with trepidation.

Then what happened?

Armed with their new-found self-belief, the following week United travelled to Celtic and came from behind to claim a point. Now the title challenge was demonstrably a genuine one and confidence was high going into 1979. However, a harsh winter wreaked such havoc that, in the days before undersoil heating, United were able to complete only three matches in the first nine weeks of the year. All were lost, among them some measure of revenge for Rangers who scored the only goal of the match at Ibrox.

That caused McLean's men to relinquish top spot momentarily, but they regained it after winning their next match and were still there – uninterrupted – three months later after drawing with Aberdeen in May to complete their league programme.

Crucially, however, the Old Firm had had even more fixtures fall foul of the conditions. The two Glasgow clubs still had four matches to play after United's season had ended and eventually both of them overhauled the Tangerines.

The critical period turned out to be April, when United faced Celtic twice and Rangers once. They did beat Celtic at home for the second time although they couldn't manage a Tannadice 'double double', as a 2-1 reverse at the hands of Rangers undermined the title challenge.

Then Celtic won by the same score in Glasgow, their only victory over United that season. After that encounter McLean commented, 'We just aren't good enough to win the league yet.' That final word was used advisedly, indicating an optimism which was to prove justified in the long term.

Ultimately, United finished four points behind Celtic and one behind Rangers, with a record against the Old Firm of won three, lost three, drawn two. Thus third place was clinched for the second time in a row, which reflected remarkable progress in the seven seasons since McLean had taken over.

The impact made by United that season was confirmed when their fellow professionals chose Hegarty as Player of the Year and Stewart as Young Player of the Year.

v Aberdeen 3-0

Scottish League Cup Final Replay
Dens Park
12 December 1979
Attendance: 28,984

DUNDEE UNITED	ABERDEEN
McAlpine	Clark
Stark	Kennedy
Kopel	Rougvie
Fleming	McLeish
Hegarty	Garner
Narey	Miller
Bannon	Strachan
Sturrock	McGhee (Jarvie)
Pettigrew	Archibald
Holt	McMaster
Kirkwood	Scanlon (Hamilton)
Manager: Jim McLean	*Manager:* Alex Ferguson

THROUGHOUT the then 70-year existence of Dundee United, back-to-back third-place finishes at the top level would have been regarded as a tremendous achievement. It would also have been regarded as an over-achievement that could not be sustained.

Jim McLean subscribed to the first of those, but not to the second – he wanted the progress made in his seven and a half-years as manager to be seen not as an end in itself, but as a means to an end. He viewed United's strong showing in 1978/79 as a springboard to greater things, specifically the club winning a major trophy for the first time.

During the close-season, McLean let it be known that he believed the addition of two players to his squad would enable United to challenge Glasgow's big two for honours. Although bringing talented players through their coaching system had been the basis of the club's growing reputation, the United boss accepted that the next step would require entering the transfer market.

It was typical of the man that rarely had he reached for the Tannadice chequebook, though when he did so his record was patchy. His most successful foray came early; within a month of his appointment, he paid just £7,000 to Hearts for George Fleming. Seven years later the midfielder was still a key component in the team, his experience an invaluable resource from which the young players benefitted greatly.

For sure, the arrival of Paul Hegarty for £27,500 in 1974 had already proved an outstanding success, albeit that he was bought as a striker before being converted into a central defender.

That created a record fee paid by the club and it was broken in 1975 and 1977 when strikers Tom McAdam (£40,000) and John Bourke (£60,000) were signed from Dumbarton. Neither justified their fees with the club delighted to accept an offer of £60,000 for McAdam from Celtic in 1977 at a time when the player was not in the team. Bourke walked out after a year with £40,000 of his fee eventually being recouped from Kilmarnock.

So when, in August 1979, McLean established another record in exchange for another striker, some supporters were a little sceptical. At least on this occasion the player was a Scotland international and a proven goalscorer at the top level, Motherwell receiving £100,000 – the first six-figure fee paid by United – in return for Willie Pettigrew. Over the next two seasons, he would more than repay that outlay.

With the club on a firm financial footing, United directors had never denied McLean the necessary cash when he identified a player he believed would enhance his squad. However, the first six-figure fee had been received when Aston Villa paid £115,000 for Andy Gray in 1975. Gray was the first of the players brought through the system at Tannadice to generate a big fee and the second was to occur less than a month after Pettigrew's arrival.

An offer of £400,000 was received from West Ham United for full-back Ray Stewart and it was, literally, one that could not be refused. It was understood to be twice the value that McLean had placed on the player, who was just 19 and had made fewer than 50 league appearances in tangerine. McLean was convinced that he had a more than capable replacement in another of his emerging young players, Derek Stark. The 20-year-old Fifer took over the number two jersey and never looked back.

McLean still required the final piece of his jigsaw and at the end of October he found it. A sizeable chunk of the Stewart fee was used to bring Eamonn Bannon back to Scotland with United giving Chelsea £165,000, £50,000 less than the attacking midfielder had cost the London club when he left Hearts nine months earlier.

At the time that was the highest transfer fee ever paid by a Scottish club and most Arabs were astounded, not just because their club had been the one to pay it, but that the normally cautious McLean was the manager who had driven the deal.

Bannon made his debut against Raith Rovers at Tannadice in the first leg of the Scottish League Cup quarter-final. By that time United had repeated their feat of the previous season and were sitting top of the Premier Division. Becoming champions of Scotland remained McLean's ultimate aim but that would involve a long haul and one of the cup competitions offered a more direct route to a first major trophy.

The League Cup was a competition in which United had never distinguished themselves. Even after almost two decades at the top level, a single semi-final appearance (in 1964) represented the peak of their achievement but, having been drawn against lower league opposition for the third time in that season's competition (Airdrieonians and Queen's Park had been eliminated in the earlier rounds) they had been presented with an excellent opportunity to claim a place in the last four.

Bannon didn't manage to find the net as United laboured to a 0-0 draw with Raith, though he did the following Saturday in a 3-0 league win at Aberdeen. Alex Ferguson's team had themselves reached the League Cup quarter-final where, having already knocked out Rangers, they were in the process of making it an Old Firm double by eliminating Celtic. United did just enough to join them in the semi-final, Hegarty scoring the only goal at Kirkcaldy as they advanced by the narrowest of margins.

For the first time in 20 years both Celtic and Rangers were absent from the penultimate stage of the League Cup, a welcome development as far as McLean and his players were concerned. But they could have been forgiven had they begun to believe that this just might be their year when the semi-final draw paired the other two Premier Division clubs, Aberdeen and Morton, leaving United to face First Division Hamilton Accies.

Dunfermline's East End Park had never previously hosted a major semi-final but it was the venue for what proved to be a historic occasion for Dundee United.

Torrential rain had made the pitch a quagmire but that didn't explain United's tentative approach; it seemed they suffered a bout of nerves, though they went in at half-time with a 2-1 lead. It was clear McLean had used the break to settle those nerves because his team overran Hamilton in the second half with a decisive 6-2 victory the outcome, including doubles for Billy Kirkwood and Paul Sturrock.

United's opponents in the final would be Aberdeen, who then sat three places ahead of them in the league table and had recent experience of a final, having won the League Cup three years earlier. For some years a friendly rivalry based on mutual respect had been developing between McLean and Ferguson. Neither had yet led their clubs to a major trophy and this was the first time they had been pitched into direct confrontation with a prize at stake.

Hampden Park was a dreich place on 8 December 1979, but that was a risk inherent in scheduling cup finals for December. The teams and the crowd of 27,156 tried their best to make the match fit the occasion but, although it contained more goalmouth action than the scoreline suggested, it wasn't exactly incident-packed.

United went on the offensive in the first quarter but Aberdeen then wrested control and retained it for most of the remainder of normal time. Had they capitalised on one of several chances they would have taken the trophy back with them to the Granite City, but United also defended competently and so the match went into extra time.

By then, the heavy conditions and the weight of the occasion had left both sides flagging, meaning the additional half-hour was characterised more by the determination to avoid mistakes than to create a winning goal.

McLean pulled no punches in his after-match comments, 'I was really disappointed with our performance. Aberdeen outplayed us, especially in midfield, though if we hold the kind of luck which helped us survive we must have a great chance of winning the cup. We didn't deserve a draw.' That was rather harsh, though doubtless it was aimed at his players as much as the world at large.

Ferguson – even then a master of the mind game – was also intent on sending a message, to his own players as well as United's, 'I don't think there is any doubt that the replay presents a more difficult challenge to us. It's probably true to say that we handed the psychological advantage to Dundee United after having so much of the play and failing to win on Saturday.'

Showing a level of common sense with which it had not often been associated, the Scottish League decided it was neither fair nor wise to expect 30,000 fans to make a round trip of up to 300 miles for a second time in four days, especially in wintry conditions.

So the replay was switched to Dens Park, where the crowd was only marginally bigger than at Hampden but, in a stadium packed to capacity, the contrast in the atmosphere generated could hardly have been greater.

They also saw an entirely different encounter. McLean had vowed his team would be much more positive than in the first match and he did not disappoint the United fans, who saw the Tangerines dominant, in control almost from start to finish on a treacherous pitch with the goalmouths particularly muddy.

Whereas 120 minutes had failed to produce a goal at Hampden, it took only 15 for the deadlock to be broken at Dens Park. Bobby Clark had to dive full-length to save a 20-yard drive from Kirkwood as United's pressure mounted, but in the next attack the Aberdeen keeper was beaten. Stark went on a marauding run down the left wing before sending a low cross into the penalty area. As Clark and Doug Rougvie became entangled, Pettigrew darted in between them to drive the ball into the net.

Despite the heavy pitch, United were playing their normal passing game with Bannon living up to his tag as Scotland's most expensive player in his role as midfield creator. In contrast Aberdeen relied on the long ball, but with Hegarty and Narey imperious that was a tactic never likely to succeed. Frank Kopel and Kirkwood again had good chances to increase United's lead but by half-time there was no change to the score.

The second half maintained the pattern of the first with much of the play in the Aberdeen half. So when United increased their lead, with a goal of genuine quality, the only real surprise was that it had taken so long. Bannon won the ball and found John Holt, who fed Sturrock on the left. Luggy beat two defenders before sending in a looping cross that Pettigrew reached before Clark to send a glancing header into the net.

Just over an hour had been played, but the brief invasion of the pitch by Arabs at the Provost Road end left nobody in any doubt that they regarded the cup as theirs already.

Such assumptions have a habit of coming back to bite those who make them but on this occasion, such was United's control of the match and the disconsolate demeanour of several Aberdeen players following the second goal that it didn't seem far-fetched.

United's players were taking nothing for granted and continued to drive forward. In the 77th minute came the *coup de grâce*. Sturrock collected the ball on the halfway line and outpaced the Aberdeen defenders, then checked back before getting in his shot. The ball seemed to be heading for Clark's far corner but it deflected off Willie Miller into the opposite one, sending United's army of fans into raptures.

It was no more than the team's performance merited and it was a more than fitting manner in which to end the club's 70-year wait for a major trophy. Dry eyes were few and far between among Arabs as captain Hegarty raised the Scottish League Cup to a huge roar of acclaim.

Never one of the more emotional managers in Scotland, McLean had allowed himself a little leeway after the third goal, leaping out of the dugout and performing a joyous dance on the touchline. With the cup still being paraded to the crowd he said, 'All the years of effort were worth it in the end. Our play tonight fulfilled all that promise, it was a magnificent performance.'

Exactly eight years after leaving his coaching job at Dens Park, the United manager made his return and the team he had painstakingly created ensured it was a triumphant one.

Then what happened?

Bannon's hugely influential display was not lost on the watching national team manager, Jock Stein. Seven days later the midfielder became the third United player to win a full cap for Scotland. It was only seven weeks after he had joined the club yet that short period had seen him win a League Cup medal and become a Scotland international.

v **Dundee** 5-1

20

Scottish Cup Third Round
Tannadice
30 January 1980
Attendance: 18,604

DUNDEE UNITED	DUNDEE
McAlpine	Donaldson
Stark	Millar
Kopel	Schaedler
Fleming	McLaren
Hegarty	Glennie
Phillip	Shirra
Bannon (Kirkwood)	Murphy (Barr)
Sturrock	Mackie
Pettigrew (Dodds)	Pirie
Holt	Sinclair
Graeme Payne	Redford
Manager: Jim McLean	*Manager:* Tommy Gemmell

WINNING a major trophy for the first time in their history was important in its own right. It cemented Dundee United's status as one of Scotland's leading clubs and showed the psychological barrier of securing that first success had been surmounted.

Further glory now beckoned, but in the eyes of Arabs the first step had been taken on the road to claiming the title of the city's 'big' club. For decades, as a part-time club, there could be no serious argument that United were cast in the shadow of Dundee FC. By 1960 the Dens Park club had spent all but two of their Scottish League seasons in the top division, while United had spent a mere four of theirs at that level.

But during the two decades since then the pendulum had swung decisively in United's direction to the extent that they had not been out of the top division while Dundee were relegated at the end of the Premier Division's first season – and had taken three years to return. The 1979/80 season saw the resumption of derbies and thus far home advantage had proved decisive, with United winning two to Dundee's one.

So in terms of recent form and the standing that flows from finishing in the upper reaches of the league table, United were certainly the pre-eminent club in Dundee as the 1980s dawned. Winning the Scottish League Cup had merely confirmed that, although supporters of Dundee didn't accept it. They pointed to the fact that their club had won the Scottish Cup (as long ago as 1910, the year after Dundee Hibernian were founded) and were champions of Scotland in 1962. Add to that three Scottish League Cup wins and it meant their supporters were able constantly to taunt Arabs that their club had won five major trophies, while United had won none.

That could no longer be said but Dundee were still some way ahead in the honours stakes and, for most Arabs, the 1979 Scottish League Cup win was a means of saying to their city rivals, 'We're coming after you.'

Needless to say, for supporters of Dundee the United triumph was unwelcome – and doubly so since it was achieved on *their* territory at Dens Park. But the draw for the

Scottish Cup now offered the chance for their club to challenge the assumption that the order of football in the city had shifted.

Although in total the clubs had then faced each other in the three major competitions on 67 occasions, they had been drawn together in the Scottish Cup only four times. The clubs were never in the same division at the time, but such was the close-fought nature of those ties they all went to a replay.

The first Scottish Cup derbies took place in 1928. In a six-goal thriller at Tannadice, United scored a late equaliser against their much-fancied neighbours but Dundee won the replay by the only goal.

A year later the venues were reversed – and so was the outcome. This time the first match was at Dens and it ended 1-1, with United then causing an upset by winning the replay 1-0.

The other two occasions came during the 1950s. The biggest crowd at a city derby – 38,000 – packed Dens Park in 1951 and saw United score two late goals to earn a 2-2 draw. This time home advantage was not enough and Dundee advanced after winning 1-0. In 1956, as usual United were given little chance but they again battled to a 2-2 draw, only to lose the replay 3-0.

But that was the only Scottish Cup tie between the two decided by more than a single goal, illustrating the intensity of the rivalry and the ability of United to use it to raise their game and often hold their own against the odds.

That, then, was the history; after a gap of 24 years United and Dundee prepared to resume battle in the Scottish Cup.

Seven weeks earlier Jim McLean's players had marked the high point in the club's history with that League Cup win, but since then it seemed they were suffering a hangover from the headiness of it all. Of the five Premier Division matches played, three had been lost and only one had been won, leaving the Terrors, incredibly, languishing second-bottom in the table. The win had come against Dundee and was the second derby success that season at Tannadice.

Harsh winter conditions meant that neither club had played for three weeks and Tannadice had been unplayable when the tie was scheduled the previous Saturday. The weather relented just enough to allow it to go ahead on the Wednesday evening and the torrid action it produced would prove more than enough to make the crowd oblivious to the bitter cold.

The Dundee tactics soon became evident. Perhaps because they knew they couldn't compete man-for-man with United their players made it clear their intent was to try and prevent the Tangerines building any kind of rhythm by resorting to a strong-arm approach.

As the tackles flew in, Stuart McLaren and Jim Murphy were shown yellow cards within the first quarter of an hour and that set the pattern for what was an intensely physical tie. Not that United lacked players who could look after themselves and the likes of Derek Stark, George Fleming and Frank Kopel certainly gave as good as they got. But it was up front, where most of the United players were less robust, that the Dundee men focussed their attention.

Meanwhile, with the emphasis on attack, United held the upper hand. But it took almost half an hour for the first goal to arrive and it came from a piece of sheer brilliance from Eamonn Bannon, who was already looking excellent value for his record £165,000 fee. He beat three Dundee men in a superb run through the middle before playing in Willie Pettigrew, who calmly placed his shot beyond goalkeeper Ally Donaldson.

Dundee now had to chase an equaliser and they thought they had done just that after 37 minutes. Peter Mackie crossed from the right and Jim Shirra dived to head the ball strongly beyond Hamish McAlpine's dive. The referee awarded the goal but United's players, led by captain Paul Hegarty, surrounded him claiming that Shirra had been offside. After consulting the linesman, the referee changed his mind and gave United a free kick. Cue pandemonium from players and fans in dark blue as they in turn protested, but the decision stood.

Peter Millar allowed his frustration to get the better of him and became the third Dens player to find his way into the ref's book as United's lead remained 1-0 at half-time.

Bannon had been United's driving force in the first half so there was some concern when he failed to re-appear for the second. A groin injury had failed to respond to treatment but Arabs needn't have been concerned because, before his replacement Billy Kirkwood had even touched the ball, the Tangerines had doubled their lead. In the 49th minute a cross from Graeme Payne reached Iain Phillip, whose shot was blocked. But the ball ran to Paul Sturrock who wasted no time in firing it past Donaldson.

The reaction of the Dundee players was to take out their frustration with a series of crude tackles. On 55 minutes Kirkwood and McLaren clashed off the ball and after the United midfielder was left rolling on the track, the Dundee man was booked for a second time and sent off.

United lost no time in cashing in on their numerical advantage. Four minutes later, substitute Les Barr handled in the box and a penalty was awarded. Sturrock took it but Donaldson pulled off a fine save, though his heroics didn't get his team off the hook. The ball hadn't left the area before it reached Pettigrew who quickly planted it in the net for his second and United's third.

That did nothing to prevent the behaviour of the men in dark blue deteriorating even further and after 62 minutes they were reduced to nine men. Eric Sinclair disgracefully threw a punch at Hegarty, presenting the referee with arguably his most straightforward decision of the whole match. Once again United quickly took advantage and six minutes later Pettigrew completed his hat-trick. Again Sturrock was involved in the lead-up to the goal, his pass to Pettigrew allowing the striker to beat Donaldson with some style.

At 4-0 with a quarter of the match still remaining and Dundee two men short the prospect of a real drubbing for the Dens Park outfit was on the cards. United certainly didn't ease off, but Dundee decided that a damage limitation exercise was their only option, bringing everyone behind the ball – and keeping them there.

It seemed their ploy had been successful until six minutes from the end, when United won another penalty. Having already been booked, Millar could consider himself extremely fortunate not to become the third Dundee dismissal of the evening when he hauled down Sturrock in the box. Luggy's miss with the earlier spot-kick would have been a factor in another player taking this one, but so too was the desire to offer Pettigrew the opportunity to increase his tally. The number nine didn't pass it up, blasting the ball into the net to become the only player – before or since – to score four times for United in the derby.

McLean then withdrew Pettigrew to enable him to receive a thoroughly-deserved standing ovation from the ecstatic United crowd.

Billy Pirie's last-minute counter was greeted with ironic cheers by Arabs who would have preferred a repeat of the famous 1965 score, but were more than satisfied with the most decisive derby Scottish Cup victory ever.

Dundee United's Greatest Games

Then what happened?

United didn't make any further progress in the competition, losing disappointingly by the only goal to Rangers at Ibrox in the next round.

From that point their league form did improve, however, and McLean's men finished the season in fourth place, above Rangers for the first time. A mere six goals were conceded at home – still by some distance their lowest in a league season.

Having played in all but one of the club's 51 competitive matches, Pettigrew completed a highly successful first season as leading marksman with 22 in all competitions, making him the second-highest scorer in Scotland. His double in the Scottish League Cup Final meant he had written himself into United's folklore.

The SFA took a dim view of Dundee's indiscipline in the cup tie and fined the club for having two men sent off and another three booked. That was the least of their worries because they finished the season ninth in the Premier Division and returned to the First Division just a year after leaving it.

v Celtic 3-0

Scottish League Cup Semi-Final Second Leg
Celtic Park
19 November 1980
Attendance: 19,700

DUNDEE UNITED	CELTIC
McAlpine	Bonner
Holt	McGrain
Kopel	Reid
Phillip	Aitken
Hegarty	McAdam
Narey	Weir
Bannon	Provan
Payne	McCluskey (MacDonald)
Pettigrew (Kirkwood)	McGarvey (Doyle)
Sturrock	Burns
Dodds	Nicholas
Manager: Jim McLean	*Manager:* Billy McNeill

WINNING a trophy for the first time naturally left everyone associated with Dundee United hungry for more. When the Scottish League Cup began its 35th season in 1980, as holders United were the team to beat. Over four months involving a total of 11 ties they did actually taste defeat – twice – although given the competition's format, with all rounds before the final played over two legs, neither proved irrecoverable.

Nobody with any knowledge of football would have predicted United's stuttering start to the 1980/81 Premier Division campaign – and it brought with it an unwanted record for manager Jim McLean. Six months earlier he was in charge when United won their first trophy in what was, as a consequence, their best season. In stark contrast, just months later he was in charge when the club made their worst start to a season in their 71-year history.

Not one of the first nine league games was won, something that had never happened before, even to Tannadice squads of much poorer quality than McLean's, which then included four full Scotland internationals.

Although only three of those opening nine league matches had been lost, such poor form had nonetheless left the Tangerines languishing in seventh position. McLean was not the type of man simply to put that dismal run down to a hangover from the previous season, not least since it stretched into the middle of October. But neither was he the type to panic and, although he did spend £75,000 to sign Partick Thistle midfielder Ian Gibson, he refused to waver in his belief in the squad, convinced it was only a matter of time before they came good again.

In fairness, it should be said that same period saw United record their biggest win in European competition. A place in the UEFA Cup was part of the reward for winning the Scottish League Cup and the first round sent United to Poland, a country not previously visited. Their opponents were Slask Wroclaw and at the time Polish football was highly regarded, particularly at international level. So after defending confidently while under sustained pressure, returning from the first leg with the score at 0-0 was a more than satisfactory outcome for McLean and his men.

The pattern of the second leg was somewhat different. Although Arabs must have believed United were capable of getting the victory that would take them into the next round, none could have foreseen a seven-goal bonanza. But some powerful attacking play allied to clinical finishing left the Poles chasing shadows as the Terrors lived up to their nickname, winning 7-2. Unfortunately, faced with better-quality opposition in the second round, United exited to Belgian club Lokeren on the away goals rule.

By then that elusive first Premier Division win had been recorded and United had progressed to the semi-finals of the Scottish League Cup. The first two rounds had been straightforward with comprehensive wins home and away against Second Division sides East Fife and Cowdenbeath, but the following two rounds, against clubs from the First Division, proved more problematic.

The visit to Motherwell was not seen as a potential banana skin with the Lanarkshire club then in the middle of a three-year absence from the top level. But the first leg of the third-round tie proved to be an uncomfortable occasion with McLean relieved at the end of it that his team had not suffered greater damage than a 2-1 defeat.

At Tannadice, United again found it difficult to get the better of their lower league opponents. Despite levelling the score, they allowed Motherwell to regain the lead and only a late equaliser took the tie to extra time.

To McLean's consternation, Motherwell promptly scored again, leaving the holders facing elimination. But the men who had taken United to that first major trophy were determined not to relinquish their hold on it and dug deep, eventually scoring twice to secure their place in the quarter-final.

That had been much too close for comfort and with Clydebank forming the barrier between them and a last-four place that seemed to offer the players the opportunity for some payback to their loyal support. But they failed to do so, again losing the away leg by 2-1 and, with United then still without a league win, that prompted media speculation as to why the team had gone off the boil.

But just four days later Kilmarnock were beaten in the Premier Division and, with the monkey finally off their backs, United began to rediscover the kind of form that had served them so well the previous season. When Clydebank came to Tannadice for the second leg there was never any question about the outcome, United winning 4-1 to set up a semi-final with Celtic.

Even though United were the holders, few of their supporters could have viewed the prospect of facing the Glasgow club over two games with much enthusiasm. Already that season United had lost 2-0 at Celtic Park in the league but it was the club's cup record against them over many years that cast a shadow over any meeting in one of the knockout competitions.

In all, the two clubs had met 14 times in the Scottish League Cup and only once had United emerged with a victory. That was in 1965 and even then it didn't do them any good, as it came in a section from which only Celtic ultimately progressed.

United had made great strides since then and, no less pertinently, the Celtic of the early 1980s did not bear comparison with the Celtic of the late 1960s. Nonetheless, the expectation by most was that, particularly with the second leg at home, Celtic were most likely to reach the final.

The first match took place on a cold Wednesday evening at Tannadice. United dominated after Eamonn Bannon gave them a first-half lead with a stunning volley but couldn't find another and a late equaliser from Charlie Nicholas came as a body blow to Arabs' hopes of a return to Hampden for the second time in a year.

The return a week later saw Glasgow shrouded in the rainy conditions and all-pervading dampness which all too often, it seems, engulfs that great city. Some United fans viewed that as an omen because exactly a year earlier those were precisely the conditions in which their team had defeated Hamilton Accies to progress to the final of the same competition.

Such optimism was commendable, though it resembled more a clutching at straws, first because the match was not being played at a neutral venue and secondly because hooped jerseys were the only thing that Celtic had in common with Hamilton.

Scottish football attendances were at something of a low ebb, yet it nonetheless seems strange that less than 20,000 thought it worthwhile being at Celtic Park for what was effectively a one-off tie for a place in the final.

McLean was upbeat prior to the match, 'We must not allow Celtic to take control and come at us. Our attitude must be as positive as theirs. We are the holders and enjoyed the taste of success last season and we desperately want to experience that great feeling again. It will be difficult, but by no means impossible.'

As it happened, the most telling of those comments was the first, because not only did United not allow Celtic to come at them, they started on the front foot and with all guns blazing.

Celtic's Ireland international Pat Bonner had to save at full stretch from Paul Sturrock after three minutes and 60 seconds later, United took the lead. Bannon gathered the ball on the left and evaded tackles before finding Graeme Payne. The little winger passed inside to Willie Pettigrew, who flicked the ball into the net, leaving the Celtic players and fans stunned.

United had quickly mastered the conditions while Celtic had not and that was not a temporary state of affairs because the Tangerines completely dominated play. Pettigrew had the ball in the net again midway through the half, but it was ruled out for offside. Another header from United's leading scorer flashed past the post with the home defence wide open and the only time Celtic threatened was just before half-time when Hamish McAlpine superbly parried a shot from George McCluskey, with Frank Kopel then on hand to clear.

Predictably, Celtic were fired up on the re-start and determined to assert their authority. But not only were they unable to trouble the United defence, they soon found themselves two behind. After 53 minutes United attacked brilliantly on the counter, winning a corner. Bannon's kick found Sturrock and he stabbed a foot in front of a defender to divert the ball into the net and send the travelling Arabs into wild celebrations.

That blow effectively sucked what resistance remained from the home side and minutes later it should have been three for United when a Payne shot smacked against the crossbar with Bonner beaten. Then a Paul Hegarty header was cleared off the line by Danny McGrain as the holders regained command.

The crowd had reduced significantly after United's second goal and with ten minutes remaining almost all of those Celtic supporters who had retained some faith decided it was time that they, too, should head for the exits. That was when Pettigrew fed Sturrock and Luggy headed for the byline before sending over a cross tailor-made for the head of Davie Dodds, who decisively sent it past Bonner for 3-0.

It was an outstanding performance by McLean's team, which contained ten of the players who had won the trophy a year earlier. On a pitch that resembled porridge, their unswerving determination to return to the final was evident from the kick-off and even the final score failed to reflect the extent to which they controlled first the pitch and then the match.

Then what happened?

Typically, McLean refused to get carried away but he revealed that his pre-match comments had been based on the confidence he had sensed in his players, 'I knew we were capable of playing this type of football and indeed have given similar displays many times. But not against Celtic and certainly not in Glasgow. We didn't change our tactics or do anything different. It was just that the players went into the tie with confidence and took the chances we had missed in the past.'

The same evening Dundee beat Ayr United on aggregate to secure their place in the final and set up the biggest city derby in history.

v Dundee 3-0

22

Scottish League Cup Final
Dens Park
6 December 1980
Attendance: 24,446

DUNDEE UNITED	DUNDEE
McAlpine	R Geddes
Holt	Barr
Kopel	Schaedler
Phillip	Fraser
Hegarty	Glennie
Narey	McGeachie
Bannon	Mackie
Payne	Stephen
Pettigrew	Sinclair
Sturrock	Williamson (Scrimgeour)
Dodds	A. Geddes (Shirra)
Manager: Jim McLean	*Manager:* Donald Mackay

T HE city's two clubs first met as far back as 1915, when Dundee beat Dundee Hibs in a friendly. The first competitive meeting didn't occur for a further ten years, by which time the Hibs had become United and the men from Tannadice had reached the First Division for the first time.

Although by 1980 the two had met 69 times in the major competitions, they had faced each other in the Scottish League Cup on only ten occasions. All but the first two of these (in 1956) were in sectional ties and United had recorded five wins to Dundee's three.

Fourteen years had elapsed without the clubs meeting in the League Cup, but when that sequence was broken it came in the form of a blockbuster. With the exception of Celtic and Rangers, a cup final between two clubs from the same city is extremely rare in Britain, even involving participants from London, which has 12 clubs.

By 1980 it had happened in the Scottish Cup only six times in the 20th century – and never without one of the Old Firm clubs being involved. The only time there had been a Hearts–Hibs final was also in the Scottish Cup but that was in 1896. In the Scottish League Cup, again excluding Glasgow's big two, there had been just two all-Glasgow clashes, both involving Celtic and Partick Thistle.

To have a major final contested by Dundee and Dundee United was not just a momentous occasion for the city, it was a momentous event in football in Scotland and, indeed, in Britain.

Mathematically, the chances of the two teams meeting in a national final were not great in normal circumstances. But in 1980/81 they were remote because the clubs were a division apart.

Dundee had been relegated from the Premier Division in May 1980 and at the mid-point of the following season they had put together a run of 17 games unbeaten in their attempt to make an instant return to the top level. Added to that, the Dark Blues had earned their place in the final by defeating reigning Premier Division champions Aberdeen at Pittodrie in the quarter-final.

A year earlier the Scottish Football League had acted with commendable common sense in scheduling the replayed League Cup Final for Dens Park. Once the two Dundee clubs had qualified for the 1980 final initial indications were the SFL regarded 1979 as a one-off, involving a replay and not the first match which, like every final since the competition began in 1946, had taken place at Hampden Park.

However, both city clubs were adamant that the match should be staged in Dundee. Jim McLean suggested that any advantage could be avoided by deciding the final over two legs, but that ran counter to the competition's rules. Eventually, the two clubs asked the SFL to toss a coin to decide which ground would host the match and the management committee agreed.

With Dens Park having been the scene of their first major trophy win, United were not too disappointed to have lost the right to stage the final but of greater concern to McLean was how the event would reflect on the city, 'First and foremost we want to win, but almost as important is that the final should be well-ordered. There is always a danger from the hooligan element.'

His comments, no doubt well-intentioned, should be seen in the context of the dreadful aftermath of that year's Scottish Cup Final at Hampden Park when a riot on the pitch involving followers of Celtic and Rangers shamed Scotland worldwide. But those events – and the sectarianism that fuelled them – had no equivalent back story in Dundee, where nobody could recall any violence before, during or after a city derby match. The fact the most important one of all was about to take place did not, to the vast majority of Dundonians, suggest any likelihood of that changing.

The match would have been a sell-out anyway but the demand for tickets was increased because ground redevelopment under way meant the capacity was 5,000 less than the 29,000 who had been at the previous year's replay. Unusually, the ground was full almost an hour prior to kick-off as both sets of fans gave full vent to their repertoire of songs. The uniquely Dundonian nature of the occasion was completed when the referee appointed was the city's own Bob Valentine.

It is frequently stated that the form book goes out the window in derbies and, in common with most clichés, it contains more than an element of truth. The same can be said of cup finals, but the general expectation that the Premier Division side would win merely heaped further pressure on the shoulders of McLean and his players.

That December is hardly the ideal time to be playing a cup final was amply demonstrated by the fact that the normal frost was compounded by snow flurries prior to the match and this left the pitch pockmarked in white and generally in a treacherous condition. That had the potential to act as a leveller, although the pressure of being favourites seemed to have a positive effect on the United players who were clearly fired up and assumed a dominance that they rarely relinquished throughout.

Despite that, the first half fell some way short of the cut and thrust expected of a final. Until the final minute of the half the nearest thing to a goal came when Dundee's Eric Sinclair had the ball in the net, but was adjudged to have fouled Hamish McAlpine before putting it there. Paul Sturrock was Dundee's tormentor-in-chief but neither he nor his colleagues were able to finish any of the chances they created.

Then, just as it seemed the first half would end goalless, United struck. Wide on the left, Sturrock received a throw-in on the edge of the penalty box and turned George McGeachie inside out before chipping an inch-perfect cross on to the head of Davie Dodds.

The striker was completely unmarked as he rose to meet the ball and he sent in a header that bounced down and quickly up off the hard surface, deceiving goalkeeper

Bobby Geddes on its way into the net. After keeping the scoreline blank until that point through disciplined defensive work, the goal must have come as a shattering blow to the First Division side.

In the second half Sturrock didn't just maintain his pace and power, he stepped it up a gear. With Graeme Payne and Eamonn Bannon running the game in midfield he saw plenty of the ball in his role of wide attacker and United never looked like relinquishing their lead. Payne came close to doubling United's advantage with a fine drive from 20 yards that Geddes just managed to turn over the bar as the Terrors turned the screw.

As for Dundee, their only real threat came when their most effective player, 17-year-old Ray Stephen, went down in the box under a challenge by McAlpine. A penalty might well have been awarded but referee Valentine saw nothing untoward; it was undoubtedly a let-off for the cup holders.

Then, with an hour on the clock, United's superiority finally told. Sturrock ended a mazy run with a shot that brought a stunning fingertip save from Geddes. Payne sent over the resulting corner and Paul Hegarty rose highest to meet the ball, heading it against the crossbar. It came down conveniently for Sturrock to nod it into the net unchallenged and at 2-0 even the Dark Blues and their supporters knew that there was no way back for their team.

The men in tangerine took their foot off the gas to some extent immediately following the goal, although from that point on Arabs were in full voice proclaiming victory theirs. It surely was, but eight minutes from the end they had another goal to cheer.

Fittingly, it was man-of-the-match Sturrock who started and finished the move. Once again he drove at the Dundee defence at pace down the right and after he entered the penalty area only a last-ditch tackle from Erich Schaedler prevented him from getting his shot away. In doing so, the defender conceded a corner, which again was taken by Payne.

Nor was that where the similarity with the second goal ended because again Hegarty was the most determined and won the ball in the air. This time, instead of hitting the bar, his header brought a save from Geddes but when the ball broke clear it was Sturrock who was on hand, this time merely to touch it into the net from close range.

The remaining few minutes were turned into a form of exhibition as United did their best to keep possession and deny their opponents so much as a chance to enter their half and all the while joyous Arabs chanted the name of their hero, Jim McLean.

At the final whistle a huge roar of acclaim from the tangerine-clad sections of Dens Park rent the cold night air before subsiding as the reality sank in for them. After waiting their entire lives for their club to win a major trophy, they had now witnessed the feat twice inside 12 months.

Although few may have recognised the detail at the time, the final had passed without referee Valentine having to show a single yellow card. The match enhanced the reputation of both clubs in terms of the manner in which it was played; although it was relatively one-sided it was fiercely contested.

When the time came for the trophy to be presented, tradition was dispensed with as captain Hegarty ushered McAlpine, the team's longest-serving player, forward to receive the League Cup. That simply added to the rapturous response from United fans and it was later revealed that, although the idea was Hegarty's, he had consulted the rest of the team shortly after the semi-final win over Celtic with his suggestion – which was enthusiastically endorsed by his colleagues.

With the celebrations still in full swing, McLean revealed his inner feelings in a way he had felt unable to do before the final, 'I always knew we had better players but in the past lack of competitiveness has been our downfall. We can't be accused of that this afternoon. The first goal was vital. If they had scored it, I feel we could have come back at them but I knew if we scored the opening goal then there was no way Dundee would beat us.'

Then what happened?

The atmosphere before, during and after the final was a credit to the city of Dundee and to the supporters of both of its clubs. There were no reports of any trouble during a Saturday evening when feelings among Dundee and United fans must have been running high, for widely contrasting reasons. In many cases glory was toasted and sorrows drowned side by side.

Liverpool is possibly the only other city where such an occasion could take place without the need for the police to flood the city centre in its aftermath.

The league season was not one to remember for United, ending with them fifth in the Premier Division, the lowest for five years. But 1980/81 will always be remembered as the first in which United reached two major cup finals. The Scottish Cup Final with Rangers ended in defeat in a replay but nevertheless marked another milestone in the club's epic journey under McLean.

Dundee did manage to win back their Premier Division place at the end of the season, though only on goal difference after finishing eight points behind First Division champions Hibernian.

Collie Martin – only four times has a Tannadice player ever ended the season as top league scorer in the division, and he did it twice.

This is our day. Bobby Ross and George Grant denying Celtic at Tannadice in 1949, in one of the all-time Scottish Cup shocks.

The 1-0 victory over Berwick Rangers that clinched promotion in 1960 was a nerve-racking affair, but some of the tension would have been eased had this point-blank header from Bobby Norris found the net.

Peter McKay, United's record goalscorer with a phenomenal 199 in 237 games in the major competitions between 1947 and 1954.

United are back! Ron Yeats is mobbed by jubilant supporters as the club returns to the top level after an absence of 28 years.

Doug Smith made more than 600 appearances over 17 years in the number 5 jersey and was never once booked. He was club chairman from 2000-02.

The long wait is almost over. Willie Pettigrew scoring the first of his two goals against Aberdeen in the 1979 Scottish League Cup Final replay.

Hands on. Eight years after leaving his job as a coach at Dens Park, Jim McLean returned and led United to the club's first major trophy.

Dave Narey, who made the greatest number of appearances for the club (866) and was the first United player to win a full Scotland cap.

The trophy retained. Captain Paul Hegarty leads the celebrations after United had beaten Dundee in the 1980 Scottish League Cup Final.

At the end of a 50-yard run, Eamonn Bannon watches the ball enter the net in the 5-0 drubbing of Borussia Mönchengladbach in 1981. It is widely regarded as one of the greatest goals ever scored by a United player.

Paul Sturrock, United's second-top scorer of all time with 170 goals in 576 appearances. He returned to Tannadice as manager from 1998-2000.

Happy Birthday, Ralph! Milne soaks up the adulation after his wonder goal in the match that saw United win the Premier Division title in May 1983.

Arabs' hearts were in their mouths as Eamonn Bannon's penalty was saved in the Dens Park championship decider, but he drove home the rebound for what ultimately proved the winner.

Champions of Scotland!

Paul Sturrock scoring the goal that earned United a 2-2 draw in the UEFA Cup tie at Old Trafford in 1984.

Before the ball has come to rest, Kevin Gallacher (far right) is celebrating after his lob had given United the lead against Barcelona in 1987, a mere 100 seconds into the match.

United on the world stage. The teams and officials take the field for the UEFA Cup Final second leg at Tannadice in 1987.

Glory beckons. The ball is in the net for the only goal of the 1994 Scottish Cup Final as the man who put it there, Craig Brewster, joins his joyous fellow-Arabs.

What Scottish Cup success feels like. Goalscorer Craig Brewster, manager Ivan Golac and man-of-the-match Gordan Petric.

Super Mo. Maurice Malpas is second only to Dave Narey in terms of appearances in tangerine (826) but he's United's leading international, having played 55 times for Scotland.

A picture speaks a thousand words. There's no disguising the elation of Derek Lilley following his late winner against St Johnstone that guaranteed United's SPL survival in 2001.

We have lift-off. David Goodwillie releasing the inch-perfect 25-yard chip shot that gave United the lead in the 2010 Scottish Cup Final.

How about that? Craig Conway looks rather pleased after scoring the second goal at Hampden in 2010.

Scottish Cup winners 2010. Captain Andy Webster leads the Hampden celebrations.

David Goodwillie raises the trophy at a packed City Square.

Andy Robertson, who was a sensation in his all-too-brief twelve months at Tannadice. The wing back became a full Scotland international at 19, was voted Young Player of the Year, played in the Scottish Cup Final and joined Hull City for £2.85m in July 2014.

Nadir Ciftci. Following his arrival in the summer of 2013 the charismatic Turk became a huge favourite with United supporters, ending the season as the club's top scorer with 17 goals.

v Rangers 4-1

23

Scottish Premier Division
Ibrox
18 March 1981
Attendance: 11,208

DUNDEE UNITED	RANGERS
McAlpine	Stewart
Holt	Miller (Cooper)
Stark	Dawson
Phillip	Stevens
Hegarty	Jackson
Narey	Bett (Forsyth)
Bannon	W. Johnston
Milne (Kopel)	Russell
Kirkwood	McAdam
Sturrock	Redford
Dodds (Pettigrew)	MacDonald
Manager: Jim McLean	*Manager:* John Greig

O VER the years, visits to Ibrox have rarely been anticipated with anything other than a sense of foreboding by United supporters. Such feelings have their roots in a record that shows success there for visiting clubs – even Celtic – is rare, but occasions when United departed with anything at all have been few and far between.

That was even more decisively the case in 1981. At that time United had enjoyed 20 consecutive seasons at the top level, the five most recent in the Premier Division. That sequence had involved 25 visits to Ibrox – and only six times had United managed to escape without defeat. There had been three wins (the most recent in 1977) and three draws, a record that hardly inspired confidence as Jim McLean prepared his team to meet Rangers in March 1981.

That said, United did have an alternative source to draw confidence from having three months earlier retained the Scottish League Cup. And entry to the final had been gained by recording the club's record win at another Glasgow ground as Celtic were beaten 3-0.

United had already met Rangers twice in league matches that season, both at Tannadice, with the clubs each winning one. United's victory was just six weeks before they travelled to Ibrox so there was no doubt the Tangerines possessed the ability to beat Rangers in their own back yard. The question for travelling Arabs was whether the players had the belief to do so.

The match should have taken place in December but was postponed because United had more important business that day – the Scottish League Cup Final against Dundee.

It would not be an exaggeration to say there was an unpleasant taste in the mouth from the meeting between the clubs at Tannadice in February. Rangers defender Gregor Stevens had been sent off for violent conduct, resulting in a four-match suspension. Ironically his return to action coincided with this particular encounter.

McLean's men went in as the form team. They had won their last seven matches in the Premier Division and the Scottish Cup and they began with a determination that suggested any previous misgivings about facing Glasgow's big two on their turf had been dismissed from their thoughts.

In front of a pitiful crowd (Rangers' average that season was only 19,000) the match got under way amid flurries of snow and on a pitch which showed little evidence of having been softened by Ibrox's undersoil heating.

Nonetheless, United started confidently and aggressively and might have gone ahead after five minutes. A slick move involving Iain Phillip, Paul Sturrock and Davie Dodds ended with Ralph Milne despatching a shot which Rangers goalkeeper Jim Stewart saved when he should have been left with no chance of doing so. The same player then tested Stewart a minute later with a header.

A fierce shot from Ian Redford which Hamish McAlpine shepherded past the post was all the home side could muster before the Tangerines forged ahead after 19 minutes. They had already carved open the home defence on several occasions but this time there was an end product. A cross from Milne was miscued by Alex Miller straight to Billy Kirkwood and the midfielder wasted no time in hammering the ball home from 12 yards.

United were well in control and could have added two more in the 25th minute alone as Stewart got his fingertips to an Eamonn Bannon header and from the resulting corner the goalkeeper was fortunate to block a Dodds shot.

As Rangers became more frustrated in their attempts to stem the tide of attacks they resorted to some heavy tackling that brought warnings, but no cards, from the referee. Such indulgence did nothing to rein in the wilder elements in the home side and on the half-hour, Dodds had to be helped off after an uncompromising challenge from Stevens.

If Rangers or their fans fancied that might have blunted their opponents' attack they would have been sorely disappointed when the replacement for Dodds was ace marksman Willie Pettigrew.

It was poetic justice that, from the free kick won for the assault on Dodds, United doubled their lead. Bannon took it and sent a low accurate shot that beat the defensive wall before nestling in the net. Minutes later Pettigrew might have made it three but he hadn't yet warmed up and his header in the six-yard box went wide.

It seemed United could create chances at will and Kirkwood and Sturrock went close before, against the run of play, Rangers pulled one back. A long through-pass from Jim Bett deceived Paul Hegarty and Colin McAdam took it into the box before toe-ending the ball past McAlpine.

That gave Rangers some hope and, as if to further enhance their chances of regaining parity, Stevens swung into action again – literally – this time bringing down Milne. His intervention had the desired effect as far as Rangers were concerned because, despite receiving treatment, Milne was unable to continue. This time the United attack was blunted because the replacement was full-back Frank Kopel.

Ibrox boss John Greig made his intentions clear with his half-time substitution, bringing on winger Davie Cooper in place of defender Miller. If that was an attempt to retrieve the situation it didn't work, as it merely allowed United to find more gaps in their rearguard. Stewart remained their busiest player and had saved efforts from Pettigrew, twice, and Kirkwood before the game was effectively ended as a contest after 58 minutes with a brilliant goal.

Receiving the ball inside his own half, Sturrock slalomed his way at first diagonally and then directly through tackle after tackle before placing an accurate low shot past Stewart. The run had carried Sturrock fully 60 yards and from start to finish demonstrated skill of the highest order.

Rangers were left punch-drunk but their punishment wasn't yet over. Just three minutes later United rubbed in their total superiority with a fourth goal and, as with the others, it was the result of clinical finishing. This time Pettigrew won the ball 25 yards out and passed to Bannon who held off a challenge before shooting strongly into the net from the 18-yard line.

There hadn't been many Rangers fans in the bright new stands when the match started but there were precious few still around after the score became 4-1 – and there was still almost half an hour to play. Arabs in the Broomloan Road stand were in full voice and anticipated an even wider margin of victory. But the men in tangerine eased off, though the final action was yet to come.

The clock read 71 minutes as Sturrock continued to torment the Rangers defence. Stevens, the man responsible for the shameful tackles that forced Dodds and Milne to leave the field with serious knee injuries, saved the worst until last. As Luggy tried to pass the defender yet again Stevens applied what in wrestling terms would be called a forearm smash to bring him down.

Sturrock described it, 'Gregor Stevens applied an elbow to my face. As I lay unconscious … with blood gushing from my face – and I have been assured by Eamonn Bannon and physio Andy Dickson that this is true – Tom Forsyth was standing over me directing verbal abuse at me for getting a fellow professional sent off!'

Stevens had been fortunate to survive that far into the match, but the red card he received was deserved for that act alone. By disposing of the entire United strike force he demonstrated he either could not or would not learn the lessons of the ban that followed his Tannadice dismissal.

With United's two substitutes already used both teams were reduced to ten men and the final 20 minutes passed without further incident, though the Tangerines continued to dominate. A Holt header almost got past Stewart and Pettigrew had two near misses near the end of a match that United would have won even more handsomely but for the display of the Rangers goalkeeper.

From start to finish they moved with menace and purpose in a display that Rangers couldn't cope with.

McLean was understandably fulsome in his praise, 'The players were magnificent. Don't forget, although we lost two players in the first half we still scored two goals in the second.

'We proved how good a team we have at Tannadice by our performance. If we have had an inferiority complex in the past, and there was never any justifiable reason why we should, surely this result and the manner in which it was achieved has ended it.'

Then what happened?

Inexplicably, in view of United's utter dominance of Rangers in that match, 17 days later United returned to Ibrox with a team showing just one change from the 4-1 victory – and lost 2-1. That turned out to be the difference between the clubs at the season's end because Rangers finished third, two places but just one point ahead of United.

Much more importantly, when the teams met the following May at Hampden in the replayed Scottish Cup Final, Rangers found the determination to avoid a second humiliation at United's hands. In a remarkable turnaround, the Glasgow club reversed the score of that March night, administering a second Scottish Cup Final defeat and denying McLean and his team what would then have been a unique cup double for a provincial club.

v Celtic 3-2

24

Scottish Cup Semi-Final Replay
Hampden Park
15 April 1981
Attendance: 32,328

DUNDEE UNITED	CELTIC
McAlpine	Bonner
Holt	MacLeod
Kopel	Reid
Phillip (Pettigrew)	Sullivan
Hegarty	McAdam
Narey	Aitken
Bannon	Provan
Milne	Conroy
Kirkwood	McGarvey
Sturrock	Burns
Dodds	Nicholas
Manager: Jim McLean	*Manager:* Billy McNeill

PRIOR to 1981 Dundee United had contested just one Scottish Cup Final and had reached the semi-finals on four occasions. Yet when progress to the last four was achieved for the fifth time the odds were only marginally against the club succeeding, despite their opponents being holders Celtic.

In what was Jim McLean's tenth season as manager the team he had developed, comprising an exciting mix of seasoned pros and homegrown youngsters, plus two six-figure signings in Eamonn Bannon and Willie Pettigrew, had already twice won the Scottish League Cup.

McLean's influence was now considerable – and it extended well beyond the confines of Tannadice. Having recognised McLean's talents, Scotland manager Jock Stein had appointed him as his assistant and the national team were already well on their way to qualifying for the 1982 World Cup in Spain.

In addition, several of his former players were utilising the ideas and methods they had absorbed while working under McLean at Tannadice and moving into management or coaching themselves: Gordon Wallace (Raith Rovers), Alex Rennie (St Johnstone), Archie Knox (assistant to Alex Ferguson at Aberdeen after success on his own with Forfar Athletic) and Andy Rolland (Cowdenbeath). The second of McLean's Scottish League Cup triumphs had occurred just four months earlier and retaining the trophy had been made possible by a comprehensive 3-0 defeat of Celtic, at Celtic Park, in the semi-final.

Facing the Glasgow club at the national stadium in the Scottish Cup held no fears for the United players who knew, man for man, they were at least the equal of their opponents. That was borne out by the Tangerines dominating a hard-fought semi-final that lacked nothing in terms of excitement, but did lack a goal. With neither side able to get the better of two solid defences and make a breakthrough, they returned to Hampden four days later.

Both teams had suffered injuries to key players in the first match. The ankle knock sustained by Celtic playmaker Tommy Burns was sufficient to place a question mark over his availability, but it was less serious than the twisted knee that initially suggested Paul Hegarty would have to sit out the replay.

That left McLean pondering a change that might have upset the rhythm of the side, which he had regarded as 'very good' in the first game, 'I think we proved on Saturday that we have the ability to beat Celtic. What we have got to do now is to be as determined again as we were in that game. We have got to dictate the match and play it the way we want to.'

Ultimately both players were declared fit for the replay, though in Hegarty's case it was only possible with a pain-killing injection before the game. McLean was well aware that, for such a crucial game, represented a real gamble; happily for both manager and captain it would prove worthwhile. Celtic were also able to recall their record signing Frank McGarvey, who had missed the first game through injury.

If Saturday's encounter had been a good one, the quality of the replay was several notches higher, producing an evening of almost unrelenting excitement. The two sides had effectively cancelled each other out initially yet the first ten minutes of the replay provided a stark contrast with three goals.

With only five minutes gone Celtic went ahead. Davie Provan sent in a deep cross that seemed destined for Burns at the far post. But just before it reached the Celtic man John Holt stuck out a hand to divert the ball for what was a clear penalty. Charlie Nicholas sent Hamish McAlpine the wrong way in what was a dream start for them. That said, what immediately followed was more akin to a nightmare.

Though going behind was a real setback for United, they didn't spend too much time feeling sorry for themselves. Not even three minutes in fact because by then they were back on level terms. Paul Sturrock used his searing pace down the wing to escape the Celtic defence before angling in a cross for Bannon to arrive with perfect timing and side-foot the ball past Pat Bonner from ten yards.

That was after eight minutes and just two more had elapsed when Bannon turned provider. Murdo MacLeod fouled Sturrock on the left and Bannon launched the free kick into the box. It eluded everyone except Hegarty and the United captain, who had made a late run that caught Celtic by surprise, found room to slot the ball in at the far post.

It was breathless stuff and, as they had done in the first match, United were dominating the midfield and playing with real dynamism. Davie Dodds squandered a chance to score a third when a precision move involving Iain Phillip and Bannon again left the striker with only Bonner to beat.

Bannon's wing play was so forceful that Celtic had no answer to him, a pattern that would continue for most of the match. Often it was impossible for the Scotland international to be stopped legally and it was remarkable that Dom Sullivan was the only man in green and white to be cautioned for bringing him down.

Celtic had taken some time to recover from their lead being cancelled out so swiftly and it was the 29th minute before they were able to test McAlpine. Nicholas took a Burns pass and forced the goalkeeper to save at full stretch but that was against the run of play.

Yet, for all their superiority, United surrendered the lead seconds before half-time. Mike Conroy sent a high lob into the goalmouth and McAlpine, challenged by McGarvey, did well to fist the ball away. Unfortunately it dropped to Nicholas on the edge of the penalty area and he shot with technical precision on the volley to send a low effort raging into the net.

That goal, not least the timing of it, took some of the wind out of United's sails and as the second half got under way Celtic gained the ascendancy for the first time. Nicholas might have completed his hat-trick had Holt not managed to block another volley, but slowly United clawed their way back into the game and regained control.

Although the action continued in a classic tie, defences held the upper hand, although both Bannon and Sturrock came close for United. The crowd would have been considering the prospect of extra time when the Tangerines broke the deadlock. There were 15 minutes remaining when they were awarded a free kick that Ralph Milne floated into the penalty area. Bannon got his head to the ball but could do no more than send it back across the face of the goal. It seemed that either Roy Aitken or Conroy would clear the danger but, under pressure from Hegarty, Aitken mis-hit the ball, allowing the skipper to turn it into the net.

Arabs celebrated no less than the players, though all were aware that more than enough time remained for the Glasgow side to fashion another equaliser. Billy McNeill's team tried all they knew to achieve that outcome but their hopes floundered on the rocks at the centre of the United defence in the shape of Hegarty and Dave Narey. The team maintained their discipline and held on without too many scary moments.

The closest Celtic came was right at the death when Nicholas beat two United men before feeding Burns. The midfielder let fly in a last, desperate, attempt but he was denied by a fine save from McAlpine at full stretch.

United recorded a famous victory to win a coveted place in the Scottish Cup Final. It was a performance that fully merited such a reward. McLean's team held the upper hand for two-thirds of a game that ebbed and flowed and in which the pace was relentless.

Although Hegarty scored two of the goals – fully justifying the risk McLean had taken in including him – the star of the show was Bannon. He gave a virtuoso performance, running the Celtic defence ragged and having an involvement in all three goals.

McLean was fulsome in his praise for the players, 'I am really proud of them. That was as good a performance as I have ever seen from a Dundee United team, even better than our defeat of Celtic in the League Cup semi-final this season.

'They are maturing and they proved their character in coming back after losing a goal after only five minutes. We have only arrived really and we can only get better. If we can keep these players together that is only the start.'

The significance of that semi-final in 1981 is underlined by it being only the second time United had beaten Celtic in the Scottish Cup; 33 years and eight attempts later the third is still awaited.

Then what happened?

That performance, together with the League Cup semi-final defeat of the same opponents plus United's 4-1 demolition of Rangers at Ibrox the previous month, meant that when the Tangerines faced the other half of the Old Firm in the Scottish Cup Final they were favourites to lift the trophy.

Proving that the bookies don't always get it right, United's return to the national stadium had no happy ending. As in the semi-final, the first match ended in a goalless draw but the replay produced a repeat of the scoreline in that league match at Ibrox – this time in the Light Blues' favour. It was a shattering disappointment and hard to explain given the assured performance in the semi-final replay.

Bizarrely, despite beating Celtic in the semi-finals of both cups in 1980/81, United lost all four Premier Division encounters with the Glasgow club that season.

v Aberdeen 3-0

Scottish League Cup Semi-Final Second Leg
Pittodrie
28 October 1981
Attendance: 20,137

DUNDEE UNITED	ABERDEEN
McAlpine	Leighton
Holt	Kennedy
Murray	Rougvie
Phillip	Watson
Hegarty	Cooper
Narey	Miller
Bannon	Strachan
Milne	Simpson (Bell)
Kirkwood	McGhee
Sturrock	Hewitt
Dodds	Weir (McCall)
Manager: Jim McLean	*Manager:* Alex Ferguson

IN October 1981 there was a determination among the players to write themselves into the history books. They had already done so in terms of the club's own history by winning United's first major trophy less than two years previously when defeating Aberdeen in the replayed Scottish League Cup Final. But they now had the opportunity of becoming the first club apart from Celtic and Rangers to win that trophy three years in succession. The 1981/82 season had started slowly in terms of league form. United had outplayed Aberdeen to win 4-1 on the opening day but by the end of October Jim McLean was unhappy that his team lay seventh in the ten-club Premier Division, having surprisingly lost to Airdrieonians, Morton and St Mirren.

But it was a different story in the League Cup where United came through a section that included Premier Division Partick Thistle as well as First Division sides Ayr United and Motherwell. Just one point was dropped and that came when the section had already been won. Another First Division club, Hamilton Accies, were demolished 9-0 on aggregate in the quarter-finals and that set up the mouthwatering prospect of home and away ties against north-east rivals Aberdeen for a place in the final.

With the first leg at home, McLean knew his men had to reproduce a performance like that opening-day victory over the Dons to give themselves a chance of advancing. But on the night it was Aberdeen who were the better side and they could have won more convincingly than by the single goal they scored.

The main man for the visitors was left-winger Peter Weir, the club's £300,000 record signing from St Mirren during the close-season. His pace, skill and clever use of the ball regularly had United on the back foot and it was fitting that he headed the winner in the 23rd minute from a Gordon Strachan cross.

Davie Dodds was off the pitch having stitches inserted in a head wound when the goal went in, but that couldn't be used as an excuse by United who were second best for much of the game and were fortunate to avoid greater damage when John McMaster sent a shot spinning over the bar right in front of the goal.

Although the clubs between them had won three trophies in the previous two seasons, the term 'New Firm' was not yet in common usage. But there was a real sense that meetings between them involved sides every bit as good as Celtic and Rangers, despite the gulf in resources enjoyed by the Glasgow pair.

Three weeks elapsed before the second leg, during which time both clubs played UEFA Cup ties, but with their one-goal advantage Aberdeen went in to the Pittodrie match as firm favourites. The Dons were also 12 matches unbeaten and lay second in the Premier Division, five places above the League Cup holders.

No team fielded by Alex Ferguson would attempt simply to preserve a first-leg lead, least of all at home, so the Dons set out seeking the goal that could end the tie as a contest. For McLean, it was a relief to have Paul Sturrock back. The attacker had missed the club's previous four matches after fracturing a bone in his hand in the first leg at Tannadice.

At Pittodrie, as United sought to assert themselves and ensure Aberdeen were not allowed to repeat their first-leg domination, a rejuvenated Luggy made an immediate impact. After just seven minutes a mistake by Willie Miller created the opening for United. When the Aberdeen captain lost possession just outside the box Ralph Milne was lying handy to feed Sturrock, who cleverly wrong-footed the defence by cutting one way, then the other, before brilliantly curling a shot past Jim Leighton.

Aberdeen were stunned by having their advantage cancelled out so quickly and, as they fought back, play raged from end to end. Hamish McAlpine had to make a smart stop from a Doug Rougvie shot and immediately Dodds swept upfield to force Leighton to save at full stretch.

Two Strachan crosses in quick succession caused difficulty for the Tangerines' defence and from the second one, after 23 minutes, Weir hit a ferocious shot which brought a courageous save from McAlpine at the feet of John Hewitt. That prevented what looked a certain goal, but Weir was injured in the melee that followed and had to leave the field. Given the winger's role in the Tannadice meeting, that was a sight no United man would have been too unhappy about. Weir did return after receiving treatment but departed for good soon after, apparently suffering from concussion.

After half an hour United should have extended their lead on the night when a Derek Murray free kick found Sturrock on his own at the far post but, with plenty of time to bring the ball down, Luggy elected for a first-time shot which went over the bar.

Though Aberdeen were doing plenty of pressing, the better chances were being created by the Tangerines and on 38 minutes they deservedly led the tie for the first time. Sturrock passed up a chance, this time from a Milne cross, but the ball reached Eamonn Bannon and when he returned it into the goalmouth Leighton was unable to reach it and Milne hammered home his team's second.

McAlpine was again called upon to dive at Hewitt's feet in the final minute of the half and United were happy to settle for a corner. McAlpine's bravery enabled his team to head for the break with their overall lead intact, which their play had merited.

Within a minute of the re-start the Dons missed a great chance to level the tie when, with only McAlpine to beat, Mark McGhee shot wide. With 65 minutes played the same player came much closer when he hit the bar as the home side, urged on by their vociferous support, threw everything into attack in a bid to retrieve the situation. The large number of travelling Arabs also contributed to a tremendous atmosphere and a tremendous cup tie.

Clearly frustrated at his team's inability to find a way through, Ferguson threw his normal approach aside and opted instead for an alien up-and-under style as high ball after high ball was lobbed into the United penalty area. But that was meat and drink for a defence magnificently marshalled by Paul Hegarty and Dave Narey and for all their pressure the Reds couldn't find a way back.

Play became more intense and Miller was booked for retaliation after a tackle by Dodds as United, in the driving seat, played with more composure while Aberdeen gradually lost theirs. Dodds shot past after good work by Sturrock and Billy Kirkwood then, with seven minutes remaining, McLean's men put the result beyond doubt.

With time running out and Aberdeen keeping a high line as they desperately sought a goal to force extra time, their commitment to pressing left them exposed to the swift counter-attack. That was United's stock-in-trade and they were not slow to take advantage, putting Leighton's charge in danger on several occasions and eventually they capitalised. Sturrock was sent through by Kirkwood and he left defenders trailing in his wake before lashing the ball into the roof of the net from 20 yards for a goal worthy of winning any cup tie. Arabs' joy was unconfined – and not just for the fans or players because, before play re-started, the referee booked McLean and his assistant Walter Smith for encroaching on to the pitch in celebration after Sturrock's shot hit the net.

Neither had been – nor would be in the future – known for expressing themselves in such a manner but on the night, given their team's recovery to reach another cup final, their elation was understandable. TV coverage of the incident revealed that McLean actually went no further than the running track but the manager was still unable to conceal his delight when he spoke after the final whistle, suggesting the return of Sturrock had been a crucial factor in the comprehensive victory, 'Paul scored two great goals, but he won the game for us simply by going on to the park, for the effect his return had on other members of the team and possibly Aberdeen's as well.'

For his part, Ferguson was magnanimous, 'We can have few complaints. United emerged as the better side at the end of the day. I thought we played well in the first half without taking our chances, but in the second half United always looked likely to score on the break.'

Then what happened?

Six months after the clubs had met in the Scottish Cup Final, United's opponents in the Scottish League Cup Final were again Rangers. As in May, United were the favourites but again the Tangerines found the occasion too much for them and they and their supporters were forced to make what was to become a familiar, painful, silent return home from a Hampden final.

On this occasion United dominated the first half but couldn't forge ahead despite Sturrock twice being clear on goal with only the Rangers goalkeeper to beat. The Tangerines did eventually take a deserved lead early in the second half through Milne and three minutes later Sturrock appeared to have scored a potentially decisive second with a spectacular 20-yard drive. The referee awarded the goal and Rangers didn't protest but a linesman indicated that John Holt had been in an offside position and it was disallowed.

That seemed to deflate United while offering encouragement to their opponents. Nonetheless, it was insufficient explanation as to why the Glasgow side should have been able to score twice to overtake McLean's team and deny them a hat-trick of League Cup wins.

The national stadium was becoming a psychological barrier to cup final success for Dundee United – and there would be further pain for players and supporters alike to suffer before it was eventually surmounted.

v Borussia Mönchengladbach 5-0

UEFA Cup Second Round Second Leg. Tannadice
3 November 1981. Attendance: 15,330

DUNDEE UNITED	BORUSSIA MÖNCHENGLADBACH
McAlpine	Kleff
Holt	Schäffer
Murray	Fleer
Gough	Hannes
Hegarty	Ringels
Narey	Matthäus
Bannon	Veh (Schäfer)
Milne	Bruns
Kirkwood	Mill
Sturrock	Pinkall
Dodds	Wuttke
Manager: Jim McLean	*Coach:* Jupp Heynckes

THE 1981/82 season marked United's coming of age in European competition. It was the fifth campaign in a row that the club had qualified for Europe and the tenth in total since their debut in 1966/67.

Over that 15-year period United had gradually learned how to adapt to the demands of European competition, which are often quite different from the domestic competitions. Although playing styles have developed in the 30 years since, even in 2014 a different approach is necessary when facing continental clubs.

In the early 1980s it was accepted that ball players were allowed more time and room to express themselves in Europe than was the case in the generally faster and more robust cauldron of Scottish football, where players were closed down sooner – and often brought down more quickly if they were perceived as major threats to defenders.

United's European debut had produced a famous double victory against Barcelona in the Fairs Cup that shot the club to prominence. However, of 14 opponents since then, the only club of note United managed to get the better of was Anderlecht, on the away goals rule in 1979. In the next round United suffered what was then the club's heaviest aggregate defeat (4-1) to Diosgyori VTK, a club unknown outside their native Hungary.

The following season saw Poland's Slask Wroclaw hammered 7-2 on aggregate before United went out on away goals to another Belgian club, KSC Lokeren. So it was clear that, under a manager in Jim McLean who looked to Dutch football for his inspiration, United were absorbing lessons from their experience and were now getting the hang of Europe and its demands.

That said, the draw for the first round of the UEFA Cup in 1981 handed the Tangerines what appeared one of the more demanding tasks at that stage of the competition, AS Monaco. Football in France was then of a comparable standard to Scotland and the first leg on the Côte d'Azur promised to be awkward. But United produced a sublime performance, dominating and using flowing attacking football to record a stunning 5-2 victory.

Any doubts as to the quality of the French club were answered when they came to Tannadice and put on an impressive away display of their own, winning 2-1. It wasn't enough to prevent United advancing but it did demonstrate what they were capable of and Monaco went on to win the French championship that season.

Emboldened by that success, Arabs eagerly awaited news of the next opponents, though there must have been mixed feelings when they were revealed as Borussia Mönchengladbach, then one of West Germany's leading clubs.

Mönchengladbach had been Bundesliga champions in five of the preceding 11 seasons and had reached four of the last eight UEFA Cup finals, winning twice, most recently in 1979. For good measure they had lost to Liverpool in the 1977 European Cup Final and were under the guidance of one of their own all-time great players, Jupp Heynckes, a member of Germany's 1974 World Cup-winning squad, now in his third season as coach.

United had never previously played a competitive match in Germany, East or West, but whichever club they faced on their first visit would have been extremely tough. Mönchengladbach initially treated their visitors with respect, coach Heynckes stating pre-match that, having beaten Monaco, 'The Scots will give us a strong test both in attack and defence.'

For the match at the Bökelberg Stadion United were handicapped by the absence of Paul Sturrock, who had a broken bone in his hand and remained at home. That didn't prevent McLean's men from attacking on the counter whenever the opportunity arose, but Mönchengladbach dominated play and there were several close shaves as the visiting defence coped manfully with what became an onslaught.

It was a gutsy display by the Tangerines and one that looked for much of the match as if it would prevent the home team from establishing an advantage. But two late goals from set pieces ultimately gave the Germans a two-goal lead to bring to Tannadice.

In his after-match comments, Heynckes's respect mask slipped somewhat. He was certain his team had done enough to make the second leg a formality, offering the arrogant opinion, 'No team in the land could give Borussia Mönchengladbach two goals of a start and beat them.'

McLean was of the view that his team were still very much in the tie, but that dismissive remark by his opposite number was one the United manager would use to energise his players for the return.

Sturrock was restored to action as McLean pledged his team would press the Germans from the start, all the while aware that conceding would leave United with a monumental task. And with Paul Hegarty and Dave Narey in form at the centre of the defence, United were able to take the game to the Germans, who were immediately forced on to the defensive.

Richard Gough (making his European debut) and Eamonn Bannon had seen attempts clear the crossbar before United won their first corner in the fourth minute. Ralph Milne took it and there was an almighty scramble in the six-yard box before the Germans cleared, only for Milne to return and send in a dipping shot that goalkeeper Wolfgang Kleff instinctively pushed over.

Such was United's domination that Hamish McAlpine did not touch the ball until the tenth minute, though that merely involved collecting a lob from Lothar Matthäus.

The tightly-packed and well-disciplined Mönchengladbach defence was proving hard to penetrate but the Germans appeared to take some satisfaction from having weathered the early storm and eventually began to assert themselves by pushing forward. However, United prevented them from getting too close and the visitors had to be satisfied with long-range efforts. That wasn't to say they were without menace though, because 25-yard efforts from Hans Bruns and captain Wilfried Hannes brought a full-length save from McAlpine in the first case, while the other thundered narrowly past.

By this time more than half an hour had passed and the Tannadice crowd were starting to become a little nervous, wondering whether a breakthrough would come. With 35 minutes played they had their answer thanks to a flash of brilliance from Sturrock. He split the Mönchengladbach defence with a precise crossfield pass into the penalty area where Milne met the ball and swept it home from ten yards.

There was relief among players and fans that all United's pressure had paid off and in all probability most would have settled for a score of 1-0 when half-time came. That seemed to be happening with just a minute of the half remaining when Sturrock collected the ball and moved towards the penalty box. Defenders crowded him out but the ball broke to Billy Kirkwood some 25 yards from goal. The midfielder didn't think twice about his options, simply letting fly with a shot that bounced once in front of Kleff before flying up and past him into the net.

That brought wild joy to the terraces and when the referee signalled half-time seconds later the crowd gave United a standing ovation as they left the pitch.

McLean admitted later that he didn't want the game to come to a halt, such was the momentum his team had established, but when play resumed so did United's high-powered assault on the creaking Mönchengladbach defence. The Germans had to find a means of attacking if they were to survive but United had no intention of allowing them to do so and Milne, Bannon and Gough all had efforts saved in the first three minutes of the half.

Another three had elapsed when Tannadice again erupted as United stormed into an overall lead. A long pass into the penalty area from John Holt was mis-headed by Norbert Ringels straight to Sturrock who wasted no time in lashing the ball past Kleff.

Although the 3-0 scoreline would have sent United through, it remained dangerous because a single strike by Mönchengladbach would have won it for them on away goals. They came very close to achieving that after 72 minutes when the ball broke to Frank Mill six yards out. Arab hearts were in mouths as the midfielder stabbed the ball goalwards only for McAlpine to extend a leg and divert it wide.

That acted as a wake-up call to the Tangerines and three minutes later they finally put the tie beyond doubt. Again the ubiquitous Sturrock was involved, this time getting his head to the ball from a corner, although he could only watch as it rebounded from a post. Happily for United, Hegarty was on hand to turn it over the line for one of the easiest – but most loudly-acclaimed – goals he would ever score.

Mönchengladbach were now in tatters but there was worse to come. Arabs hadn't stopped cheering when Bannon worked a one-two with Sturrock on the halfway line and set off on a mesmerising run. He weaved his way half the length of the pitch with the Germans in his wake before prodding the ball past Kleff for United's fifth goal – and the *coup de grâce* for the celebrating crowd.

The word 'brilliant' is over-used in football yet it's doubtful whether it is adequate in describing that goal. Many seasoned United supporters – this one among them – maintained then and still do more than 30 years later that it was the greatest by a Dundee United player they have ever witnessed.

Despite holding an unassailable 5-0 lead, rather than count down the clock for the remaining 14 minutes United continued to attack and could have scored more. The most notable occasions were when Davie Dodds powered in a shot that Kleff just managed to push over the bar and then, from the resultant corner, Gough had the ball in the net but was adjudged to have been offside.

Suffice to say neither he nor his team-mates protested too strongly and soon after that the final whistle sounded on a match and an evening nobody who was there would forget – particularly those from Mönchengladbach.

The 15,330 people privileged to be there cheered United to the rafters and would not allow the players to leave the pitch. It was a performance of the highest quality from a team that – leaving aside Hamish McAlpine – had an average age of 22-and-a-half.

It was very much McLean's team and he commented, 'They did Scotland proud. People talk about West German football, Dutch football and all the rest but I think we showed tonight that Scotland aren't bad either.'

That was a view endorsed by the watching Scotland manager, Jock Stein, who described it as, 'A tremendous display. It must do Scotland's image good for one of our clubs to beat a top German club so overwhelmingly'.

To his credit, Heynckes didn't hide from the media and, though he didn't explicitly admit that his prediction had been completely trashed, it was implicit as he admitted, 'It was catastrophic for us. United were a wonderful team and we cannot possibly complain. We couldn't get out of defence.'

Then what happened?

For the first time, Dundee United had survived two rounds in Europe and their next opponents were Winterslag. The Belgian club had beaten Arsenal in the previous round and so a goalless draw in the away leg on a gluepot of a pitch was a satisfactory result for McLean's men.

The crowd for the return was even bigger than for the Mönchengladbach match and those supporters of other clubs who joined Arabs in hoping for a repeat were not disappointed. On another evening of high-powered attacking play, another 5-0 thrashing was handed out as United marched into the quarter-finals.

When that tie came round three months later, despite a 2-0 first-leg defeat of Yugoslav side Radnicki Nis at Tannadice, the return leg proved the end of the road with a 3-0 reverse.

Though disappointed to exit at the hands of what he regarded as the least accomplished of the four clubs his team had met in Europe that season, McLean was aware that he had brought the name of Dundee United to a much wider audience and had enhanced the club's reputation immeasurably.

v PSV Eindhoven 2-0

UEFA Cup First Round Second Leg
Philips Stadion
28 September 1982
Attendance: 12,500

DUNDEE UNITED	PSV EINDHOVEN
McAlpine	Doesburg
Phillip (Malpas)	van Aerle (Jung Moo Huh)
Stark	Wildschut
Hegarty	Brandts
Narey	Stevens
Gough	Poortvliet
Bannon	W. van der Kerkhof
Milne	Lokhoff (Landsbergen)
Kirkwood	R. van der Kerkhof
Sturrock	Koolhof
Dodds	Thoresen
Manager: Jim McLean	*Coach:* Thijs Libregts

UNITED'S European adventure of 1981/82 had taken the club into the hitherto uncharted territory of the quarter-finals of the UEFA Cup, but Jim McLean and his players had merely had their appetites whetted. They wanted more of that – and they wanted to progress further.

Victories over clubs from such established footballing nations as France, Germany and Belgium (while scoring five times in a match against each one) meant United had a growing reputation on the European stage.

When the next season began the draw for the first round of the UEFA Cup was eagerly anticipated. In the days before seeding or preliminary rounds the draw was all-in and it handed United a tough test in PSV Eindhoven. It was made even tougher with Tannadice hosting the first leg, traditionally regarded as a disadvantage in such situations.

In many ways, the Netherlands had been *the* European footballing nation of the 1970s. The national team were runners-up in two World Cup finals while Dutch clubs won the European Cup four times, more often than any other country. Those were major achievements for a country of only 15 million people yet they are not the main reason Dutch football was held in such high regard worldwide in 1982.

Dutch teams didn't just play fast, exciting, effective, winning football, they played what had become known as 'Total Football' – a system in which any outfield player could take over the role of any team-mate that was pioneered by the wonderful Ajax sides of the early 70s.

It was a fluid system with success dependent largely on the adaptability of each player, in particular the ability to quickly switch positions depending on the on-field situation. The Dutch understood it and operated it effectively although, perhaps because it placed high technical and physical demands on players, it was never widely adopted elsewhere.

Perhaps the most famous example was seen in the 1974 World Cup Final. Johan Cruyff kicked off and the ball was passed between his team-mates 13 times before it returned to Cruyff, who then went on a run that ended when he was brought down in the penalty box. Johan Neeskens scored from the spot-kick to give the Netherlands a 1-0 lead with just 80 seconds played and without a German player having touched the ball. West Germany eventually won 2-1.

When McLean was appointed United manager in 1971 he had already been to the Netherlands to study their training methods and tactics, although he no doubt appreciated that attempting Total Football at Tannadice was probably a bit ambitious. But he did impart much of what he had learned and he remained a firm advocate of United trying to play a passing game with as much movement and flexibility as possible.

PSV Eindhoven had also been part of the footballing revolution in their country and it had brought them success. During the 70s they were Dutch champions three times in four years and also won the UEFA Cup in 1978. As the previous season's runners-up and current leaders of the Eredivisie they formed formidable opposition for United while presenting different challenges to those the Tangerines had faced the previous campaign.

United had made a positive start to 1982/83, winning all six of their sectional ties in the Scottish League Cup. Although those opponents were from the First Division, the only two Premier Division matches played had produced a home win over Aberdeen and a draw with Rangers at Ibrox so United had reason to feel confident as they prepared to host PSV.

McLean had stated beforehand that his only doubt concerned whether to play Dave Narey – who had made a big impact for Scotland in the World Cup in Spain – in defence or midfield. In the event McLean decided on the former, aware of the need to guard against conceding an away goal.

United drove forward from the start, refusing to allow the Dutch to play the patient possession football their coach, Thijs Libregts, had stated they would aim for. Goalkeeper Pim Doesburg was the man who kept PSV in the game during a first half in which his goal was peppered with shots as United sought the breakthrough. Seven minutes from half-time Davie Dodds was the man who got it, though from a suspiciously offside position, a decision that enraged the Dutch.

Hamish McAlpine had been largely redundant for the first 45 minutes but PSV changed their tactics and began to make the goalkeeper work. However United still held the upper hand and spurned reasonable chances before the Dutch struck on the counter-attack. With 68 minutes played Willy van der Kerkhof outpaced Paul Hegarty then beat McAlpine to score a goal that silenced Tannadice and came as a serious blow to United.

Further efforts to re-establish a lead came to nothing but, despite having left themselves with a harder task than they would have liked, United players could reflect that they had outplayed a side supposedly superior to them – at least in technical terms – and were capable of doing so again. That optimism was reflected with 600 Arabs preparing for the trip to Eindhoven.

A visit to the Philips Stadion was a daunting prospect for any club. PSV had lost just once in 36 home European ties stretching back to 1955, though United might have been able to derive some encouragement as the club who prevented that record from being unblemished were Scottish: Rangers had won 3-2 in 1978.

Libregts had called for an early goal and he got it – though hardly as he had imagined. PSV were of a much more attacking frame of mind than at Tannadice and for most of the first five minutes play was confined to United's half. But the Dutch were contained by the United defence and then the Tangerines broke with devastating effect. Paul Sturrock carried the ball down the left wing before finding Eamonn Bannon. His cross into the penalty box reached Billy Kirkwood who expertly chested the ball down before blasting it into the net.

PSV were clearly rattled and put the United defence under pressure, though McAlpine was equal to any efforts that reached him. Not many did, though, because Narey and Hegarty were forming a formidable barrier.

Soon United re-asserted themselves and began to use the passing style more often associated with Dutch teams. This led to scoring opportunities, most notably when Richard Gough powered in a header which Doesburg saved at full stretch. Then the keeper had to be even more alert to touch a Davie Dodds shot over his crossbar as United took advantage of a remarkably shaky home rearguard.

Such was the extent to which the Tangerines had grown in the game that it was no surprise when they extended their lead. It began with PSV defenders floundering as they tried to contain a probe down the left and Bannon was able to reach the byline before sending in a low cross that was intelligently dummied by Ralph Milne. That wrong-footed the PSV defenders, allowing Hegarty to sweep the ball in.

Only 29 minutes had been played and the PSV fans left their players in no doubt as to their disapproval by whistling and jeering. More noise, however, was coming from celebrating Arabs, who must have been close to hoarse already with less than a third of the match played.

It was clearly not in McLean's instructions for his players to attempt to protect their lead because they maintained a pressing game and five minutes after the second goal they had the ball in the net again. PSV were caught out at the halfway line as Kirkwood, Bannon and Sturrock raced away, faced by only two defenders. Eventually Bannon shot home but a linesman had flagged him offside as he received the ball.

The home side began the second half in a manner suggesting they hadn't given up hope but Narey was in imperious form, often moving forward into midfield to break up attacks or stifle a PSV player trying to find space. The result was that the Dutch increasingly had to resort to long-range efforts, which were comfortably dealt with by Hegarty, Narey and McAlpine.

The nearest PSV came was when a powerful 30-yard drive from Piet Wildschut was deflected over the bar by Frank Kopel. But there was no real indication of any revival and United remained cool and in control.

McLean's team continued to break at every opportunity, stretching the home defenders whose frustration began to show with some heavy tackling, though only substitute Jung Moo Huh had his name taken.

In the 68th minute United came within a whisker of increasing their lead. Bannon ran at the PSV defence and let fly from just inside the penalty box. Doesburg stuck out a leg to divert the ball but the goalkeeper could only watch as it ran to Sturrock, whose shot rebounded off the post.

Then another Bannon effort from 25 yards whistled inches wide as United emphasised their superiority in a manner that nobody would have predicted.

The travelling Arabs were in full voice – or at least what voice they still retained – when the final whistle sounded with United on the attack, where they had been for much of the 90 minutes. To their great credit, the PSV supporters acknowledged the quality of their opponents' play by applauding as United left the field of play.

It had been a stunning display by Hegarty and his colleagues. Almost throughout the match they had been in control, demonstrating they had become attuned to the manner in which away ties in Europe had to be approached.

McLean had been sufficiently confident in what the team was doing for him to feel it unnecessary to use either of the two substitutes available. But the manager was typically subdued post-match, simply stating, 'My players did the job I had asked. This was one of our finest performances in Europe and we thoroughly deserved our win.'

What he might have said was that he had a group of players who had matured at home and in Europe to the point where they were reaching the height of their collective powers. Hegarty and Narey at the back, Bannon and Kirkwood in midfield and Sturrock and Milne up front were sublime on this occasion and to be able to enter the country associated more than any other with controlled football and depart convincing winners was a tribute to the coaching and tactical skills of their manager.

Then what happened?

In the second round United were paired with Viking Stavanger. After the level of performance reached in both matches with PSV it was never likely that the Norwegian part-timers would halt their progress. So it proved, though the 3-1 aggregate score by which the Tannadice men advanced was identical to that against PSV.

This time victory opened the door to an altogether more demanding test in the next round where Werder Bremen awaited.

v **Werder Bremen** 1-1

UEFA Cup Third Round Second Leg
Weserstadion
8 December 1982
Attendance: 37,500

DUNDEE UNITED	WERDER BREMEN
McAlpine	Burdenski
Stark	Kemp (Bohnke)
Malpas	Otten
Gough	Gruber (Schaff)
Hegarty	Fichtel
Narey	Moehimann
Bannon	Sidka
Milne	Siegmann
Kirkwood	Völler
Sturrock	Okudera
Dodds (Holt)	Meier
Manager: Jim McLean	*Coach:* Otto Rehhagel

BY the end of 1982 Jim McLean's United had established a European pedigree that demanded respect. The elimination of PSV Eindhoven was the latest addition to a list of clubs of the calibre of Anderlecht, Borussia Mönchengladbach and AS Monaco.

So when the draw for the third round of the UEFA Cup paired Dundee United with another Bundesliga side in Werder Bremen, the prospect fazed neither the manager nor his players. That said, they were under no illusions as to the scale of the task they faced to reach the quarter-finals, particularly with the second leg to take place in the West German city-state.

Bremen were not one of the Bundesliga's big clubs. After winning the title in the competition's second season (1964/65) they generally finished mid-table or lower until they suffered relegation in 1980. But they made an immediate return to the top level and followed that with their best Bundesliga season in 15 years, finishing fifth and earning a UEFA Cup place.

As Bremen's visit beckoned, McLean could reflect that the season was progressing well as far as United were concerned with his team lying second in the Premier Division, having lost just one of their opening 12 league matches. The only blip was the 3-2 aggregate defeat by Celtic in the semi-final of the Scottish League Cup.

The first leg against Bremen was played on a muddy Tannadice pitch and it was clear from the start that passes would have to be hit with twice the normal velocity to reach their intended destination. United grasped this quickly and began their pressing game, forcing four corners in the first six minutes as they sought an early lead.

It took until only the 15th minute for the opening goal to arrive. Davie Dodds and Eamonn Bannon worked a neat one-two before Bannon's pass was finished first-time by Ralph Milne.

That set an already noisy Tannadice alight, but the fans were aware the Germans were as adept as United at employing the counter-attack. On one occasion the always-dangerous Rudi Völler broke free and had only Hamish McAlpine to beat, but Arabs' favourite cult figure further enhanced his reputation by spreading himself brilliantly to avert the danger.

When Völler was again through one-on-one in the second half he learned from the first occasion and went round McAlpine, then unaccountably hesitated long enough to allow Maurice Malpas time to scramble the ball off the line.

But the Germans were showing genuine aggression and they were rewarded on 65 minutes when Paul Hegarty blocked another Völler effort but Norbert Meier was on hand to score from the rebound.

As had happened against PSV Eindhoven in the first round, there was an audible sound as hearts sank among Arabs. An away goal is often priceless but the United players didn't noticeably wilt, not least because it appeared that Bremen, having got their goal, retreated to some extent as if determined not to concede another.

John Reilly replaced Bannon as United redoubled their efforts and the young striker missed a golden opportunity when he sent a free header straight at Dieter Burdenski. It began to look as though they would have to settle for a draw – until seven minutes from the end, when they were rewarded for their energy and determination with a winner.

It came from an unlikely source as Dave Narey, perhaps not seen as a threat by the visitors and therefore able to find space, received the ball from a Milne free kick and sent in a cute chip that Burdenski touched but couldn't keep out.

Though it wasn't a classic United performance, they had done enough to establish a narrow lead to take to West Germany. In one sense, 2-1 was no better than 1-1 as a single-goal win for the West Germans would take then through in either case. But the goal they had scored made Bremen favourites to progress and the simple fact facing United as they contemplated the second leg was that setting out their stall for a draw was unlikely to prove successful. Realistically, to reach the quarter-finals they would almost certainly need to score in Bremen.

McLean was assiduous in his preparation and spent the 11th anniversary of his appointment as manager in the Weserstadion, watching Bremen beat Eintracht Frankfurt 3-0. Eintracht is the German word for united and McLean, though impressed, was determined his United would achieve a much better outcome four days later.

The manager's spying mission had given him an idea as to how he might gain an edge on his Bremen counterpart, Otto Rehhagel, and he surprised his opponents and the travelling United fans by playing Richard Gough, Billy Kirkwood and Ralph Milne on the left rather than the right. Kirkwood's very presence was a surprise because, in what appeared to be mind games on McLean's part, the midfielder had not travelled on the club's charter flight with the official reason given as 'flu symptoms'. But those symptoms soon flew away, as did Kirkwood himself on a scheduled flight the day before the game.

Everyone associated with United knew their team would face an onslaught and the question was how the players, particularly their well-established back four, would respond. The Germans needed a single goal to advance but everyone associated with United was aware all that would change should they succeed in registering an away goal of their own. And that's precisely what they did.

Packed to capacity, the Weserstadion was a cauldron of noise, at least for the first three minutes. Then United won a corner which Milne swung over and Hegarty rose highest in a crowded six-yard box to power a header past Burdenski.

Just as they had done in Eindhoven three months earlier, the Tangerines had silenced the home crowd early on and they now held a 3-1 aggregate advantage. The good news emanating from that was that the Germans now required at least three goals to win; the bad news was that they had 87 minutes in which to score twice and take the match into extra time.

It was immediately apparent that the Bremen management and players had not foreseen such an eventuality. The home side took most of the first half to re-discover their confidence and establish some momentum but, although McAlpine was called into action a couple of times, the nearest thing to another goal came at the opposite end two minutes before the break when Dodds ought to have doubled United's lead from six yards and was kept out only by the legs of Burdenski.

Bremen re-emerged for the second half a different team. Firing on all cylinders they went on the offensive and, just as United had done in the first half, scored within three minutes. Völler beat McAlpine and that ratcheted up the already deafening volume inside the stadium by several more decibels.

Even more so than at Tannadice, Völler was proving a real thorn in United's side as the Germans attacked relentlessly, trying everything to get the goal which would give them the lead on the night and possibly the platform for a decisive third. As shots peppered McAlpine's goal the woodwork was struck no less than five times, three of them from the boot of Völler.

To describe United's situation as backs-to-the-wall scarcely tells half the story; it became a desperate rearguard as they were subjected to wave after wave of attacks.

In the 75th minute it seemed the breakthrough had come with Völler again at the heart of it. He broke clear just inside the United half and, as McAlpine advanced to meet him at the edge of the penalty area the striker expertly lobbed the ball over the advancing goalkeeper who, like everyone else inside the stadium, waited for it to drop into the net.

Well not quite everyone because Hegarty certainly hadn't given up the ghost. In a heart-stopping moment for all those watching he raced back and stuck out a leg to claw the ball out from underneath the crossbar just as it was about to cross the line.

The excitement up to that point had been intense but the incident capped everything that had preceded it and as the United defence regrouped and cleared the ensuing corner, there was a collective feeling that the denial of what had seemed certain to be a goal might have sapped the confidence of the German team.

Among the United players that great escape virtually conferred upon them a sense of invincibility, a feeling that it was their night, that a place in the quarter-finals was meant to be theirs.

The cacophony from the crowd intensified and there was no respite in Bremen's efforts, but they never again threatened the United goal to any great extent. When the final whistle sounded McLean's men sank to their knees, almost too exhausted to celebrate. They had been put through the mincer in 90 minutes of unrelenting drama but they had survived, which, as in any knockout competition, was all that mattered.

McLean revealed that during the nail-biting second half he had had no option but to put the emphasis on defence, 'It's the first time I can remember doing that deliberately. We planned to defend just inside our own half but Bremen pushed us back and I admit we were as hard pressed as we have ever been. You obviously don't get the same satisfaction winning by that tactic but all credit to the players for the way they battled it out successfully.'

Man of the match Hegarty, who scored and saved a goal, said, 'I had what I would consider was one of my best ever games, though probably because I was always in the thick of the action.'

Then what happened?

Having reached the quarter-final stage for the second successive season United had no need to fear any of the other seven clubs remaining in the competition – even though they included previous winners of European trophies in Anderlecht, Benfica and Valencia.

In the event their opponents were the unheralded East Europeans, Bohemians Prague. With the first leg to be played in the Czech capital, United were favourites to reach the last four for the first time.

But one aspect of the beauty of football is that it frequently refuses to follow logic, form or reputation. There was a three-month gap before the tie was played and the first leg was one that United had the chances to win and certainly ought not to have lost. But, on a gluepot of a pitch, their opponents scored the game's only goal, though that still left the outcome of the tie in United's favour with home advantage in the second leg.

A fortnight later, a crowd of 21,336 demonstrated that the will to see United reach the semi-final had attracted the interest of people throughout Scotland, but it was not to be. Against a side the equal of neither PSV Eindhoven nor Werder Bremen, United pushed but simply could not find a way through in a match reminiscent in many ways of the Weserstadion in December. The difference was that on this occasion United didn't prevail.

At the time – not least because that same evening Aberdeen had beaten Bayern Munich in the European Cup Winners' Cup to reach their semi-final – it was a huge disappointment. Two months later, many Arabs would come to the conclusion that it was actually a blessing in disguise.

v Dundee 5-3

Scottish Premier Division
Tannadice
12 March 1983
Attendance: 13,448

DUNDEE UNITED	DUNDEE
McAlpine	Geddes (Mackie)
Stark	McGeachie
Malpas	McKimmie
Gough	Fraser
Hegarty	Smith
Narey	MacDonald
Bannon	Ferguson
Milne (Reilly)	Bell (McLelland)
Kirkwood	Sinclair
Sturrock	Scrimgeour
Dodds (Holt)	Kidd
Manager: Jim McLean	*Manager:* Donald Mackay

A S the 1982/83 season approached its climax, Dundee United had everything to play for. Well not literally. Defeat by St Mirren in the Scottish Cup for the second successive year was disappointing but United were still in with a chance of achieving two club 'firsts' – a Premier Division title and a European semi-final.

With the exception of a single week in September, Jim McLean's team had been in the top three all season, while carefully plotting a route through the early rounds of the UEFA Cup. PSV Eindhoven, Viking Stavanger and Werder Bremen had been beaten and in the first week of March the visit to Prague resulted in a narrow first-leg loss to Bohemians by the game's only goal.

United were now anticipating a Tannadice double-header and for once the derby did not take pride of place. That was because the season's third city derby would be followed four days later by the return meeting with the Czechs. Arabs had almost come to expect that derbies would be followed by a joyous and raucous walk to the pub, where they could 'commiserate' with their Bluenose counterparts. The difference between the clubs since the Premier Division began eight years earlier had been decisive: of 14 clashes, United had won eight and Dundee three. Perhaps more pertinently, Dundee had won just one of the previous ten matches and hadn't managed to score in the first two meetings of that season, won 1-0 by United at Tannadice and 2-0 at Dens.

Secure in mid-table, the Dark Blues were managed by former United goalkeeper Donald Mackay. In the build-up to the latest meeting Mackay indulged in a spot of what might be termed mind games, suggesting McLean and his team would be more focussed on the UEFA Cup tie than on the derby.

McLean was robust in his response, 'There's no way my players will be looking over their shoulders and thinking about Wednesday when we play Dundee.' Then, deliberately playing down United's role in the league race, he added, 'We are in with an outside chance of winning the Premier League and we know only too well that we have to win every game to do so. Draws are no good to us in our situation.'

Of the 25 Premier Division games United had played to that point only three had been lost and the race to be crowned champions was a three-way contest between Aberdeen, Celtic and United, all separated by a single point with Aberdeen having played one game more. Draws would be damaging, though less so at that time when a win produced only two points. Whether or not Mackay actually believed his team might enjoy some kind of advantage through United being distracted by their upcoming European encounter, the Dark Blues were soon plunged into a distraction of their own – very much unforeseen.

The match got off to a bad start for them when goalkeeper Bobby Geddes succumbed to a freak injury after only six minutes. He damaged his collar bone in a collision with Jim Smith and played no further part in the match. In the days when only two substitutes were allowed it was rare for clubs to have a goalkeeper on the bench so midfielder Brian Scrimgeour donned the cap and gloves. He had never previously done so, but revealed after the game, 'I was the only one to offer.'

For quite some time Dundee protected Scrimgeour effectively and despite dominating the game it took half an hour for United to go ahead, Richard Gough drilling home an unstoppable shot after a corner had not been cleared. Despite their disadvantage, Dundee were not without their own chances although they failed to trouble Hamish McAlpine. In what was not shaping up as one of United's vintage performances, Ralph Milne hit the side netting from a promising position and the score remained 1-0 at half-time.

Early in the second half, Dundee complained to the referee that Davie Dodds was guilty of over-robust challenges on their stand-in goalkeeper and the official agreed, issuing the striker with a stern warning, though no yellow card.

But Dodds played no part after 50 minutes when United doubled their lead – and Scrimgeour was largely at fault. An Eamonn Bannon corner was touched on to the crossbar by Paul Sturrock and, with Scrimgeour slow to react, Gough was unchallenged as he headed home the rebound. The stand-in had been more than holding his own until then but it was a goal Geddes would probably have prevented.

Facing rivals without a recognised specialist between the sticks, Arabs contented themselves that the game was over and it was now simply a question of how many their team would score. It seems some of the players may have adopted a similar mindset because within two minutes Dundee were back in the game. Gough went from saint to sinner when he was penalised for holding Eric Sinclair in the box and Iain Ferguson netted from the spot.

The play was more even thereafter with both sides creating good chances, but tempers were becoming heated and Sturrock, Bell and Malpas were all cautioned for over-zealous challenges within the space of three minutes. It was now much more typical of a derby as play raged from end to end, although events between the 70th and 75th minutes still came as a shock.

Dundee equalised with what can only be described as a freak goal. Albert Kidd cleverly rounded Bannon in the United penalty box before unleashing a shot that McAlpine should have saved. But the ball evaded his dive, hit the post then rebounded off the prostrate goalkeeper and rolled into the net. Technically it was an own goal but no United player – least of all McAlpine – was keen to deny Kidd the credit.

Then, before the men in tangerine could come to terms with that setback, against all the odds the Dark Blues forged ahead. Sinclair fed Cammy Fraser 25 yards out and the midfielder let fly with a shot that went past McAlpine like a rocket.

For a team in their situation to turn a two-goal deficit into a lead was, to say the least, remarkable and Dundee's sudden burst of energy had taken United by surprise. Mackay immediately replaced a midfielder, David Bell, with a defender, Chic McLelland, in an attempt to hold on to the lead, while McLean bided his time as United sought to regroup and then regain control of a match that should not have been allowed to slip from their grasp.

With ten minutes remaining McLean decided to replace the tiring Milne with John Reilly, a 20-year-old striker who had been used mainly from the bench but had netted six league goals during the season.

Reilly waited only three minutes before making that seven, hitting the equaliser with a crisp shot from the edge of the box that Scrimgeour allowed to slip under his body. Again it was one that Geddes would have expected to save, but with points vital in the chase for the title nobody of a United persuasion gave a moment's thought to expressing anything resembling sympathy.

Both sets of fans were by now in full voice but the momentum was very much back with the Terrors and on 85 minutes they regained the lead. Scrimgeour had covered himself in glory on several occasions and had done the opposite on others (many fewer, it should be said) but he was powerless to prevent Paul Hegarty restoring United's advantage, the captain turning Bannon's cross in at the back post.

Sturrock almost made it five with three minutes remaining when he brilliantly volleyed a Gough flick on to and over the bar, but another goal was not long delayed. In the final minute, Dodds was on hand to bullet a header past Scrimgeour from a Billy Kirkwood cross.

Despite their understandable anguish, Dundee fans joined in the ovation given to both sets of players at the end of one of the most pulsating city derbies ever. It was not to be forgotten quickly by anyone who was there, none of whom could have known then the points that United wrested from their local rivals would prove crucial come the end of the season.

McLean was a relieved man, 'I was satisfied with the end product ... but not the overall performance. Our passing and general build-up play deserted us and our below-par display almost gave Dundee victory.'

Then what happened?

At Tannadice the following Wednesday, United battered the Bohemians defence relentlessly for almost the entire 90 minutes but could not find a way through and their interest in the UEFA Cup ended for another season.

Disappointing as that setback was for McLean and his players – not least because they knew they were more than capable of eliminating the Czechs to reach the semi-final – it did permit all their efforts to be concentrated on challenging for the Premier Division title.

There was also a form of bonus in that United's two fellow challengers, Aberdeen and Celtic, were unable to give that contest their undivided attention. The pair were due to meet in the semi-finals of the Scottish Cup while the Dons had also reached the same stage of the European Cup Winners' Cup.

Three days after their UEFA Cup exit, McLean's men travelled to Pittodrie and won 2-1 against one rival, at the same time as Dundee were helping out by beating the other, Celtic, at Dens Park.

The next city derby was scheduled to take place across the road on the final day of the season ... and the rest is history.

v Celtic 3-2

30

Scottish League Premier Division
Celtic Park
20 April 1983
Attendance: 23,965

DUNDEE UNITED	CELTIC
McAlpine	Bonner
Stark	Sinclair (McCluskey)
Malpas	Reid
Gough	Aitken
Hegarty	McAdam
Narey	MacLeod
Bannon	Provan
Milne	McStay
Holt	Nicholas
Sturrock	Burns
Dodds	McGarvey
Manager: Jim McLean	*Manager:* Billy McNeill

THOUGH the sense of disappointment at United's failure to reach the semi-finals of the UEFA Cup was keenly felt in the Tannadice dressing room, it was not permitted to linger long.

Jim McLean later recalled there were suggestions the following day that the team's season was as good as over because United lay three points behind leaders Aberdeen and two behind Celtic. Even though a win was then worth two points, it seems ludicrous that with the club so close to the top two and with ten Premier Division matches remaining – more than a quarter of the programme – such a suggestion could have been made.

Yet it was. Just two weeks earlier (and two days after returning from Prague) United had visited Motherwell, and convincingly beaten the home side 4-1. That drew this remark from the *Sunday Mail*'s reporter, 'United kept their slim championship hopes alive with a fine victory at Fir Park.' Support of the theory was hard to find, though journalists from that and other newspapers made the effort.

Underpinning their flimsy analysis was a deep-seated suspicion that United simply didn't have the staying power for the final straight of a title chase, with events in 1978/79 cited as 'evidence'. That ignored the fact that in the intervening four years United had progressed quite significantly under McLean and, in case nobody had noticed, had won two trophies while showing great strength and maturity in Europe.

And, of the ten league matches remaining after their UEFA Cup exit, six were away – three involving visits to Pittodrie and Celtic Park. Further, in three Premier Division meetings already that season with Aberdeen and two with Celtic, United had managed just one win.

The last point did at least have some validity as, despite beating Aberdeen 2-0 at Tannadice on the opening day of the season United had been thrashed 5-1 at Pittodrie in October and had done little better when the Dons visited Tannadice for the second time, going down 3-0. The meetings with Celtic, both at Tannadice, had ended with honours even.

Now, a supposedly despondent United had to make a return trip to the Granite City on the back of their European exit to face an Aberdeen team buoyant following their elimination of Bayern Munich.

McLean wasn't fazed by all of this and used it as reverse psychology on his players. Of course their season was not over, though another defeat at Pittodrie would undoubtedly seriously damage their title challenge. As they prepared for one of the most demanding games they would face that season, McLean called on his players to show character – and that's certainly what they did.

Determined to look forwards not backwards, the Tangerines seized the initiative from the start and midway through the first half had their reward when Ralph Milne scored twice within five minutes. Aberdeen pulled a goal back in the second half and then, with less than 20 minutes remaining, Milne turned from saint to sinner when he was sent off.

How easy it would have been for United to crumble, allowing the Dons to equalise, or worse. But sheer refusal to countenance that, allied to the strength of their defence, saw them hold out for two crucial points.

On returning to the dressing room they received the news that Celtic had lost – at Dens Park, of all places – meaning that United now lay just a point behind Aberdeen and ahead of Celtic on goal difference, though the Glasgow side had a game in hand. Season over? It was just taking off.

Next up were two home games and although drawing with struggling Hibernian was careless, a week later Rangers were beaten 3-1. Remarkably, with seven games left, United were guaranteed a place in Europe because Rangers were now too far adrift to catch them. Now for the crunch – the first of two visits within a fortnight to Celtic Park.

Over the years, the famous stadium in Glasgow's east end had rarely proved a happy hunting ground for United. It was not until their 11th journey on league business that the club managed to record a win there in 1967 and the 22 visits since then had produced just one more.

The first part of the double-header took place on 6 April and the fact it attracted a midweek crowd of 34,508 – 11,000 more than their season's average – demonstrated the importance of the occasion in the eyes of the Celtic support. It was a hard-fought, physical encounter with nothing between the teams, reflected in the scoreline remaining at 0-0 after an hour. Then something quite uncharacteristic happened – Paul Hegarty made a mistake, which allowed McGarvey to give Celtic the lead. Nicholas didn't require any assistance to add a brilliant and decisive second and there was no further score.

That came as a blow to United. It meant the Tangerines trailed Celtic by three points and, although they were level with Aberdeen, the Pittodrie side now had a game in hand.

McLean and his players had a heart-to-heart the next day, the manager spelling out that with just six games remaining there was room for no further slip-ups. United beat St Mirren 2-1 at Paisley the following Saturday and ten days later made their third consecutive journey to the west coast for the return visit to Celtic.

Despite the defeat they had suffered a fortnight earlier, McLean demonstrated the confidence that he had in his players by sending out the same team. Some might have suspected that redemption or revenge would be the motivating factor for United, but it was not: something more tangible and much more important dominated their thoughts. All that mattered was a win because that would have the effect of a four-point shift in the dynamic at the top of the table.

Given that, it was perplexing that the crowd was significantly down on the earlier meeting. Perhaps some Celtic supporters regarded that first victory as decisive, although there were plenty of Arabs present to ensure their team were in no doubt the league race was far from over.

With Dave Narey operating in a central midfield role, it was United who did the bulk of the early pressing. Several corners were forced, although initially none troubled Pat Bonner in the Celtic goal. However, with 14 minutes played the latest one led to United seizing the lead. Two weeks earlier, Hegarty had been responsible for an error in the lead-up to Celtic's first goal. Now it was the turn of the home defence to make a mistake – and how appropriate it was that Hegarty should be the man to benefit.

Eamonn Bannon's corner was not one that should have caused Celtic problems. No United player was close to the ball as Bonner and his captain Roy Aitken rose to meet it. That was the key, because they got in each other's way with the result that the ball spun off Aitken's head to the unguarded opposite side of the goal, where Hegarty was required to do no more than extend his right leg to send it in.

Already this game had shown signs of being as closely-contested and as uncompromising as the first. But with less than 15 minutes played, there was a crucial difference – United were ahead.

Celtic's mantle as champions was not one that was ever likely to be removed easily and they appreciated the scale of the task that faced them. As the men in hoops stepped up the pressure, Narey and Bannon were in superb form, as were Milne and Paul Sturrock, who stretched Celtic whenever they received the ball. At the back, Richard Gough was playing with much more maturity than someone just turned 21, particularly as he was partnering Hegarty in central defence rather than occupying his normal role as an attacking full-back.

Despite their best efforts, Celtic had not troubled Hamish McAlpine but they hauled themselves back into the game via the penalty spot. Seven minutes of the first half remained when Davie Provan, who had been the home side's most dangerous attacker, fired in a cross that United failed to clear. The ball landed at the feet of Tommy Burns, who was barged to the ground by Derek Stark. The referee's decision was a straightforward one and Nicholas was clinical with his kick.

Over the piece the half-time score was a reasonable reflection but McLean must have delivered a powerful team talk because when his players emerged for the second half it was immediately clear they had raised their game.

Gough was booked for an uncompromising tackle on George McCluskey as United served notice that they were unwilling to play second fiddle. After 52 minutes a ball into the box was collected by Davie Dodds, who was then pulled to the ground by Murdo MacLeod. Another clear penalty and another no-nonsense kick saw Bannon restore United's advantage.

That caused an already fiery encounter to become even more intense and six minutes later things reached boiling point. After Provan and Gough squared up to each other, sparking a general melee, the referee cautioned the Celtic man but sent Gough to the dressing room, presumably due to his earlier booking. That meant United faced more than half an hour with ten men and, with Narey pulled back into defence, they were left exposed in midfield.

That was not to say McLean told his men to concentrate on defending their lead, although the extent to which Celtic launched an all-out assault on the United goal more or less made that the de facto response. Pressure had been building when the strong-running McCluskey turned quickly and lost the two defenders tracking him. He then squared the ball to Burns who swept it high past McAlpine and into the net.

Seventeen minutes of the match remained; 17 minutes that would come to define United's season. Players and supporters were only too aware that, while a draw would not be too damaging, a defeat would bring to an end their hopes of becoming Scotland's champions for the first time.

It is not clear at which point the players (it seems they and not McLean made the decision) reached the conclusion that attack was the best form of defence. With forward players of the talent – and energy – of Bannon, Milne and Sturrock, United keeping Celtic occupied in their own half whenever possible had the double benefit of reducing the chances of losing another goal while maintaining the possibility of making the decisive strike themselves.

It was a high-risk strategy that paid off in sensational fashion. With 84 minutes played, Bannon drove at the Celtic defence down the left before crossing to Milne. In a display of brilliant technique, Milne controlled the ball on his chest before lobbing it over the heads of three Celtic defenders and beyond Bonner.

It was a goal of quite stunning quality and it seemed to suck the life out of Celtic because they never seriously threatened a third equaliser as United held out for a glorious win over their rivals, against the odds and with only ten men – just as they had done when they went to Aberdeen.

The victory at Celtic Park left United just one point behind Celtic with Aberdeen four adrift, albeit with two games in hand.

Rarely one to over-enthuse, McLean described it as, 'Probably the best performance away from home since I became manager.' It certainly turned out to be the most important because without it United would not have won the league title.

Then what happened?

Four days later, Aberdeen beat Celtic at Pittodrie while United were defeating Kilmarnock at Tannadice. So, with three games remaining, United were the leaders for the first time that season. It was a position they never relinquished.

v Dundee 2-1

31

Scottish League Premier Division
Dens Park
14 May 1983
Attendance: 29,106

DUNDEE UNITED	DUNDEE
McAlpine	Kelly
Stark	Glennie (Mackie)
Malpas	McKimmie
Gough	Fraser
Hegarty	Smith
Narey	MacDonald
Bannon	Ferguson
Milne	McGeachie
Kirkwood	Sinclair
Sturrock (Holt)	Stephen
Dodds	Kidd
Manager: Jim McLean	*Manager:* Donald Mackay

THERE is a saying in football that the only time it matters which club occupies top spot in the league table is after the final match of the season has been completed. The thrilling victory at Celtic Park on 20 April proved to be a pivotal moment of 1982/83 for United. As they headed for the dressing room that evening they knew collectively that they could win the league. Before that they had believed it was a possibility; now they knew it was within their powers, if not yet quite within their grasp.

Three days later United beat Kilmarnock 4-0 at Tannadice to assume leadership of the Premier Division for the first time that season. They had three matches remaining and, providing they won each of them, could not be prevented from winning the title and becoming champions of Scotland.

Most of the football journalists who had poured cold water on that idea had changed their tune. The *Sunday Mail* was typical, 'Dundee United's skill and ability has never been in doubt. Now they've added self-confidence and belief to those attributes, they'll take some stopping in their challenge for the Premier flag.'

The next two matches, against Morton at Cappielow Park and Motherwell at Tannadice, were also won 4-0, demonstrating that the Tangerines had found their best form at the right moment. That burst of 12 goals without reply had not just established United at the top of the table, one point ahead of Celtic and Aberdeen. It gave them a goal difference superior to their rivals and, with one match still to play, they had already exceeded the record number of goals scored in a Premier Division season.

Jim McLean's team were top on merit – all they had to do now was deliver the *coup de grâce* and the title would be theirs. As the final day of what had been a long season approached the manager acknowledged that neither formal training nor detailed tactical planning was necessary. Through their collective efforts McLean and his players had taken United to the cusp of the greatest achievement in the club's 74-year history.

So he largely left his men to their own thoughts, reasoning, 'With what the players are going out to play for, there is no talking I can do. They know that they'll achieve near immortality if they win the league championship and if that doesn't make them play, then nothing will.'

It was such a huge occasion that the fact it involved a visit to their oldest and fiercest rivals couldn't increase the pressure any further. In any case, Dens Park was a ground, to United's players and supporters, associated with nothing but success.

Over the past four seasons it had been the scene of both their Scottish League Cup triumphs while the previous three league derbies there had ended in two-goal wins for the visitors, the most recent four months previously. It was no exaggeration to state that United were almost as comfortable playing at Dens as they were at Tannadice.

In retrospect, it seems astonishing that a match of such importance was not made all-ticket. They were required for the grandstand – then the only seated part of the ground – but for all other areas it was pay-as-you-go. The Scottish League Cup Final between the clubs in December 1980 was all-ticket with a safety limit of 24,700 set. Although Dundee had nothing to play for in what was a Premier Division decider, it was never likely that their supporters would boycott the match while for those of a United affiliation, being there to witness the club becoming Scotland's champions was an even bigger enticement than seeing the League Cup retained.

It was, surely, predictable that the number of people wanting to get into Dens Park would exceed the safety limit and that was what happened. Although the attendance figure released after the match was precisely 25,000, it later emerged the actual number who had paid for entry was 29,106, almost 4,500 above the safety limit. Even that wasn't sufficient to meet demand because people were seen perched on the roofs of buildings behind the east end of the ground, where the bulk of the United supporters were.

Although Tayside Police seemed as relaxed about that as they were about the safety limit being breached, they did issue encouragement to supporters to arrive early to minimise congestion outside and inside Dens Park and that advice was heeded.

In Scotland it's normal for fans to arrive as close to the start of the match as possible but this time the ground was well-filled an hour before kick-off, continental-style. The persistent rain made no difference to the spirits of both sets of supporters, who offered up their full repertoire of songs.

On a heavy pitch, the match began at a brisk pace as both teams won corners. Tension was very much in the air for Arabs, anxious that their players should settle quickly; they knew United were the more skilful team and if they played to form, they would win. But football is rarely as straightforward as that so the best way for nerves to be settled – on and off the park – is with an early goal. Few, though, could have envisaged it coming as early as the fourth minute.

Just inside his own half, Paul Sturrock controlled a pass from Dave Narey before swivelling round then releasing the ball for Ralph Milne to run on to. Seeming to skate over the greasy surface the striker used his pace to skip past an attempted tackle by Stewart McKimmie and then spotted that goalkeeper Colin Kelly was off his line. Contemptuously, he sent a sublime chip over the stranded Dundee man from 25 yards.

Although there were more compelling reasons for having finished in such outstanding fashion, it was nonetheless a belated birthday present to himself, having turned 22 the previous day. Dundee-born and bred, he would later confide that it was, 'Probably the best goal I've ever scored...undoubtedly the most important.'

Having made a habit of scoring vital goals during the season – not least the winners at Pittodrie and Celtic Park in the run-in – Milne had now given his team the perfect springboard from which to close in on the championship.

Having built their challenge for the title with incisive attacking play, there was never any doubt United would continue driving forward for a second goal. That they should succeed may not have been unexpected, that it should come just seven minutes after the first probably was.

Arabs were still celebrating Milne's monumental strike when Narey, playing in midfield, moved on to a flick from Sturrock inside the penalty area. Iain MacDonald made a rash challenge which brought the United man down and the referee had no hesitation in awarding a penalty.

The official had to get involved before the kick could be taken, as Kelly insisted on jumping around on his line with the intent of breaking the concentration of Eamonn Bannon as he prepared himself.

Kelly eventually calmed down and made a fine save when the kick was taken. Then his luck ran out as the ball broke away from him and Bannon had little difficulty in scoring at the second attempt.

Eleven minutes had been played and United were two ahead; had they scripted the match themselves they could hardly have envisaged a more positive and uplifting start. That said, everyone in tangerine would have been far happier had that second goal hit the net 11 minutes from the end of the game, but United were in control.

The pride that is inherent in a derby would never have allowed the Dundee players to adopt the role of spectators as their rivals strolled to victory. So it was perfectly understandable that the Dark Blues began to come into the game more, although United twice more came close to increasing their lead.

Midway through the half, Sturrock sent in a lob that deceived Kelly, who could only touch it on to his crossbar and he was mightily relieved that Bobby Glennie was on hand to clear. Minutes later United again hit the woodwork and this time came even closer to making the score 3-0. Bannon reached the by-line before cutting the ball back to Dodds who side-footed it against the underside of the bar, from where it bounced down on, but not over, the line.

If that was a let-off for the home side they wasted no time in capitalising on it as, within a minute of United's lead almost being stretched to three, Dundee had cut it to just one. Eric Sinclair headed a cross down to Iain Ferguson who lashed the ball into the bottom corner of the net from 15 yards, well out of the reach of Hamish McAlpine.

That came after 28 minutes and for a period immediately following it the game's dynamic shifted. With Dundee re-invigorated, United lost their grip on the play and with it went their early ascendancy. Dundee had much more influence and most Arabs were relieved to hear the half-time whistle, anticipating that McLean would use the time in the dressing room to settle his players and map out their route through the second 45 minutes.

The second half was a more even contest, though the 45 minutes began to feel like as many hours as the tension increased. United were still intent on using attack as the best form of defence but now the Dundee midfield was benefitting from the wet conditions, which slowed play down. Shortly before the hour-mark Sturrock came close, cutting in from the left before firing in a shot that the diving Kelly just managed to push over the bar.

That was one of few opportunities fashioned by either side and two minutes later Sturrock, who had suffered a recurrence of a hamstring strain, limped off to be replaced by John Holt. Luggy was later to reveal, 'If ever I am unlucky enough to develop ulcers...the last 30 minutes of this match could well be the root cause, because the pressure of having to sit and watch the remainder of that game from the dugout was almost unbearable.'

McLean also made some positional changes, bringing Narey back to his usual position at the heart of the defence, with the tough-tackling Derek Stark joining Holt in a more robust midfield.

The message was clear – Dundee were to be halted in their tracks when they attempted to come forward, but should they manage to do so the formidable pairing of Narey and Paul Hegarty would provide a barrier.

Dundee continued to make life difficult but they were able to create just one chance which caused anxious moments for United. On 72 minutes a Cammie Fraser free kick reached Albert Kidd and the diminutive winger was allowed a free header. Fortunately for United Kidd seemed taken by surprise, sending the ball over when it seemed easier to score.

That caused McLean to abandon his normal place on the bench and for the remainder of the match he was constantly out of the dugout, roaring instructions, most of which must have gone unheard by the United players in the cauldron of noise that was now at its peak.

As the minutes ticked slowly by, Arabs stopped singing and resorted to emitting shrill whistles as if to encourage the referee to release the only one that mattered. In those final minutes Bannon had a free kick touched round the post by Kelly but that went almost unnoticed as, from a United perspective, the most important fact was that the ball was in the opposing half and out of danger.

Finally, referee George Smith signalled the end of the match and a tumultuous roar exploded from those parts of Dens Park coloured tangerine and black. Fans were shouting, cheering, leaping into the air, hugging their neighbours and, in more than a few cases, breaking into tears. All behaviour which, in the circumstances, was as justified as it was understandable, because their club were now officially the best in the country. Dundee United were champions of Scotland.

Then what happened?

As the players celebrated on the pitch, they soaked up the joy emanating from supporters who had followed their club for so many years, barely daring to hope they might one day experience a moment like this.

As there was no trophy to be presented the players eventually headed for the dressing room but the roars of the crowd brought them back and they then raised McLean on to their shoulders, which allowed iconic pictures to be taken, soon to adorn the wall of many a home or workplace.

In the latter part of the season, McLean had said, 'I feel that, year by year, the club is making progress. We could win the league. We have a stronger pool than we had when we almost won it four years ago.'

Yet, even with that achievement just one win away, he reverted to type, refusing to allow champagne to be bought in anticipation of victory. With corks popping all around him he revealed, 'We had to send out for this at time up. It's not our style to pre-judge anything.'

Much champagne was consumed that night by celebrating supporters as they partied late into the night. As, deservedly, did the players, many ending up at the home of Frank Kopel, for so long one of them, but who had left the club the previous year.

The following day the players played a testimonial match at Forfar before returning to Tannadice, where the league trophy had now arrived. They then boarded an open-top bus that headed for the city square.

Despite persistent rain, a huge, happy, singing crowd was there to greet them, almost lifting the roof off the city chambers as the trophy was paraded by the players. The bus then toured the city to let as many people as possible see the trophy, almost as if there was a need to prove to them that, however improbable it seemed, Dundee United really were champions of Scotland.

It is apposite that the last word on a memorable triumph should go to the man who, above all others, made it possible. McLean said, 'For the first time in 12 and a half years as manager I couldn't speak to the players in the dressing room. I was shaking with emotion after dying a thousand deaths in the Dens dugout. I'm sure very few people will grudge us the championship. There's no way we should be champions, though, because we really only have 12 players and they've had to sustain us for 55 matches.'

He was exaggerating, though only slightly. In winning the Premier Division United had ten players who played in more than 30 of the 36 matches, while another two played 26 and 28. Only two more reached double figures in appearances and it was that solid core that enabled United to find the consistency that made them champions.

Never one to blow his own trumpet, McLean did not say that of the 13 players at Dens Park on the last day of the season only Hamish McAlpine was not signed by him, while ten of them – including McAlpine – had emerged through the United ranks to become champions.

The indomitable spirit of the squad was the cornerstone of that triumph and it stemmed from having 11 of the players steeped in the fabric of Dundee United, as shown by their overall appearance records: two played more than 800 games for the club; another three made 700+, 600+ and 500+ respectively; two played over 400 and another two almost 400, while two more played more than 250. It is no surprise that three later became United managers.

It would be impossible to overestimate the influence that McLean had on Dundee United becoming such a force in Scotland and Europe. His achievements made every supporter immensely proud to be an Arab – and still do.

v AS Roma 2-0

32

European Cup Semi-Final First Leg
Tannadice
11 April 1984
Attendance: 20,543

DUNDEE UNITED	AS ROMA
McAlpine	Tancredi
Stark	Oddi
Malpas	Righetti
Gough	Nela
Hegarty	Di Bartolomei
Narey	Maldera
Bannon	Conti
Milne	Cerezo
Kirkwood	Pruzzo
Sturrock (Coyne)	Chierico
Dodds	Graziani
Manager: Jim McLean	*Head coach:* Nils Liedholm

THE summer of 1983 saw United's players and supporters slowly drift back down to earth following the ultimate high of the final day at Dens Park. Gradually, thoughts began to turn to the new campaign and the prospect of United flying the flag for Scotland in the European Cup. The original and the most prestigious of the three UEFA tournaments, the European Champion Clubs Cup had begun in 1955. In that first season Scotland's representatives were Hibernian, not because they were champions, but because they were then the only club whose ground had floodlights suitable for staging the ties.

United became the seventh club to enter the competition as Scotland's champions and they could fairly claim to have served a proper European apprenticeship on the way there, having played 46 matches from 11 qualifications since 1966.

The European Cup was the premier tournament but, with only one club per country eligible to enter, the strength in depth was less than in the UEFA Cup. As United had reached the quarter-finals of that competition in the two previous seasons, it was with some justification that Jim McLean and his players believed they were well prepared for the challenges awaiting them.

The opening round presented United with a relatively straightforward introduction by pairing them with the champions of Malta, Hamrun Spartans. Two 3-0 victories opened the door to a more formidable opponent in the shape of Standard Liege. It was the second time United been drawn against the Belgians; five years earlier the clubs had met in the UEFA Cup with Liege advancing after scoring the only goal of two closely-contested legs.

This time it was different. United had grown up in European terms since then and a controlled and disciplined performance in Belgium secured a 0-0 draw. But at Tannadice the Tangerines let rip with 90 minutes of scintillating football. Liege were pulled apart as Ralph Milne produced another outstanding performance, scoring twice in a 4-0 win that again brought Dundee United to the centre of the European stage.

That meant United had reached a European quarter-final for a third consecutive season, although no one at Tannadice would have suggested that this occasion was as worthy as the others. The next opponents were Rapid Vienna but, because there were fewer clubs involved in the European Cup, there followed a gap of four months before the ties were played.

If style had been the passport to the quarter-final, true grit was required for progress beyond that stage as the Austrian champions proved hard nuts to crack. After a series of narrow escapes in the first leg by the Danube, Derek Stark scored to give United the away goal that would be worth its weight in gold. But Rapid mounted a strong second-half offensive which finally had its reward with two late goals and Arabs there that evening were not too dissatisfied with a final score of 2-1.

Two weeks later an expectant crowd of 18,865 assembled at Tannadice and they were not disappointed. Although the popular view was that all United had to do was to score once to claim a semi-final place, there was a rather important caveat to that – they must also ensure they didn't concede.

In the event, things worked out well. Davie Dodds scored after 21 minutes and, although Rapid put the home defence under pressure as they went for what they believed would be the decisive goal, United held out to become one of only four clubs remaining in the European Cup.

Now came the crunch because the other three were AS Roma, Dinamo Bucharest and Liverpool. This wasn't the first time that the city had provided a European Cup semi-finalist – Dundee had been there in 1963. They lost to AC Milan and, in a remarkable parallel 21 years on, United also drew Italian opposition.

There the similarities ended, though, firstly because United would play the first leg at home and secondly because Roma did not have a reputation to match that of AC Milan.

Although Roma had won the Inter-Cities Fairs Cup in 1961 they did not have a great European pedigree and, like United, were first-time participants in the European Cup. That said, any club crowned champions of Serie A represents formidable opposition and Roma had in their ranks two members of Italy's 1982 World Cup-winning team, Conti and Graziani, as well as two Brazilians, Cerezo and Falcao, who had represented their country in those finals.

A further factor increased the task facing United. Before the competition began it was known that the Stadio Olimpico would host the final and having the rare opportunity to compete for Europe's top prize at their home ground had to be a powerful motivating force for Roma.

There was tremendous interest in the tie and tickets reflected both that and the occasion itself. Prices were doubled to £5 standing and £10 for the stand, producing record Tannadice receipts of £120,000. There was some adverse reaction to the prices but the club had looked after their regular fans by allowing free entry to ticket holders to the following weekend's Premier Division match with St Johnstone.

The occasion would not easily be forgotten by those privileged to be there. The absence through injury of Falcao was not mourned by Arabs but the Italians quickly demonstrated they didn't intend to employ a containing game. In fact, they were the first to threaten when Odoacre Chierico made room for a shot that flew narrowly wide.

After seven minutes it was United who came close to opening the scoring. Milne sent a free kick towards the near post but somehow Paul Sturrock failed to get the touch which would have produced a goal.

The tackling was uncompromising by both sides with some challenges not for the faint-hearted, though not for the first time Hamish McAlpine provided some light relief – or perhaps it was merely relief – when he raced 30 yards from his goal to head the ball away from the advancing Roberto Pruzzo, then nullified any threat by delivering a neat pass.

Play was more even than McLean would have liked and he must have been concerned in the 25th minute when the next near miss came from Roma, because it was very near indeed. Chierico floated a delicate cross in from the left and Francesco Graziani reached it ahead of Richard Gough to send a header against the bar. The danger was cleared but the warning to United was unambiguous – Roma were determined to get a crucial away goal.

The remainder of the first half saw the two sides cancelling each other out and for McLean the interval provided the opportunity to instil in his players the importance of increasing their tempo to a level that the Italians were unaccustomed to.

Straight from the re-start the Tangerines injected a level of pace that Roma couldn't handle and during that opening phase the first goal was created. Paul Hegarty had just headed narrowly over when United regained possession. Gough drove down the right, evading tackles before sending over a cross to the back post that was missed by the Roma defence. It reached Eamonn Bannon, whose angled drive struck a defender and broke to Sturrock. Showing razor-sharp thought and reflexes he touched the ball back to Dodds, whose low shot slid inside the post.

That came after 48 minutes and brought the crowd alive while leaving the Italians exchanging accusing glances and, in some cases, words. United wisely seized the opportunity to build on their momentum, mounting sustained pressure which 12 minutes later paid off handsomely. Again Sturrock was the instigator, collecting the ball on the touchline near the Roma penalty area before pushing it into the path of the advancing Stark. The full-back took a few paces before unleashing a blistering drive from 25 yards that dipped and swerved as it deceived goalkeeper Franco Tancredi and hit the net with Tannadice erupting in an ear-splitting roar.

Those goals were scored in front of the 1,000 hitherto-noisy Roma fans and understandably had the effect of silencing them. Roma were now rocking as United maintained the tempo and might well have added to their tally.

Milne had been largely anonymous in the first half but was making up for it in the second and he had a fierce shot from just inside the penalty area beaten away for a corner. He took the kick himself and from it Hegarty had another header frantically tipped over the bar by Tancredi.

The fact that Chierico – their best player – was booked for a wild tackle on Bannon illustrated the extent of the Italians' eclipse. That there was no further scoring was due to a damage-limitation exercise by them that ensured they were still in the tie when the final whistle sounded.

McLean explained what lay behind United's second-half performance, 'I told the players at half-time that they were out of the tournament the ways things stood and that they might as well relax in the second half. They did just that … we scored two really good goals but deserved more and now we're just 90 minutes away from absolute glory.'

Roma coach Nils Liedholm looked and sounded shattered by the result, 'We missed Falcao but I thought my players were beginning to put things together, until United hit us with those goals.' But he added ominously, 'Falcao should be able to play in Rome and he will make a big difference.'

Such was the power of United's second-half display that the Roma president actually suggested the men in tangerine had been on drugs. Given the more languid style of Italian football it was understandable the Italians might have been taken aback by United's pace but there was real venom in their post-match comments, a trend that was relentless in the run-up to the second leg – and didn't even let up after it.

Then what happened?

It is tempting to say 'don't remember' but the events at the Stadio Olimpico were, for very different reasons, as unforgettable as those at Tannadice.

For a match second only in importance in the club's history to the Premier Division championship-clincher the previous year, McLean enlisted the advice and assistance of a man who knew not just how to reach a European Cup final but how to win one. Scotland manager Jock Stein travelled with the United party to Rome – and into an atmosphere even he had not previously witnessed.

In the cauldron of the Stadio Olimpico the 500 United fans there had to be moved by the police to another part of the ground for their own safety before kick-off and when the players emerged pre-match they were pelted with oranges and less yielding objects. It would have been strange had they not been at all intimidated by the wave of hatred that swept down from the terraces. It was little less intense from the Roma players and their bench. It is not in any way an indictment of United to suggest the determination to reach the final was greater among the home players, because for them the prize was to play it on home turf, something that they regarded as their destiny.

Not that the United players didn't give their all but it simply wasn't one of their better European performances and there's no doubt that they were simply outplayed on the day.

Yet McLean's men might well have extended their overall lead to three early on when Bannon crossed and the ball was missed by Dodds, but arrived unexpectedly at the feet of Milne. He could have steadied himself but chose to shoot first-time only to see it spin over the bar.

That was pretty much United's only opportunity of the match. Roma had tied the aggregate score before half-time with goals in the 21st and 38th minutes and a penalty midway through the second half proved the decisive strike.

The improbable appearance of Dundee United in the European Cup Final did not come to pass. In the event, the Romans were unable to translate home advantage into victory in the final. Liverpool were just a bit too world-wise and perhaps a bit too mentally tough to be swayed by the kind of intimidation suffered by United and the match ended 1-1 after extra time.

To the unrestrained delight of everyone associated with United, the English club won the penalty shoot-out, leaving the Italians with precisely what they deserved – nothing.

The gauntlet of hate that McLean and his assistant, Walter Smith, had to run, perpetrated by Roma players, officials and fans alike – as they returned to the dressing room was a disgrace and largely attributable to a smear campaign fuelled by the Italian press following the first leg.

The manager later said the experience had left him scarred; not literally, though it might well have done.

It was no better for the players. Sturrock recalled, 'As we left the park we were subjected to a torrent of abuse and hatred by their players and management. We were all spat upon until we reached the sanctuary of the dressing room.'

And that thuggery came from winners – the response had the Italians been losers can barely be imagined. Anyone doubting that should consider this comment by a man not known for exaggeration, 'There are times I feel that if we had been the team in the final then I might not be alive today,' said McLean.

Though in retrospect nothing associated with United's Italian experience should have come as a surprise, the revelation two years later that a Roma official had attempted to bribe the French referee, Michel Vautrot, before the second leg still retained the ability to shock. UEFA suspended director Riccardo Viola from all UEFA activities for four years and the club itself was handed a one-year ban from European competition.

Typical of UEFA's weak-kneed approach to dealing with the bigger clubs, the latter was subsequently commuted to a fine, which even *Gazetto Dello Sport* described as 'a scandalous decision'.

There was no evidence Vautrot had accepted the bribe and, equally, there was no evidence during the match he had been influenced by the offer. He disallowed a Roma 'goal' in the first half because of a foul in the build-up and the award of their penalty was not contentious.

Shocking as those events were, it was to McLean's great credit that he refused to seek solace in them, stating unequivocally the reason United lost was simply that the players proved unable to rise to the occasion in Rome, 'All I know is that we did not play well. We played well at Tannadice. Possibly we deserved even more than we got from the first game – but we got what we deserved in the Olympic Stadium. Probably, ten out of our 11 players didn't reach their normal standards. That is what cost us our place in the European Cup Final.'

Nonetheless, though that episode left an unpleasant taste in the mouth it was merely one strand of the nastiness that United experienced. But the controversy over the Italians' despicable conduct tended to obscure the achievement of reaching the semi-final of Europe's premier tournament at the first attempt.

v **Morton** 7-0

33

Scottish League Premier Division
Tannadice
17 November 1984
Attendance: 8,562

DUNDEE UNITED	**MORTON**
McAlpine	Adams
Malpas	Wilson
Holt	Holmes
Gough	O'Hara (McClurg)
Hegarty	Mackie
Narey	Duffy
Bannon	Robertson
Taylor (McGinnis)	Docherty
Coyne	Gillespie
Sturrock	Clinging
Beedie	Pettigrew
Manager: Jim McLean	*Manager:* Willie McLean

AFTER the demoralising defeat in the European Cup semi-final, for most Dundee United players and supporters the 1983/84 season could not come to an end soon enough. While drawing a line and moving on was understandable, given the circumstances, until that fateful day in Rome it had been often exhilarating, both at home and abroad.

Yet a final league placing of third was disappointing. As champions United were the team to beat and for the most part they responded well to that challenge. They were never below third throughout the season, yet never rose above it after November. They dealt well with one major rival, avoiding defeat against Celtic, but fell short in crunch games against Aberdeen, who ultimately won the title with ten points more than United.

During the summer of 1984 Jim McLean resolved to refresh his squad for the new campaign, using some of the resources produced by those electric European Cup nights at Tannadice. He brought in Scottish international goalkeeper Billy Thomson from St Mirren for £70,000 and attacking midfielder Stuart Beedie from St Johnstone for £90,000.

Those additions to an already strong squad had some pundits pointing to United as being capable of returning the Premier Division championship to Tannadice; but that was some way removed from the reality of 1984/85. By the end of October they were not even in the top half of the table.

The first three months had seen a continuation of the excellent form in the Scottish League Cup, with Celtic and Hearts eliminated en route to United's fourth final in six years. Yet six of the opening 11 Premier Division matches had been lost and already pretensions of a title challenge had all-but evaporated.

It was a stuttering start and unfortunately the inconsistency then spread to the Scottish League Cup as the form that had seen United reach the final was absent when that occasion came around. Opponents Rangers were in comparative doldrums and would end the season in fourth, nine points behind United. But they claimed the only goal at Hampden with the scorer being Iain Ferguson, who would join United in two years.

The final was sandwiched between the two legs of a 7-2 aggregate UEFA Cup second round defeat of LASK Linz from Austria, which followed the first-round dismissal of AIK Stockholm. The prize was a mouthwatering tie against Manchester United and the very prospect appeared to revitalise the Tangerines' league form. The first two matches in November produced wins over St Mirren and Dundee and the following week Morton were the visitors at Tannadice.

With the Greenock club propping up the table and United having won 3-0 at Cappielow Park two months earlier, the outcome was not difficult to predict. What gave the match extra intrigue, however, was that it featured a confrontation between managers who knew each other rather well – because they were brothers.

Jim McLean was the middle one of three footballing siblings from the Lanarkshire village of Ashgill, all of whom played and managed at senior level. The youngest, Tommy, had the most illustrious playing career, earning Scotland caps and winning league championships with Kilmarnock and Rangers. The achievements of the eldest, Willie, were more modest although he had been Motherwell's manager during the Premier Division's first three seasons in the 1970s and returned to the top level with Morton in the summer of 1984 – replacing brother Tommy.

The McLeans are a close-knit family and the three all stated they never enjoyed being pitted against one another, though with Scottish football forming what is a relatively small pond, such scenarios were not uncommon from the 1960s to the 90s. It may have been more than coincidence, then, that Jim opted to forego this particular family reunion, travelling instead to Old Trafford on a spying mission 11 days before he was due to take his team there for the first leg of the UEFA Cup tie. The English club were returning the complement with one of their coaching staff present at Tannadice.

Prior to relegation in 1983, Morton had spent five seasons in the Premier Division but they bounced straight back a year later. It is more than possible they already wished they hadn't bothered by the time they travelled to meet United at Tannadice. Because, after winning their first two matches they managed just one more out of the 12 that followed and were bottom of the table for almost two months.

The day was to turn into a personal triumph for a player who had reached the very top of his profession. Since making his first-team debut for United at the age of 17 in 1974, Paul Sturrock had won the Premier Division and had been part of two Scottish League Cup-winning teams. For good measure he had won 15 caps for his country and had been a member of the Scotland squad at the 1982 World Cup. Just prior to the tournament he had enjoyed a further accolade when the Scottish football writers voted him their player of the year.

With 1984/85 three months old, United had played 19 matches in all competitions and Sturrock had started every one. Nicknamed Luggy in his youth because of protruding ears, he had recently voiced his concern at what he felt was a lack of protection provided by referees to flair players like himself. He claimed he often spent half the time between games on the treatment table because of tough tackling from defenders – a situation so serious he said it had forced him to consider leaving Scotland.

One of the most exciting attacking players United had ever produced, Sturrock had twice ended a season as United's leading scorer (one of them shared with Davie Dodds) though he also created many goals for his strike partners. He had only once managed to score a hat-trick – against Morton, at Tannadice, in 1981.

Perhaps that ought to have been a warning for the men from Greenock but rather than heed it manager Willie McLean decided that was the day to hand a debut to 19-year-old goalkeeper Craig Adams. At the other end of the age scale was a player who, despite appearing in blue and white hoops, received a tremendous reception from the United supporters. Now 31, Willie Pettigrew remained a Tannadice hero having scored in both of the club's Scottish League Cup triumphs.

The match began as it was to continue, with United on the attack. Richard Gough and Tommy Coyne both scorned opportunities to open the scoring before that honour fell to midfielder Alex Taylor. That occurred 18 minutes into the game when he found space in the box to meet an Eamonn Bannon cross and neatly flick the ball home.

United were dominant and Sturrock should have doubled the lead when he fired in a shot from 12 yards that Adams did well to turn over the bar. But in the 24th minute Luggy did get his name on the scoresheet. Dave Narey lofted a free kick into the danger area where Gough met the ball perfectly, heading down to the waiting Sturrock who hammered the ball past Adams from 12 yards.

Despite the difficult conditions caused by driving wind and rain, United were producing some excellent football and Sturrock could easily have had his hat-trick before half-time but for some fine saves by Adams. The interval arrived without any further score.

The resumption of play saw the one-way traffic continue and only five minutes into the second half Tannadice witnessed one of the goals of the season. Sturrock was not known for his tough tackling but he won the ball in midfield and exchanged a slick one-two with Beedie before escaping the defence to advance into the penalty box, where he rounded Adams and slid the ball into the unguarded net.

Now 3-0 behind and looking bedraggled, Morton succumbed to a fourth goal six minutes later. This time Maurice Malpas was handily placed to score his first of the season when he rose to head in a Bannon cross.

It was surprising that a further ten minutes elapsed before goal number five, though when it came it was similar to the third. Only Sturrock winning the ball in midfield was missing because Beedie again fed the ball through and Luggy again took it round Adams before completing his hat-trick.

No sooner had Arabs begun chanting 'we want six' than Sturrock delivered just that as only 90 seconds after his third he was on target again. Morton failed to deal with a Bannon free kick and they paid the price as Sturrock converted the loose ball as it bounced across the face of goal.

With four goals, that meant Luggy had equalled the Premier Division scoring record and one of the four other players who had also managed that feat was present to see it happen. Pettigrew, who by that stage must have been willing the match to come to an end, was quick to congratulate his former team-mate.

Now the demand from the terraces was 'we want seven' and with ten minutes remaining they again got their wish. A through ball reached Coyne, who had worked tirelessly in his attempts to get his own name on the scoresheet but had been denied. When a high ball reached him he flicked it on for Sturrock to run onto and this time, rather than round Adams, he lashed the ball in from 12 yards.

Now Sturrock was out on his own in terms of the scoring record and he was still looking for more at the final whistle. It was a fine team performance from United but it was a quite outstanding individual performance from Luggy, as close as he could hope to come to perfection.

Sturrock revealed he had been inspired by Scotland's great 3-1 win over Spain in a World Cup qualifying group match three days earlier, 'I took a great lift from just being part of the big occasion win for Scotland. Even though I didn't play I can assure you there was no one at Hampden more excited at the way the side played.'

Shell-shocked Morton boss Willie McLean could only utter, 'What can I say after that, we were simply overrun.'

Then what happened?

Although four players have since scored five goals in the Premier Division or SPL, none has bettered Sturrock's feat that day.

For the second time in five years United reached both domestic finals in the same season. Sadly the Scottish Cup Final saw the Old Firm complete the double over United as that trophy, too, remained in Glasgow.

Morton were relegated, finishing bottom of the Premier Division and conceding 100 league goals in the process – 18 of them in their four meetings with United. At the time of writing, they have not since returned to the top level.

v Manchester United 2-2

UEFA Cup Third Round First Leg
Old Trafford
28 November 1984
Attendance: 48,278

DUNDEE UNITED	MANCHESTER UNITED
McAlpine	Bailey
Malpas	Gidman
Holt	Albiston
Gough	Moses
Hegarty	McQueen
Narey	Duxbury
Bannon	Robson
Dodds	Strachan
Kirkwood	Hughes
Sturrock	Whiteside (Stapleton)
Beedie	Olsen
Manager: Jim McLean	*Manager:* Ron Atkinson

THROUGHOUT the summer of 1984, United's players and supporters tried not to dwell on the crushing disappointment of losing out on a place in the European Cup Final the previous May. The very fact they had reached such a stage in the premier European competition was remarkable, although the players' inability to protect a two-goal lead – despite extreme provocation in various forms – made the defeat harder to accept.

But when the new season got under way and the time came to resume visits to foreign fields, Jim McLean's men had re-focussed. That was shown by how they confidently dealt with the challenges of AIK Stockholm (3-1 on aggregate) and Linz ASK (7-2) to reach the third round of the UEFA Cup.

The draw produced a Scotland–England clash that saw two Uniteds going head-to-head. Inevitably the media dubbed it the 'Battle of Britain' and Dundee United were given next to no chance of gaining the upper hand over the two ties.

That wasn't simply because of the vast gulf in resources between the two clubs. The tie represented the 18th occasion that teams from either side of the border had met in the various European competitions – with Scots having eliminated their English opponents just five times. However, writing Dundee United off in such a matter-of-fact manner failed to take account of the European pedigree McLean had been building over the previous five years. Knocking out Anderlecht, Borussia Mönchengladbach and PSV Eindhoven (each of whom had recently won European trophies) plus clubs of the stature of AS Monaco, Werder Bremen and Standard Liege suggested the Tangerines were not naive when it came to understanding what worked in Europe.

Equally telling, had any journalist bothered to do the necessary research – although Manchester United had reached the European Cup Winners' Cup semi-finals six months earlier, that was the first occasion since 1969 they had progressed beyond the second round in Europe. The 1984/85 season was just the sixth one in which they had even qualified during those 15 years.

That said, while McLean had brought the vast bulk of his squad through the ranks at Tannadice – only Eamonn Bannon (£165,000) and Paul Hegarty (£27,500) commanded fees – Ron Atkinson had spent more than £5m on just half the team that would face McLean's men at Old Trafford.

Bryan Robson's transfer from West Bromwich Albion in 1981 established a British record of £1.5m, while Frank Stapleton, Remi Moses, Gordon Strachan, Gordon McQueen and John Gidman each cost … well, a lot more than £165,000.

Although Dundee United had been competing in Europe since 1966, there had not been a great tradition of Arabs following the side to foreign fields. Even the Fairs Cup visit to Newcastle in 1969 had seen just 2,000 venture south, but the run to the European Cup semi-finals the previous season had fired enthusiasm and many who had travelled, having enjoyed the experience, were hungry for more.

Even had the pairing with Manchester United been the club's very first European sojourn, there would have been a frenzy of activity among Arabs eager to ensure their presence for the first leg at one of the most iconic stadiums in the world. The allocation of 5,000 tickets was rapidly taken up, leading to an invasion of Manchester which began two days before the match.

The atmosphere was nothing but good-natured and matchday saw the city's Albert Square a sea of tangerine and black as bemused Mancunians – not least those peering down from the Town Hall – cast their eyes over what was not a common sight, despite the many big games the city's two clubs regularly staged.

There was an electric atmosphere inside Old Trafford as the teams appeared. The home fans outnumbered Arabs by eight to one but you wouldn't have known it, with the Scots in great voice. Two years before he would become boss of Manchester United, Alex Ferguson watched from the stand in his role as assistant to Scotland manager Jock Stein, who was also present.

As was expected of the home side, Manchester did most of the early pressing and United suffered a blow after just nine minutes with two of the three Scots in the Reds' line-up involved. Gordon McQueen rose to meet a Gordon Strachan corner and, with the ball goalbound, Maurice Malpas stretched to palm it away. Robson quickly knocked the ball in but the home supporters' celebrations were cut short as Bulgarian referee Bogdan Dotchev pointed to the penalty spot, claiming he had blown his whistle before Robson shot.

Two things about that sequence of events signify changes in the way rules are interpreted 30 years on. The advantage rule would be applied, meaning Robson's goal would stand. However, if a penalty was awarded then Malpas would have been shown the red card for a deliberate handball that denied a goalscoring opportunity, leaving United to play more than 80 minutes with ten men. In the event, Malpas wasn't even cautioned.

Before the match, Strachan – who had been signed from Aberdeen for £500,000 three months earlier – had claimed he would rather not take a penalty as Hamish McAlpine knew his technique so well. Atkinson must have overruled him because Strachan did take it, sending McAlpine the wrong way to put the home side ahead.

The Tannadice men then defended doggedly, though that was hardly a novel experience for a club now accustomed to absorbing and counter-attacking when possible. Atkinson's team were dominant during the first half with McAlpine the United hero, dealing with all they could throw at him.

Manchester might have been two ahead after 30 minutes when Robson had the ball in the net, only for it to be ruled out for a foul by Norman Whiteside in the build-up. But there was no question the Reds were good value for their lead at the break.

Whatever McLean said to his men in the dressing room, it was certainly effective because they emerged revitalised and no sooner had the second half got under way than the scores were level.

Hegarty was always a threat at set pieces with his heading ability making opponents wary. So when he stationed himself at the edge of the box as Malpas floated in a free kick, if the home defence were aware of him at all they probably sensed little threat. But when Richard Gough knocked the ball down to Hegarty the United captain led by example as he hammered his shot past goalkeeper Gary Bailey.

It is doubtful few who had witnessed a rather one-sided first half had seen that coming, but as Arabs erupted in celebration United were now back in the game. Perhaps not for long, though. If one United captain had led by example, the other was prepared to settle for no less and Robson rose to the challenge.

The visitors had been conceding free kicks in their own half on a regular basis and from one of those Manchester's lead was restored just three minutes later. Jesper Olsen flighted the ball towards the six-yard box, where Mark Hughes opted for the spectacular with an overhead kick. He missed the ball completely but it ran to the in-rushing Robson who prodded home.

Hegarty and his men had been unable to survive the period of a game when a team is at its most vulnerable, just after scoring. They then regrouped and steadied the ship, although with 59 minutes on the clock came the incident that could well have seen them dead and buried as far as the tie was concerned.

For the second time the home side were awarded a penalty – and again it was for handball, this time against Hegarty. Like Malpas, he was not shown a yellow card, although he had earlier received one for a challenge on Hughes. This time Atkinson might have wished he had listened more closely to the fears expressed by Strachan because McAlpine, already the hero of the hour, produced a superb save to deny his fellow Scot and keep the score at 2-1.

That seemed to give the Terrors and their travelling support a boost because within two minutes they equalised for a second time. Again utilising their counter-attacking game, Stuart Beedie received the ball and advanced down the right before sending in a low cross behind the defence that Mike Duxbury ought to have intercepted. But he failed to do so and the ball continued on its way to Paul Sturrock who ran in and guided it confidently into Bailey's far corner. Most of Old Trafford was silenced, but the Arab contingent certainly wasn't and they urged their team on.

The second half was much more even and it was a full-blooded and pulsating cup tie. With parity restored, United looked the likelier to add to the score. Manchester came close to losing their unbeaten home record in Europe on 73 minutes when, in an incisive attack, Sturrock and Bannon combined brilliantly to set up Davie Dodds, who couldn't quite apply the finish the move deserved.

Atkinson brought on Frank Stapleton in an attempt to win the match but the Irishman hardly touched the ball, such was the domination at that point of the Hegarty–Narey defensive partnership. Perhaps surprisingly, McLean didn't see the need to call on fresh legs as United ended the 90 minutes in the ascendancy.

That was quite a turnaround given the pattern of play in the first half, but the 'plucky' Scots – despite the pundits' expectations – had kept the tie alive with home advantage to come.

Arabs celebrated defiantly, airing their full repertoire of songs until the police had to ask them to leave as they were the only ones remaining in the ground. No Dundee United supporter at Old Trafford will ever forget the pride they felt for club and country that night.

It was a great European night of the kind United were becoming used to experiencing, based on a performance that was a heady mixture of high-energy skill and a never-say-die spirit.

Then what happened?

Two weeks later the Uniteds reconvened in the rather more prosaic surroundings of Tannadice, which was bursting at the seams.

Any team scoring four times against Manchester United over two legs – particularly with two goals away from home – would establish a strong case for advancing. However, despite equalising four times over the tie, an own goal and a cruel deflection for what proved the winner in the second leg saw the English club advance 5-4 on aggregate.

v Rangers 3-2

Scottish League Premier Division
Ibrox
16 August 1986
Attendance: 40,948

DUNDEE UNITED	RANGERS
Thomson	Woods
Malpas	Nicholl
Beaumont	Munro
Gough	Souness
Hegarty	MacPherson
Narey	Butcher
Bowman (Holt)	Fraser
Gallacher	West
Clark (Bannon)	McCoist
Sturrock	Durrant (Ferguson)
Redford	Cooper
Manager: Jim McLean	*Player-manager:* Graeme Souness

THREE years after being crowned as champions of Scotland, rightly United were judged by high standards – by their manager and by their supporters. There is therefore no other description that could be attached to 1985/86 than a disappointment. Semi-final defeats in the domestic cups to Aberdeen and Hearts were compounded by the extra-time UEFA Cup third round exit to Neuchatel Xamax, a club United would have despatched without ceremony had they instead met on the way to the 1987 final.

Perhaps most concerning of all was that the challenge for the Premier Division title, in which United had been involved amid great excitement, ended in anti-climax. The final-day drama, when Hearts needed only a draw to become champions yet let the title slip from their grasp with Celtic poised to profit, created such a welter of media coverage that there was scarcely a mention of the fact that, right up until the third-last week of the season, there were three clubs in the gripping race.

United were the other but points then were unaccountably dropped in a draw with Clydebank and a defeat by St Mirren and this prevented the season ending in an unprecedented three-way points tie at the top of the table. Celtic became champions by a margin of three goals but had United won those two games Jim McLean would have been celebrating a second championship in four seasons. That fact quickly disappeared into the mists of time, but the title race really was that close and Arabs also reflected ruefully that United had taken seven out of eight points from their meetings with Celtic over the season.

A ringing endorsement as to the quality of the players McLean had developed came when Scotland's squad for the World Cup in Mexico was announced. In the wake of Jock Stein's tragic death, Alex Ferguson had been appointed as interim manager and he included Eamonn Bannon, Richard Gough, Maurice Malpas, Dave Narey and Paul Sturrock in his 22. That was one more than he named from his own club, Aberdeen, and it equalled the record established when Leeds United provided five of Scotland's players for the 1974 finals.

The close-season saw three prominent departures from Tannadice. After 12 years (in two spells) as a player, Walter Smith was offered a coaching role by McLean when injury brought his playing career to a premature end. The manager regarded him as a natural and Smith was such a success that on McLean's advice he was appointed assistant manager. As his reputation grew and it became clear other clubs were increasingly aware of his potential, the Tannadice board had made him a director of the club in February 1986.

Transparently, the aim was to bind Smith to United for the long term and in normal circumstances that would almost certainly have been achieved. However, circumstances at Rangers at the time were abnormal.

They were languishing in mid-table (and would eventually finish fifth, 12 points behind United), leading to the appointment in April 1986 of Graeme Souness as player-manager. Rangers decided Souness needed an assistant who could bridge his lack of knowledge of Scottish club football and, possessing such experience in spades, Smith was identified as that man. Having been a Rangers supporter in his youth, it was not an offer Smith felt he could decline.

Three years after winning the Premier Division only one of the players centrally involved in that triumph had departed Tannadice. Little more than a year later, injury had cruelly cut short Derek Stark's career at the age of 26 but the summer of 1986 saw two more leave the club, though in return for six-figure transfer fees.

Davie Dodds had again ended the season as United's leading scorer (shared with Bannon) and the impression he made in the UEFA Cup against Neuchatel Xamax prompted the Swiss club to offer £200,000 for him. McLean was of the opinion the time was right for Dodds to move on and he felt the same in relation to Billy Kirkwood, whom Hibernian signed for a fee of £100,000.

The cash that those moves generated – and quite a bit more besides – was used to secure midfielders Dave Bowman and Jim McInally from Coventry City. Injury kept McInally on the sidelines for the first month of the season but United made a promising start by defeating Aberdeen at Tannadice, though returning from New Kilbowie Park, Clydebank, four days later with just a point was less impressive.

That still left them a point ahead of Rangers as McLean and his men prepared for the visit to Ibrox – a ground where United had recorded only four wins from a total of 42 league visits.

Souness had introduced three major signings during the close-season. Bringing in Chris Woods from Norwich City and Colin West from Watford didn't cause huge waves but securing the services of Terry Butcher certainly did.

It has never been regarded south of the border as a sensible career move for a leading English player to join a Scottish club and Butcher was then captain of Ipswich Town and a regular in the England team. The culture shock involved meant none of the three – plus Souness himself – had fully acclimatised to their new surroundings by the time they faced United. The Rangers fans seemed to have been enthused, though. United's last visit to Ibrox eight months previously had been watched by less than 17,000; there were two and a half times as many this time.

From the start United found themselves on the back foot, scarcely able to enter the Rangers half for sustained spells. Although not known for his goalscoring, it was Souness who came close to doing so when he let fly with a piledriver though Billy Thomson was the equal of it.

Despite applying considerable pressure it was 25 minutes before the home side were able to breach United. A corner from Davie Cooper appeared harmless with no Rangers players close to it but the defenders in tangerine hesitated rather than clearing and Ally McCoist was quickest to react, stabbing it into the net.

In an attempt to contain the flow, United then began to operate with a flat back four. The aim was to try and defend further up the park but seven minutes before half-time that plan was in tatters as a Souness pass penetrated the backline, sending McCoist through one-on-one with Thomson. The contest had a predictable outcome and United's protests that McCoist was offside proved futile. With a two-goal lead before half-time the home team appeared to be well in control.

McLean apparently didn't regard United's cause as lost, however, because in what looked like a bold move he made a substitution, replacing striker John Clark with winger Bannon. McLean wanted United to make greater use of the full width of the big Ibrox pitch and with Bannon on the left, complementing the foraging Kevin Gallacher on the right, they had greater ability to stretch Rangers.

That said, for the first 20 minutes of the second half United's attempt to change the course of the match hadn't had any noticeable effect. Rangers were seen less as a driving force although perhaps that merely reflected that they already regarded victory as secure. If so, such complacency was brought into sharp focus when United did reduce the deficit after 68 minutes, assisted by dithering in the home defence.

Bannon's probing down the left was beginning to concern his opposite number, the experienced Jimmy Nicholl. Bannon moved inside the full-back before releasing a pass towards Gallacher, though it didn't appear the ball would reach the youngster. However, Butcher and Stuart Munro got in each other's way and the ball broke to Gallacher who quickly dispatched it behind Woods.

Suddenly, it was 'game on' as Rangers attempted to re-impose the control they had established in the first half. But the play was now more evenly balanced with most of it taking place in midfield and little activity inside either penalty area.

As the game entered its final ten minutes Rangers became noticeably tentative, presumably with the aim of holding on to their lead. United had other ideas, however, with Gallacher the main threat to the home defence.

With just seven minutes left the balance shifted again as United equalised. Ian Redford gained possession and pushed the ball into the path of Gallacher as the front man entered the box. Before the Rangers defenders could react Gallacher had bulleted his shot home for his second goal and the game was level.

If there was some irony in Redford being at the centre of the move, it would be nothing compared to what transpired five minutes later. The forward had spent five years with Rangers and won four trophies – three when United were opponents in cup finals. He had departed to join United for £70,000 a year earlier.

The Ibrox crowd was by now restless and Souness appeared to be caught in two minds as to whether to push for a winner or hold on for a point. In the event they got neither as United attacked down the right and won a free kick which was taken quickly to Bannon, and the winger floated over a cross that Woods intended to claim. But Redford spotted his chance and rose brilliantly to reach the ball ahead of the goalkeeper and direct it into the unguarded net.

The cheers from the travelling Arabs had scarcely been heard after the first two goals but such was the shock around Ibrox that the Rangers supporters were silenced and the singing from the section where the United fans were was clear for all to hear.

United had little difficulty in seeing out the remaining two minutes for a famous victory – and one the bookmakers must have been offering long odds on after an hour.

Dundee United's Greatest Games

The much-vaunted 'Souness revolution' would, in good time, come to pass, but for now the troops had been effectively confined to barracks.

Then what happened?

That dramatic victory at Ibrox was Gough's last match in tangerine. Two days later, he was transferred to Tottenham Hotspur for £750,000.

For United the season was to be characterised more by their exploits in Europe as they marched to the final of the UEFA Cup. One of their conquests were Borussia Mönchengladbach, who had beaten Rangers at an earlier stage. But the Ibrox club were focussed on the Premier Division and at its conclusion Souness's first season saw Rangers regain the title from Celtic, with United third.

v Barcelona 2-1

36

UEFA Cup Quarter-Final Second Leg
Camp Nou
18 March 1987
Attendance: 42,000

DUNDEE UNITED	BARCELONA
Thomson	Zubizaretta
Holt	Gerardo
Malpas	Manolo
Clark	Migueli
Hegarty	Moratalla
Narey	Victor
Gallacher	Caldere (Urbano)
McInally	Roberto
Ferguson	Lineker
Sturrock	Hughes
Redford	Marcos (Rojo)
Manager: Jim McLean	*Coach:* Terry Venables

D EMONSTRATING the benefit of ten consecutive years of competing in Europe, the progress made by United through the first three rounds of the 1986/87 UEFA Cup was solid rather than spectacular. Jim McLean's team had used their experience to overcome tough opponents from reputable footballing countries, though none were household names.

Having earned the status of a seeded club, United might have anticipated a less demanding opening to their campaign than a visit to France. Racing Club Lens were not one of the country's famous clubs but French football was still basking in the reflected glory of the national team becoming European champions in 1984 and the tie was potentially awkward for United.

They had goalkeeper Billy Thomson to thank for being able to emerge from the first leg in Lens only 1-0 behind, though the French side were unable to live with United's power game at Tannadice. With Ralph Milne on top form the necessary two goals were scored and that brought a clash with Universitatea Craiova. A decisive 3-0 lead was built at Tannadice and it never looked likely to be overhauled, even though the Romanians did score the only goal of the second leg.

In European terms, Hajduk Split were the most experienced opponents United had faced thus far and having to play the second leg in Yugoslavia increased the scale of the challenge. Once again, though, a dominant performance at Tannadice carved out a lead – 2-0 – with the visitors denied an away goal. The return leg in the city which is now part of Croatia was not without its tricky moments, but United again drew on their knowledge of how to stand their ground on foreign soil and the match ended goalless.

There then followed the customary three-month hibernation of the European competitions and during that period one of the most outstanding attacking players to emerge during McLean's tenure as manager left the club. Milne was transferred to Charlton Athletic, then playing at the top level, for £125,000 and the size of the fee revealed that the winger, still only 25, had failed to maximise his sublime skills.

147

He was the sixth member of the championship-winning squad to depart after Davie Dodds, Richard Gough, Billy Kirkwood, Hamish McAlpine and Derek Stark. But, just as Milne was leaving, Kirkwood made a welcome return after only six months at Hibernian.

Now into the quarter-final stage in Europe for the fourth time in six seasons, the quality of the competition was ramped up. It could hardly have gone higher than the club that emerged as United's next opponents: FC Barcelona.

The world-renowned Catalans would have been a huge draw in any circumstances but interest was heightened by the their British connection in the shape of coach Terry Venables and his £6m strike force of England's Gary Linker and Mark Hughes of Wales.

Anyone at Barcelona who recalled that United had won home and away when the clubs met 21 years earlier probably put it down to the Scottish upstarts being taken too lightly by the mighty Barca, who were then the holders of the Fairs Cup.

The same description could hardly be attached to a club that had come within a goal of the European Cup Final three years previously but the news they would face United, with the second leg at the Camp Nou, can hardly have induced sleepless nights in the Catalan capital. With Tannadice a cauldron of noise United employed the now well-established tactic in European home matches of coming out of the starting blocks at a super-charged rate, aiming to catch their opponents cold before they had found their feet.

It didn't always meet with success but on this occasion it brought about a stunning opening to the match. A mere 100 seconds were on the clock when Paul Sturrock gathered the ball midway inside the Barcelona half and pushed it forward to Kevin Gallacher. The 20-year-old winger sent what looked like a curling lob into the penalty box with the outside of his foot and then watched incredulously as the ball soared over the poorly-positioned Andoni Zubizaretta and finished in the far corner.

Tannadice erupted and United had what even the term 'dream start' barely begins to describe. The goal was also eerily similar to the tremendous one scored by Billy Hainey from almost the same position in 1966.

United generally looked more likely to score again than to concede, although there was one howler of a miss by Lineker after 40 minutes that could have completely altered the game – and the tie. But the new golden boy of Europe hung his head in dismay while Arabs cheered almost as loudly as if their team had scored a second.

With Sturrock at his tantalising best, his tireless running and constant stretching of the Spanish defenders meant they often had no legal means of halting him. Midway through the second half this brought United some benefit when Francisco Carrasco, the driving force of Barcelona's midfield, received a yellow card for one foul too many on Sturrock, meaning he would be suspended for the second leg.

Although they might have added to their lead, United could take great heart from a disciplined performance that maintained their attacking style but also their record of not conceding a home goal in that season's competition.

Venables stated candidly, 'It will be a hard game in Barcelona and we'll be taking nothing for granted against this team. They are good.' His striker Mark Hughes and Jim McLean concurred. Hughes said, 'It's a worry for us that we didn't get an away goal. We believe we can score twice at Camp Nou, but we're also concerned that United are capable of scoring there.' McLean added, 'You can take it we'll give Barcelona a lot of trouble in the second match.'

United didn't exactly enjoy a morale-boosting send-off because four days prior to the tie they drew 2-2 in the Scottish Cup against part-timers Forfar Athletic at Tannadice – achieved only through a late penalty.

The Camp Nou's width and its lush green surface made for a game perfectly suited to United's well-developed counter-attacking style, with one up front and five in midfield. Continental teams tend not to be geared to all-out attack, which meant McLean's men had often been able to dominate defensively and in midfield. However, Eamonn Bannon, a key component of that style, was out injured in what was a serious blow, although the team was not short of battle-hardened players who were unfazed neither by the aura of the Camp Nou nor by the task before them.

On the plus side, Paul Hegarty was now restored to the team after almost five months out with injury. With United playing a zonal marking system, neither he nor his defensive partner Dave Narey had a specific responsibility, but Hegarty recalled them discussing the twin threat of Lineker and Hughes, 'We gave them respect, but no more. After all, if you give someone too much respect you give them an advantage. Our determination was that they wouldn't get the opportunity to show how good they were... and they didn't. I recall Lineker saying to me over there, "If you score we will fold." How right he was.'

Barcelona had to force the pace in search of goals and that they were largely restricted to shots from outside the penalty area was a credit to the resolute United midfield. When they did get through, they were met by the wall that was Hegarty and Narey, and behind them Thomson, all of whom were immense.

Thomson was helpless, though, to prevent the goal which levelled the tie five minutes before half-time. A corner taken by Marcos was half-cleared by John Clark and the ball travelled only as far as Ramon Caldere 15 yards out. The midfielder's shot took a deflection which carried it into the net beyond the goalkeeper.

The Barca fans saw that as the breakthrough with the second half certain to bring further goals, but at no stage after the break did United allow themselves to be pegged back in defence. The midfield again formed a formidable barrier. John Holt and Jim McInally were everywhere, harrying as they broke up attacks and even managing to forge forward themselves on occasion. Complementing these two was Ian Redford, whose industry and skill made sure that the speed on the wings of Gallacher and Sturrock was utilised to take pressure off the United defence. Iain Ferguson carried out his role as the lone front man, preventing Barcelona from committing too many players forward.

United actually created as many chances as their rivals in the second half. After 50 minutes Gallacher set up Sturrock, whose shot was deflected wide. Twenty minutes later Redford found Ferguson in the box but the striker was unable to make good enough contact.

As the game entered the final ten minutes of normal time, Barcelona relaxed the urgency in their play, suggesting they were prepared to wait until extra time to strike the killer blow. They would soon pay for that complacency when that blow was struck – against them.

In the 85th minute full-back Fernando Garrado committed the latest in a string of fouls against the tireless Sturrock. Redford took the kick, swinging over a measured ball. Though some of United's front men might have been intimidated by the bigger Barca defenders, Clark certainly didn't come into that category. It is doubtful he had been either intimidated or outmuscled at any stage in his career and the big man rose utterly determined that nobody would prevent him from reaching the cross. He did so, using all his power to bullet a header that entered the net via the underside of the bar for the equaliser.

Except it wasn't just the equaliser. It was effectively the winner because the Catalan team now had to score twice in the remaining five minutes, which United knew – as did the Barcelona players themselves – simply wasn't going to happen.

The Barca fans accepted that the game was up when Clark scored. Many began booing their team and waving white handkerchiefs as a sign of derision, actions that increased ten-fold three minutes later.

For the home team the final whistle couldn't come quickly enough but the United players were exuberant and had no intention of trying to run down the clock. In any case, attack is always the best form of defence and in the penultimate minute an already memorable match became a momentous one.

Using as a launchpad the same left wing that had been the source of Clark's goal, Sturrock set off again, this time avoiding the attentions of Garrado. He advanced into the penalty area before chipping the ball to the far post where Ferguson met it with his head, directing it down and in for the winning goal.

When the final whistle was blown the United players danced joyfully around the turf while their illustrious opponents sank to their knees in dismay. The Catalan fans sportingly gave the men in tangerine a standing ovation and the players responded by applauding them, as well as their own tremendous travelling support.

It was impossible to choose a man of the match from such a display and it would have been unfair even to try. These men – and their manager – were heroes, the best of ambassadors for their club, their city, their country and its football. It was without doubt one of the best performances by a Scottish club on foreign soil.

It also produced a statistic that was stunning then and has lost none of its ability to take the breath away today: Dundee United had faced FC Barcelona four times in Europe – and had won each match. One measure of the scale of United's achievement in 1987 is that Barcelona did not lose both legs of a European tie again until 2013.

Then what happened?

It was the night no United supporter there will ever forget. Those passionate Arabs roared on their team from first to last and the celebrations went on long after the final whistle as the raucous band in the highest tier of the vast Camp Nou simply refused to leave.

The stadium resounded to their full song repertoire as the supporters cheered the players' after-match warm-down and only allowed their thoughts to turn to leaving as the floodlights began to be switched off. Back in the city centre, the Ramblas knew all about it as the celebrations continued until dawn.

For the second time in three years, a European semi-final beckoned.

v Dundee 3-2

Scottish Cup Semi-Final
Tynecastle Park
11 April 1987
Attendance: 13,319

DUNDEE UNITED	DUNDEE
Thomson	Geddes
Holt	Forsyth
Malpas	McKinlay (Glennie)
McInally	Shannon
Hegarty	Smith
Narey	Duffy
Ferguson	Rafferty
Bowman	Brown
Bannon	Jack (Angus)
Sturrock	Coyne
Redford	Wright
Manager: Jim McLean	*Manager:* Jocky Scott

THE rivalry between Dundee's two clubs has always been passionately felt but its product has also been generally beneficial, both in terms of the financial benefits of their meetings but also – and arguably more importantly – the spirit which has characterised them on and off the pitch.

Crowd trouble before, during or after derbies is almost unheard of, although it's highly improbable that Arabs would be spotted at Dens or Bluenoses seen at Tannadice on any other occasion. Intense though it undoubtedly is, and not just on matchdays, the rivalry is characterised much more by banter than hatred, which is not a claim that can be made of any other city derby in Scottish football.

Probably the best illustration of the relationship was provided on the occasion of the most high-profile derby of them all, the Scottish League Cup Final of 1980. Despite the fact that one of Scottish football's major trophies was at stake, the celebrations by United's supporters rarely strayed into anything more forceful than mockery while the reaction of the Dundee supporters (who must have found the comprehensive 3-0 defeat extremely difficult to thole) was admirably controlled and contained more than a share of magnanimity.

Although the clubs had met more than 150 times in all competitions, they had been drawn together in the Scottish Cup on only four occasions: 1928, 1951, 1956 and 1980. All but one had required a replay so when Dundee and United emerged from the hat when the draw for the 1987 semi-finals was made the immediate question on the lips of supporters of both was – at which of the two grounds would the tie be staged?

The clubs advocated a repeat of the common sense that was applied when they had contested that final seven years earlier, with a toss of a coin deciding where the match would take place.

That, though, was a competition run by the Scottish League; the Scottish FA were adamant that their competition would not depart from the long-established tradition of semi-finals being decided on neutral territory.

That apart, why the SFA dug their heels in on the matter was not clear. The rationale behind a neutral venue is surely to deny either team an advantage, yet both clubs – and their supporters – had made it clear they would be quite content to cross the road if that was how the coin landed.

With the crowd split evenly there would be little advantage at all and as the first to emerge from the hat, Dundee would have been allocated the home dressing room even if Tannadice had been chosen as the venue. Regarding Dens Park, with United having won two League Cups and a Premier Division championship there, that ground carried only positive memories and Arabs would have welcomed the opportunity to create more.

But the SFA authorities were adamant tradition was of greater importance than considering the wishes or needs of supporters so Tynecastle was named as the venue. That meant fans being unnecessarily required to make a 130-mile round trip to the capital, which the committed would undoubtedly be willing to do. But the 20,000-plus crowd that would have filled either of the city grounds was not realistically achievable in Edinburgh.

By the beginning of April United had already played 52 competitive matches during 1986/87 and at least a further 11 remained.

That was a sign of the level of success achieved by the club under Jim McLean and, having already reached the semi-final of the League Cup (in which they succumbed 2-1 to Rangers), the Tangerines were now preparing for three more last-four ties, the first two within days. Borussia Mönchengladbach were due at Tannadice for the first leg of the UEFA Cup semi on 8 April, while the Scottish Cup equivalent was scheduled three days later.

That gave the players little time to shake off the effects of what was a physically and emotionally draining European night, while Dundee had the luxury of a full week's rest.

Interest in the Scottish Cup meeting was predictably high within the city, though it was not anticipated that the attendance at Tynecastle would exceed that at any of the four league meetings between the clubs that season when most supporters were required to do little more than roll out of bed and head for the match.

However, the lure of a Scottish Cup Final had clearly been underestimated and 13,319 made the trip for what remains the only Dundee derby match to have taken place outside the city.

United lay two places, but 13 points, above their neighbours in the Premier Division table, although those league derbies – two of which took place in the month before the semi-final – had been close-fought, with both sides winning once and the other two ending even.

Perhaps more pertinently from their viewpoint, Dens boss Jocky Scott had seen his team embark on a run of just one defeat in their 16 games prior to the Tynecastle clash. Add into the mix the cliché that 'the formbook goes out the window in derby matches' and it can be seen that only the committed or reckless would have predicted the outcome with confidence.

As the teams appeared, the noise and clamour emanating from the Tynecastle terraces would have done justice to a much bigger gathering and perhaps at first the occasion got to some of the players because both sides made a tentative start. There were few efforts on target until midway through the half when Bobby Geddes was tested by a Paul Hegarty header, but with 29 minutes played United spectacularly broke the deadlock.

After a slick passing move the ball reached John Holt, who beat two opponents before finding Iain Ferguson. The striker, who began his career at Dens Park, showed no sympathy for his former employers by lashing a fierce right-footed shot beyond Geddes from the edge of the penalty area.

That was a major setback for the Dark Blues who took some time to pick themselves up, though when they did it was with a vengeance. That it was Tommy Coyne who was at the centre of their revival was not without some irony because he was another player who had swapped city allegiances – or 'crossed the road' as the local parlance has it. The striker had made 14 appearances for United during the season before Dundee paid £75,000 for him just four months earlier.

Perhaps he was determined to show McLean that he had made an error in allowing him to leave, but Coyne certainly made a powerful statement in the ten minutes before half-time, scoring one and setting up another as the lead dramatically changed hands.

With 35 minutes on the clock he came hurtling in at the back post to slot in the equaliser from close range and before United had settled to the game's altered dynamic, Dundee struck again. Five minutes of the half remained when Coyne received the ball and made a strong run down the left before crossing into the danger area where Keith Wright found the space to head decisively past Billy Thomson.

Now it was United's turn to deal with a setback but at least the interval was close. The evidence shows that McLean clearly used his half-time team talk to good advantage because from the moment play resumed United were the dominant force. For the first 30 minutes after the break they outplayed and outfought Dundee, who nevertheless played their part in a torrid second half that lived up to the slogan 'Be all you can be' of the Scottish Health Education Group, that season's sponsors of the competition.

Producing the kind of inspirational leadership every manager looks for from his captain, Hegarty led by example. Equally impressive was the grip that United's midfield quartet of Jim McInally, Dave Bowman, Ian Redford and Eamonn Bannon exerted as they went for the equaliser. It took them just ten minutes to fashion it, as fine work by McInally and then Bowman set up Ferguson who fired home both his and his team's second goal of the tie.

The running power of Ferguson and Paul Sturrock now had Dundee on the back foot and they struggled to contain the seemingly tireless United front men. Their defence was at sixes and sevens on 65 minutes when Sturrock sent over a free kick and Hegarty had a free header as he powered home what would prove to be the winner.

The Dens men did begin to mount some pressure in an attempt to get back into the game and Thomson was twice called on to make top-quality saves at full stretch from John Brown. Although McLean decided not to bring on any substitutes, Scott used both of his in the final ten minutes in a desperate attempt to force an equaliser.

But the international class and experience of Hegarty and his fellow defenders Dave Narey and Maurice Malpas capably dealt with all Dundee could throw at them and United held out for a famous victory – and a Scottish Cup Final place for the fourth time in 13 years.

McLean felt the midweek exertions against Borussia (that game had ended 0-0) had taken their toll on his players initially but concluded, 'We knew at half-time we had a real fight on our hands and I asked the players to rise to the occasion, bearing in mind how much it meant to our supporters.'

Scott was magnanimous in defeat, stating, 'In the second half we were second to every ball and didn't start playing again until we went 3-2 behind. Over the piece, United's experience of big-game situations saw them through.'

Then what happened?

Despite being favourites to capture the Scottish Cup for the first time, United lost the final in extra time by the only goal to St Mirren. Having swept past Borussia Mönchengladbach to become the only Scottish club to reach the final of the UEFA Cup, that too ended in disappointment with a 2-1 aggregate defeat by IFK Gothenburg.

Defying the law of averages, the two Dundee clubs would also be drawn together in the Scottish Cup in the following four seasons with United progressing each time. Yet, since 1991, the clubs have not met again in the competition.

v Borussia Mönchengladbach 2-0

UEFA Cup Semi-Final Second Leg. Bökelberg Stadion
22 April 1987. Attendance: 33,500

DUNDEE UNITED	BORUSSIA MÖNCHENGLADBACH
Thomson	Kamps
Holt	Winkhold (Jung)
Kirkwood	Frontzeck
McInally	Herlovsen
Hegarty	Hochstätter (Krauss)
Narey	Borowka
Ferguson (Clark)	Bruns
Bowman	Rahn
Bannon	Thiele
Sturrock (Gallacher)	Lienen
Redford	Criens
Manager: Jim McLean	*Coach:* Jupp Heynckes

DEFEATING Barcelona home and away was the outstanding achievement of the entire UEFA Cup in 1986/87 – but even that was not enough to make United favourites to win the trophy. The other semi-finalists were Borussia Mönchengladbach, IFK Gothenburg and Swarovski Tirol and, as both the West German and Swedish clubs had already won the trophy during the 1980s, they were seen as possessing the experience to repeat their success.

When United were paired with Mönchengladbach it immediately set the pulses of supporters racing. Memories were still vivid of the phenomenal performance that saw the Germans swept aside 5-0 at Tannadice five and a half years previously. Both managers then were still in their jobs, although Jupp Heynckes had already given notice that he would be leaving to take over as coach of Bayern Munich in the summer.

Of the players involved in 1981, six of United's were still there, although only two of Mönchengladbach's (Bruns and Rahn) remained.

One difference from 1981 was that United had the first leg at Tannadice, though Jim McLean refused to accept this put his team at a disadvantage. In his programme notes he declared, 'I do believe that nowadays the nature of European football is such that ties can be won away from home. In other words, we must look to reproduce our Barcelona form, not only at Tannadice but also in Germany in a fortnight.'

With eight, McLean's men had already equalled the most European matches played by the club in one season and April 1987 was a month when the games came thick and fast – eight in total, in three competitions.

United lay third in the Premier Division and the meetings with Mönchengladbach were not the only semi-finals to be faced because three days after the first leg at Tannadice there was the small matter of a Scottish Cup derby with Dundee at Tynecastle.

These were hugely exciting times for Arabs and the UEFA Cup quarter-final was keenly anticipated. So after the heights reached against Barcelona it came as a disappointment that the match – shown live on TV throughout the UK as well as what was then West Germany – ended goalless and was arguably United's least impressive European performance of the season.

Despite the Germans being without their playmaker Uwe Rahn through injury, in the first half the Tangerines couldn't find their rhythm and were fortunate to be level at the interval.

There was a marked improvement thereafter with Kevin Gallacher replacing John Clark, a change aimed at injecting more pace and width to the attack. After 50 minutes it seemed United had broken the deadlock when Iain Ferguson sent the ball high into the net, only for Paul Sturrock to be ruled offside. Corner followed corner as United controlled the play, though the technically gifted Mönchengladbach side were always dangerous on the counter-attack.

Ferguson's disallowed effort had not been the subject of much protest by the United players but that was not the case five minutes from the end when they again had the ball in the net. Again Ferguson was the 'scorer' and again a flag was raised to signal offside. Ferguson himself was the culprit, though few inside Tannadice could follow the reasoning.

The sense of frustration was merely compounded by the referee's failure to award a penalty when John Holt was bundled off the ball and then, with almost the last kick of the game, Ian Redford saw his drive rebound from a post. It seemed it wasn't to be United's night.

Not that the Mönchengladbach players cared; they were seen punching the air as they left the pitch, clearly believing they had completed the hard part of their quest for a place in the final.

United had maintained their season's record of not conceding a goal in the competition at Tannadice, containing and then dominating a Mönchengladbach side that had eliminated Rangers earlier in the competition. McLean commented, 'Over the piece a draw was a fair result and if it had to finish level, then 0-0 is better for us than 1-1.'

Heynckes was pleased with the outcome, 'We improved on Barcelona's effort at this ground and, having done this, it is up to us now to complete the job.'

When United set off for the return two weeks later they were certainly not lacking in confidence. Memories of the Camp Nou triumph were fresh and for good measure Dundee had been beaten 3-2 to set up another Scottish Cup Final. The only sour note was that a foot injury suffered in the draw at Celtic on the Saturday meant Maurice Malpas was absent. Mönchengladbach had more time to prepare, not having played for ten days.

McLean certainly sounded bullish on the day of the match, stating, 'We are good enough and we couldn't be going into the game better prepared, apart from the Malpas injury. Some of our teams in the past have had more ability but this one has more grit – and grit is going to be vital. If we get a goal we should be OK.'

Around 1,000 Arabs travelled to the Rhineland and they were joined by at least twice as many in the shape of servicemen and women from British armed forces stationed in the area. Inside the Bökelberg Stadion, those backing United were struck by the prominent notices listing prices for the home leg of the final, together with travel deals for the away leg. With Gothenburg holding a 4-1 first leg lead the destination was not in serious doubt, but hopes were expressed that the same level of presumptuousness would permeate the home dressing room.

Irrespective of the outcome of the first leg, it was not in McLean's nature to send his team on to foreign fields with a policy of merely containing opponents. The avoidance of an early goal was paramount in what everyone knew would be an initial assault by the

German team. That was precisely what happened, and Mönchengladbach – with Rahn restored to his key role in midfield – clearly believed they would gradually wear down United's resistance.

Building methodically from the back, the home side attacked relentlessly and crosses were regularly whipped in from both wings. But, marshalled superbly by Paul Hegarty and Dave Narey, the United defence repulsed them, while Billy Thomson dealt confidently with any attempts that reached him.

United were dealt a blow after half an hour when the Portuguese referee – who was erratic throughout – deemed a simple tackle by Ferguson on Hans Bruns to be worthy of a booking. The effect was that the striker would now have to sit out the first leg of the final, should United prevail. That apart, McLean's plan was still intact as half-time approached with the scoreline blank.

The man who was about to break the deadlock was Ferguson, whose entry to United's European campaign had been delayed because he was signed from Rangers for £145,000 after the UEFA deadline for registering players for the first three rounds of the competition had passed. He made his European debut against Barcelona at Tannadice and then famously scored the goal in the Camp Nou that sealed United's 2-1 triumph.

That had been with his head and Ferguson now repeated the trick at the Bökelberg. The extent of the pressure that United had been under is demonstrated by the fact that when they won a corner with 43 minutes played it was their first of the match. Sturrock sent over an inswinger which goalkeeper Uwe Kamps got a fist to, but the ball went only as far as Eamonn Bannon.

With the home defence anticipating the United man sending it back towards goal, Bannon outsmarted them by instead nodding the ball sideways to Ferguson, who in turn sent a diving header into the net. It was his 26th goal of the season.

The Germans were shocked and their raucous fans were temporarily silenced as the realisation sunk in that they required two goals to turn the tie around. In the second half they certainly didn't lack effort in their attempts to do so but United were never likely to make the mistake of setting out simply to defend their lead.

That said, Ferguson was withdrawn into a deeper role, leaving Sturrock as the lone front man and the target whenever United got hold of the ball, with instructions to hold up the play to alleviate pressure on the defence.

Redford was also superb, his marauding play allowing the Terrors to be more prominent than had been possible in the first half as they began to produce their counter-attacking game. After 62 minutes a slick move ended with a Redford–Sturrock one-two that saw the former sending in an angled shot that beat Kamps and ran across the face of the goal but scraped past the post. Soon after that Sturrock himself had the ball in the net, only to receive a yellow card for what the referee saw as time-wasting because he had already blown for an infringement.

The Germans' best chance of getting back into the game came seven minutes from the end when Thomson was also penalised for time-wasting and a free kick was awarded just inside the United box, directly in front of goal. Bizarrely, as Mönchengladbach were deciding what to do with the kick the referee's obsession with time-wasting led him to book Rahn.

It was a situation fraught with danger and everyone associated with United was hugely relieved when Uli Borowka's shot hit the base of the post before being scrambled clear. That was the last real opportunity the Germans were able to create in their bid to salvage the match.

Dundee United's Greatest Games

With Sturrock having run himself virtually to a standstill, McLean replaced him with Gallacher for the final five minutes and the younger man's fresh pace was to lead to a glorious end. With the stadium clock showing 91 minutes and the United fans' shrill whistles piercing the darkening night, Gallacher turned his covering defender and raced 20 yards into the Borussia penalty area. Rather than try for goal, he unselfishly squared the ball to Redford, who coolly rounded Kamps before scoring decisively.

That brought the normally implacable McLean out of his seat in celebration – and why not? A two-goal victory was a stunning result and it represented only Mönchengladbach's second home defeat in European competition in 20 years – the other one had been to Inter Milan.

As the manager, his coaching staff, the players and the fans on the terraces all celebrated wildly, the quality of United's play and their ability once again to master the tactics required in the away leg of a European tie was clear for the widespread television audience to admire.

Mönchengladbach coach Heynckes had underestimated United when the clubs met in 1981 and McLean felt his opposite number had failed to learn the lessons from that heavy defeat, 'He was convinced he would take his team to the final, but we had other ideas. We knew we had to play them at their own game and I think the Germans felt we could not do that. Instead, it was a game that suited us.'

Looking forward to the final – where United's opponents were to be IFK Gothenburg, who had completed a 5-1 aggregate defeat of Swarowski Tirol – McLean commented, 'We have not had an easy way through, but we have made it. We need worry about no one now and I know the players know that, because of what they have achieved.'

Then what happened?

As a mark of that achievement, three days later the players were given a guard of honour by their opponents and warmly applauded by the home crowd as they took to the pitch for the Premier Division match with Falkirk at Brockville Park. That was won 2-1, as were the other two league games United played before the first leg of the UEFA Cup Final on 6 May.

Meanwhile, with that match in Gothenburg set to take place a mere two weeks after the glory in Mönchengladbach, Arabs began the scramble to make travel arrangements to ensure that as many as possible would be there for part one of the biggest occasion in the club's history.

v IFK Gothenburg 1-1

39

UEFA Cup Final Second Leg
Tannadice
20 May 1987
Attendance: 20,911

DUNDEE UNITED	IFK GOTHENBURG
Thomson	Wernersson
Holt (Hegarty)	Carlsson
Malpas	Hysen
McInally	Larsson
Clark	Fredriksson
Narey	R. Nilsson (Johansson)
Ferguson	Tord Holmgren
Gallacher	Andersson
Kirkwood	Tommy Holmgren (Mordt)
Sturrock	Pettersson
Redford (Bannon)	L. Nilsson
Manager: Jim McLean	*Coach:* Gunder Bengtsson

THE march of United to the UEFA Cup Final had caught the excited attention not just of Scotland but of the whole of the UK. That wider interest was, to a significant extent, the result of English clubs being in the second year of a five-year ban from European competition as punishment for the dreadful scenes at the Heysel Stadium in Brussels before the 1985 European Cup Final, when 39 fans tragically lost their lives.

Live transmissions of both ties against Barcelona, plus the away legs in Split and Mönchengladbach, had given United a prominence beyond Scotland that until then had been unimaginable. Coverage of the build-up to the final, quite apart from reportage of the matches themselves, multiplied that several fold.

In becoming the first Scottish club to reach the UEFA Cup Final and the fourth to reach a European final (after Aberdeen, Celtic and Rangers), United were maintaining a proud tradition. Since European club competition began in 1955, Scotland had consistently punched above its weight. Thirty-two years later no country with a population the same size or smaller had produced a finalist in one of the three competitions (and that remained the case in 2014) yet three times Scottish clubs had lifted European trophies and on another three occasions had contested finals.

By a coincidence, the country with the next best record – in terms of its size – over that period was Sweden. Only twice had clubs from that country reached a final, with one of those enjoying success. But for United the good news ended there because that club was IFK Gothenburg. And it was the UEFA Cup. And it was only five years previously. And six of the players involved then were also in the squad preparing to meet United in the 1987 final.

United were the first Scottish club to stage a European final on their own ground. Given that UEFA brought an end to home-and-away finals in 1998 that's a record the club will hold permanently.

Highlighting the need for further caution in the minds of those who dismissed the Swedes as being of a lesser standard than United's two previous opponents, Gothenburg had eliminated Inter Milan in the quarter-finals and had reached the semi-final of the European Cup 12 months earlier, beating Aberdeen on the way.

Despite the shortage of time between the semi-final and the first leg of the final in Gothenburg some 4,000 Arabs managed to be there. Without ever indulging in excess, for two days they illuminated Sweden's second city and were among a crowd of just over 50,000 in the Ullevi Stadium for an occasion that, for most, was suitable compensation for United being denied a European Cup Final place three years earlier.

That occasion was certainly not enhanced by the state of the pitch. Almost unbelievably, just days before the match the stadium had been used for a concert by Bruce Springsteen which – predictably, you would have thought – had left the surface rutted and patchy. That is not to suggest that *per se* it offered Gothenburg an advantage but it did so indirectly as it made playing United's normal passing game much more difficult.

Whereas the tactically brilliant victories in Barcelona and Mönchengladbach had been achieved on smooth and lush grass, a different approach had to be employed by Jim McLean and his coaches at the Ullevi. That meant United were denied the option of using their tried-and-tested European style of sitting back and playing the kind of possession football where the opposition are tempted forward, allowing the Tangerines to get in behind them with counter-attacks. The more direct approach they were now obliged to use was one which left the players feeling less comfortable and that had a consequent effect on the quality of their play.

That apart, United were unsettled by an injury to Billy Thomson after just five minutes when he took a heavy knock while making a save. The ensuing concussion was bad enough but he also sustained a wound behind the ear that required stitching and for some time he was groggy.

It is probable that remained the case when Gothenburg took the lead after 38 minutes because it seemed Thomson remained rooted to his line when he would normally have come to collect a corner. Stefan Pettersson rose to meet the ball and sent it downwards where it took a sharp upward trajectory off the uneven pitch into the roof of the net.

Although the Terrors suffered another injury in the second half when Paul Hegarty had to be replaced by John Clark, they were relatively comfortable in containing the Gothenburg attack and Thomson seemed restored to full strength, which was fortunate as he had to be alert on several occasions.

As it happened, the nearest thing to a goal came from United midway through the half when, from a Dave Bowman cut-back, Ian Redford sent in a vicious shot that Thomas Wernersson did well to turn over the bar.

The consensus after the final whistle among the media was that, despite not being able to register an away goal, it was well within United's capabilities to overturn the deficit at Tannadice two weeks later. Pettersson himself was quoted as saying that one goal would not be enough and his team would not win unless they also scored in Scotland.

Unfortunately, any post-match analysis failed to allow for the unforeseen factor, something which, given United's record in Scottish Cup finals, ought to have been given at least some weight.

Four days before the return leg United faced St Mirren in the Scottish Cup Final. They had finished the Premier Division season four places and 26 points ahead of the Paisley club having won three of the four meetings with them. McLean's team were clear favourites, current status and form being judged by most to carry more weight than the fact that St Mirren had won four of the five Scottish Cup ties between the clubs over the past decade.

There was also the fact that, having lost all three of their previous Scottish Cup finals, plus two Scottish League Cup finals, questions had been asked as to whether United had a psychological problem with big games at the national stadium.

The underlying reasons (if, indeed, there were any) are of no great importance now; all that needs to be recorded is that United did not play well in the final and lost in extra time to the game's only goal.

McLean later reflected, 'No one could know… just how much that defeat would drain the last ounces of courage and determination from a team who had met so many demands on so many occasions.'

Maurice Malpas recalled, 'Apart from the terrible disappointment… the Hampden defeat left the players fearing they might win nothing, which increased our nerves.'

That was a reaction foreseen by the Gothenburg coach, Gunder Bengtsson, whose attention to detail had seen him attend each one of the six domestic matches United played since becoming his club's opponents. Emerging from Hampden, he observed merely, 'I was happy to see the game go to extra time.'

The second leg of the UEFA Cup Final would be the 67th match of United's season while Bengtsson's players were just two months into their domestic campaign.

The atmosphere at Tannadice on 20 May 1987 was electric, with the attention of people across Europe focussed on the city of Dundee. A television audience estimated to be around 70 million absorbed the spectacle of a modest stadium packed to capacity, now a cauldron of noise and a blaze of tangerine and black, tinged with a defiant section coloured blue and white which contained those from Sweden.

As the teams emerged side by side every United supporter was aware that, whatever transpired over the next two hours, this was a day in their lives they would cherish forever.

McLean again turned to the 4-3-3 pattern that had brought such success on previous European nights and United immediately went in search of the early goal that would give them the initiative. They might have achieved just that only five minutes in, had a slice of luck been earmarked for them. But when Billy Kirkwood reached a pass from Kevin Gallacher his shot hit the face of Wernersson, who knew nothing about his 'save' but the ball was cleared and the chance was gone.

Thomson was the busier goalkeeper during the first half as the Swedes served notice that they were determined to add to their first-leg advantage. He had to look sharp to deal with efforts from the scorer of that goal, Pettersson, as United were unable to control the pace of the game as they intended.

The Tangerines had not conceded a goal at Tannadice in five ties en route to the final but that record ended after 22 minutes. The build-up was controversial as United had been awarded a free kick in the opposing half, which was taken by Redford. His intended target was Paul Sturrock, who appeared to be deliberately blocked as he moved to receive the ball, which broke to Tord Holmgren.

He quickly moved the ball to Lennart Nilsson on the counter-attack and the striker's diagonal run left him in a position where he was able to rifle in a shot from just inside the penalty area which escaped Thomson and entered the net just inside his near post.

Although only a quarter of the game had been played, that came as a devastating blow to everyone wearing tangerine because the effect was that United had to score three times if they were to win the trophy.

They took some time to recover from the goal but McLean's men did come close to equalising in the 33rd minute. Sturrock sent in a teasing cross that Iain Ferguson reached first, only to send a glancing header agonisingly over the bar with Wernersson beaten.

Sturrock later recounted the mood at half-time, 'The combination of...defeat in the Scottish Cup Final and losing that goal mid-way through the first half certainly left the dressing-room a very silent and sombre place at the interval.'

McLean used the time to lift spirits and also to change the formation, bringing on Hegarty to operate in a three-man defence, releasing Clark to strengthen the attack.

With Sturrock using his pace down the left, United were much more of a positive force as the second half progressed. It was clear they were going to give everything in a desperate effort to turn the game round and they struck on the hour with a superbly-executed goal.

Ferguson made a determined run down the right before checking back and finding Clark with a pass on the edge of the penalty area. Clark showed he hadn't forgotten his forward skills as he controlled the ball with his right foot, then turned with a nimbleness that ought to have been beyond someone of his size while transferring it to his left before despatching a shot that swerved away from Wernersson and high into the net.

Tannadice exploded in a mighty roar and United then turned up the heat in an attempt to capitalise before Gothenburg had regained their composure. But, marshalled by the dominant Glenn Hysen at the heart of their defence, the Swedes stood their ground.

Eamonn Bannon was introduced for the last 20 minutes but the closest that United came after that was when Gallacher ran on to a flick by Clark and his lob went over Wernersson, but also the crossbar.

The match ended soon after as United's players sank to the turf in bitter disappointment and exasperation that their best efforts had not proved enough. To end such a momentous season with no tangible reward was a cruel fate to befall a team who had given not just their own supporters but all of Scotland so many highs during their thrilling run to the final.

Then what happened?

Twenty minutes after the final whistle, scarcely anyone had departed Tannadice. The Gothenburg players had been warmly applauded following the presentation of the trophy by those who had held such fervent hopes of it bearing tangerine and black ribbons. That was not to be, but Arabs had demanded the return of their players to allow them to receive due appreciation of all they had achieved and to ensure they were aware the fans felt they had nothing to be ashamed of; quite the contrary.

Huge pride was the overwhelming emotion felt by the supporters, who as the season progressed had seen the development of a strong bond, a common purpose with the players. The sense of togetherness that had taken the club to glory in varying parts of the continent and now to the very brink of a European trophy would not be allowed to dissipate. Victory would have been shared; defeat was to be treated no differently.

Eventually, their continued refusal to leave the scene brought the re-appearance of Jim McLean and he, too, acknowledged and reciprocated the warmth of the crowd's embrace. Only then did people begin to drift away from the most momentous occasion in the club's history, in the knowledge that they would never see its like again.

v Rangers 1-0

40

Scottish Cup Final
Hampden Park
21 May 1994
Attendance: 37,709

DUNDEE UNITED	RANGERS
Van de Kamp	Maxwell
Cleland	Stevens (Mikhailichenko)
Malpas	Robertson
McInally	Gough
Petric	McPherson
Welsh	McCall
Bowman	Murray
Hannah	I. Ferguson
McLaren (Nixon)	McCoist (D. Ferguson)
Brewster	Hateley
Dailly	Durie
Manager: Ivan Golac	*Manager:* Walter Smith

OOTBALL fans worldwide would confirm that, while semi-final defeats in cups are disappointing, final losses are devastating. Dundee United supporters need no lessons on coming to terms with those.

Between 1974 and 1991 they travelled in hope to Hampden Park for the Scottish Cup Final on six occasions only to discover – or be reminded – that the return journey feels three times as long when accompanied by shattering anti-climax.

Just for good measure, the Scottish League Cup finals of 1981 and 1984 had similar outcomes which made it natural – well, easy – for journalists to suggest some kind of hex existed when it came to United and the national stadium. The term 'Hampden Hoodoo' was born.

For United supporters the summer of 1993 was special because it represented a new experience: for the first time in 22 years they faced a season in which their club was not under the wise and dynamic leadership of Jim McLean.

In June McLean had signalled an end to his long reign as manager, though he remained as club chairman. In that role he was instrumental in appointing as his successor Ivan Golac, the first foreign national to manage a Scottish club.

Having played at the top level in England and his native Yugoslavia before managing Partizan Belgrade, the new man had plenty of attributes and he certainly knew how to sell them.

In terms of personality and management style, a greater contrast to McLean could hardly have been imagined and Golac stated at the outset he wanted his players to combine Scottish aggression with continental skill. That much sounded credible; less so was his claim he would bring a trophy to Tannadice in his first season.

Unfortunately, as the Premier Division campaign progressed his philosophy brought mixed success. Golac paid Raith Rovers £250,000 to bring former schoolboy signing Craig Brewster back to Tannadice and United did make a promising start. Although the new striker had then to find the net they were unbeaten after eight games, but thereafter form was patchy and along the way the Tangerines made their exit from both the Scottish League Cup (a narrow semi-final defeat to Hibernian) and the UEFA Cup (on away goals to Danish side Brondby).

Golac had stuck largely with the players bequeathed to him by McLean but in November he made his second big signing. It was rather more than 'big', because the £600,000 paid to Partizan Belgrade for central defender Gordan Petric didn't just exceed the existing record fee paid by United, it almost doubled it. The Serb would prove a sound investment and the only other flourish of the chequebook occurred in December when winger Jerren Nixon arrived at a cost of £200,000.

When the time came at the end of January for United to join the fray in the Scottish Cup, they were in something of a rut in mid-table and no doubt welcomed the diversion the main knockout competition offered. They probably also welcomed what looked like a straightforward visit to Arbroath, though it proved much more demanding than that.

Golac's men made heavy weather of defeating a club that would finish the season third-bottom of the Second Division (then the lowest) but the feature of the match was a stunning goal by Brewster from 35 yards.

The striker was fully into his stride and his two goals in the next round seemed to have taken United past Motherwell at Tannadice until a last-minute equaliser forced a replay at Fir Park which was a thriller, ultimately settled by a single goal, brilliantly executed by defender Brian Welsh. Satisfaction at reaching the last eight was tempered, though, by the broken leg suffered by attacking midfielder Scott Crabbe, who had just established himself under Golac.

The quarter-final sent United back to Lanarkshire where First Division Airdrieonians proved resilient and the match ended goalless. That was an outcome United were prepared to settle for after Brewster received a red card, but even without him his team-mates comfortably won the replay 2-0.

For the fourth time in ten years the semi-final saw a clash of the New Firm. Aberdeen were clear favourites, largely because Golac's men had managed to take just a single point from the four league meetings with the Dons. But, as the manager cheerfully pointed out to those who raised that as an issue, 'That's the league; what has it got to do with the cup?'

His response was equally dismissive when invited to comment about the match being played at Hampden, hardly United's favourite venue.

The Tangerines fell behind after just seven minutes but, in a battling display, they were undiminished in their determination as the match entered its final two minutes and they got the reward they deserved when Welsh again came to the rescue. In the replay three days later, Jim McInally chose the perfect occasion to score his only goal of the season and it proved enough to secure a place in the Scottish Cup Final.

Rangers were to be their opponents, but in the meantime the Tangerines still had to secure their place in the Premier Division. That seemed an odd situation given that United were sixth out of 12 in the table in mid-January and never moved from that position in the remaining four months of the season.

But with the top flight about to be reduced to ten clubs, three would be relegated and it wasn't until their win at Motherwell on 3 May that United were mathematically secure. Ultimately they finished four places, but just two points, above relegated St Johnstone.

The win at Motherwell came at a heavy price. Midfielder Billy McKinlay had been in sparkling form throughout the season, a fact recognised when he won his first full Scotland cap in November. Cruelly, a yellow card shown after an innocuous tackle at Fir Park took him over the points threshold for suspension – and out of the final.

On the face of it, there was no reason for any rational person to arrive at a conclusion other than that Rangers would collect yet another trophy at Hampden. The bookmakers certainly thought so with Rangers typically quoted at 4/5 and United at 6/1. Bookies don't deal in emotion, just facts. The Ibrox club had spent millions in assembling a multi-national squad of players that had just achieved a sixth successive Premier Division title. Having won all three domestic trophies in 1992/93 they had retained two of them and required the Scottish Cup to complete back-to-back trebles, unprecedented in Scottish football.

Then there was their Scottish Cup record against Dundee United. Ten times the clubs had met in the competition and eight times Rangers had emerged victorious, with the other two drawn. As United prepared for the final they did so in the knowledge that their club had never beaten Rangers in the Scottish Cup.

The 'Hampden Hoodoo' was certainly a hot topic in the media in the days before the final although, naturally, no one at Tannadice would give it any credence. Brewster summed up the players' view, 'What has happened in the past will have absolutely no bearing. Apart from anything else, it's a new-look Hampden and a new-look United with myself, Jerren Nixon and Gordan Petric not to mention the manager, who weren't involved in previous ties the club has played there.'

That comment was actually made prior to the semi-final – and that hadn't gone too badly. The reference to a new-look Hampden reflected the makeover the national stadium was receiving, though it was only three-quarters complete and as a result the crowd was restricted to 38,000. Rangers were allocated 19,000 tickets and United 12,000 with the remainder going to other clubs and the tournament's sponsors.

Golac was unambiguous in his approach to the final, 'My philosophy is to try and enjoy life and to do that you must be relaxed and positive in your outlook. Our problem all season has been inconsistency but on the occasions we have played well we have shown ourselves more than capable of winning the big matches. If we get our act together on Saturday I cannot see Rangers stopping us getting the trophy.'

Golac's determination to ensure his players were devoid of tension involved a typically idiosyncratic decision. Having checked into their East Kilbride hotel on the day before the final the United players went to the races. McInally revealed, 'I love horse racing and when we went to Hamilton racecourse it was too good to be true.'

Later, players of both clubs were interviewed at their hotels for a BBC preview of the final and it was obvious from the body language which group looked more at ease.

McInally recalled, 'I believe that many of the doubters who saw us on the programme may have been convinced that this time we could do it. We had a long chat before the game and it was clear that every player was determined to prove a lot of people wrong. The manager instilled in us the notion that we were good enough and much of the credit must be put down to Ivan, whose management skills were second to none.'

When the big day arrived, the scene that greeted the United players as they emerged from the tunnel was stunning, both visually and audibly. Even before the kick-off the volume was greatest from the sections coloured tangerine and black. Christian Dailly remembered, 'From the moment I walked out on to the pitch I realised the fans really believed in us. You'd never have known they were outnumbered.'

As expected, Ivan Golac brought in David Hannah to replace McKinlay. Together with Dailly and Andy McLaren, Hannah was one of three 20-year-olds in the team with substitute Nixon the same age.

It was immediately obvious that Golac had set out to take the game to Rangers. Far from defending and hoping to find the space to hit on the break, United pushed the holders back with a three-man front line. Perhaps that was simply recognition that United had to score first – because they hadn't won once during the season after falling behind.

Rangers were hardly content to find themselves on the back foot and soon began to display the quick, accurate passing that had brought them such success. They were first to produce a serious threat and might well have taken the lead as early as the ninth minute. Gordon Durie sent over a corner which towering defender Dave McPherson met with a firm header that beat Guido van de Kamp. Arabs, with hearts in mouths, breathed again as McInally headed the ball off the line before it was booted to safety by Petric.

Two minutes later United broke up an attack and moved the ball quickly into the Rangers half. Brewster set up Alex Cleland with a clever reverse pass and the full-back raced into the penalty area where he hit the turf after having his heels clipped by Ian Ferguson for what seemed a clear penalty. It wasn't clear to referee Dougie Hope, though, as he waved play on despite furious protests from Golac and his players.

The ebb and flow of the match was relentless and after 16 minutes it was United's turn to have an effort cleared off the line as Brian Welsh rose to meet a McLaren corner but saw his header hooked clear by Stuart McCall.

Both sides created chances almost every time they attacked, though in the remainder of the half only two were turned into what might be termed near things. On 28 minutes Mark Hateley, who was being effectively policed by Welsh, ran into the box to meet a McCall through ball and his low shot skidded inches past the post with van de Kamp unable to reach it.

Two minutes before half-time Brewster came desperately close to breaking the deadlock, when he received a pass from McInally and cut inside McPherson before unleashing a goalbound effort from 20 yards that Ally Maxwell pushed round the post at full stretch.

The crowd must have welcomed the break almost as much as the players after a frenetic first half with scarcely a lull in play. But the second was to have an explosive start, one that would ultimately decide the destination of the cup.

There can be few Arabs who are unfamiliar with the sequence of events that unfolded in the 47th minute. They were there in person, watched it on TV or have had it told and re-told to them by those in the first two categories.

Just inside the box, McPherson tried to shepherd the ball back to Maxwell but, under pressure from Dailly, was forced to play it to his goalkeeper from close range. Maxwell then had to rush his clearance, which rebounded off the advancing Dailly, seemingly into Maxwell's arms.

But he failed to gather it, allowing Dailly to collect the ball before attempting to find the net from the narrowest of angles. He almost succeeded but the ball hit the far post before rebounding perfectly for the inrushing Brewster to turn into the gaping goal.

There is a – now iconic – picture which captures the moment when the ball crosses the line, but has not yet come to rest in the net. Despite that, the vast majority of the massed ranks of Arabs behind the goal are already in the air acclaiming the goal with a gigantic roar that rose to the roof above them before cascading down and dispersing in every direction around the stadium.

Once a semblance of order had returned, the common view among Arabs was, 'It's far too early!' Few would later admit to recalling with any semblance of accuracy the subsequent 43 minutes of play.

Rangers reacted like any wounded animal and fought furiously to restore their pride, as well as their foothold in the game. But, hard as they tried, their efforts largely foundered on the superb United midfield of Dave Bowman, McInally and Hannah. When Rangers did succeed in advancing beyond them, they found Petric and Welsh imperious at the heart of the defence and van de Kamp confident in dealing with anything that came his way.

Despite their second-half pressure, Rangers forced the goalkeeper to make just two saves. On 54 minutes Alexei Mikhailichenko let fly from just six yards and watched in disbelief as van de Kamp leapt breathtakingly to divert the ball over the bar. After 71 minutes Hateley found space to shoot from 20 yards and the Dutchman allowed the ball to squirm from his grasp before dropping on it.

Both sides introduced fresh legs with Nixon and the former United striker Duncan Ferguson joining the fray, but the Tangerines' defence stood firm as Rangers' frustration saw them progressively run out of ideas.

Most United supporters had been whistling for full time for at least ten minutes before it finally arrived. At that point, most didn't know whether to laugh or cry – so they did both.

After six attempts spread over 20 years, the boundless joy was accompanied by a huge wave of relief. Not simply relief that, at last, United had won the Scottish Cup; but relief that the return journey would be one of celebration and not recrimination.

Calmer reflection led to satisfaction that it was the product of a faultless performance by their team and their manager. The cup had been won by United, not lost by Rangers.

Then what happened?

Something that had never happened before – a Dundee United captain was presented with the Scottish Cup. Fittingly, Maurice Malpas was that man; already a club legend, the final was his 626th game in tangerine. It was particularly satisfying for Maurice because on four previous occasions he had trudged up the Hampden steps to collect his runners-up medal before watching the Scottish Cup being presented. Not this time and he raised it aloft with visible pride.

The celebrations went on long into the night and the following day the centre of Dundee was a mass of tangerine and black as the cup was paraded from the City Chambers. That came at the end of an open-top bus tour to the acclaim of wildly cheering crowds, many of whom had never been to a football match in their lives but wanted to express their sense of civic pride.

For Golac it was a case of job done, 'I said when I took over at the start of the season we were good enough to win a trophy. I'm delighted I was able to keep my word. This is a magnificent achievement, given how young the side is.'

Journalists chose Petric as the official man of the match but Golac picked out Hannah, 'You'd think he had played at this level all his life; he was quite superb.'

Among Arabs who had so often suffered crushing disappointments at Hampden there was consensus that every man had played his part in the triumph. But the orchestrator, an eccentric from the Balkans, had made it possible. To every United supporter, Ivan Golac had delivered the Holy Grail.

v Partick Thistle 2-1

Premier Division Play-Off Second Leg
Tannadice
16 May 1996
Attendance: 12,120

DUNDEE UNITED	PARTICK THISTLE
Maxwell	Walker
Shannon	Milne
McQuilken	Watson
Pressley	Smith
Welsh	Slavin
Dailly	Welsh
Winters (Johnson)	R. McDonald
Bowman	McWilliams (Dinnie)
McSwegan (Coyle)	McCue (Henderson)
Brewster (McKinnon)	Cameron
McLaren	Lyons
Manager: Billy Kirkwood	*Manager:* Murdo MacLeod

RELEGATION in May 1995 – just 12 months after that first Scottish Cup triumph – came as a painful jolt to the system at Dundee United. To surrender top-flight status after 35 years was bad enough, but the thought of the revenue loss through smaller gates and the absence of television income compounded the price to be paid.

As it happened, the drop in gate receipts during 1995/96 was limited due to the tremendous level of support maintained by Arabs in the First Division. Despite the absence of visits from Aberdeen and the Old Firm, the league average at Tannadice of 7,283 was down just 1,200 on the previous season and was higher than all but six clubs in the Premier Division.

Nonetheless, Billy Kirkwood and his players were in no doubt that a return to the top level was absolutely essential.

Kirkwood had been appointed in March 1995 following the end of the tenure of Ivan Golac. An iconic figure to all United supporters due to his role in that Scottish Cup triumph, Golac had proved unable to ride the wave of success and United failed to occupy a place in the top half of the Premier Division in the following season. That said, the decision to dispense with Golac and appoint Kirkwood with just seven matches remaining was a strange one. A legend as a player, Kirkwood had no managerial experience and, to nobody's great surprise, could not prevent relegation.

No blame could be attached to the new manager and he was given the full backing of the board – to the tune of £2m – which he used to re-shape his squad by bringing in ten new players. The most expensive was Steven Pressley, who cost a club record £750,000 from Coventry City – still a record in the summer of 2014.

It took some time for the team to gel but from mid-December United were never out of the top two in the First Division, with Dunfermline Athletic, Greenock Morton and St Johnstone their main challengers. Automatic promotion went only to the champions, with the second-placed club facing a play-off with the club finishing second-bottom of the Premier Division.

As the season reached its climax, the Terrors were in pole position and faced Dunfermline at Tannadice in the penultimate match knowing a win would seal the championship. A crowd of 12,384 saw the eagerly-awaited clash, but the Fife club claimed the game's only goal, taking United's fate out of their own hands and condemning them to a nailbiting visit to Greenock on the final day.

Just how tight the promotion race was is demonstrated by the fact that United could have ended that day anywhere in the top four. Another crowd of more than 12,000 saw a thriller at Cappielow Park end 2-2, after Kirkwood's men had twice led. That left the two clubs on the same points with United earning the play-off position by a superior goal difference.

The prize – though it didn't feel like that to many Arabs – was a home and away meeting with Partick Thistle for the right to play at the top level the following season. Promotion/relegation play-offs had been re-introduced a year earlier, for the first time since 1915. They were not popular but without them United would have been facing at least another season in the First Division. The players were informed that a £100,000 bonus was available to be distributed among them should Premier Division status be regained.

The first leg at Firhill was played in an atmosphere that reflected the thrilling sense of occasion attached to a match of such importance. Thistle drew first blood when, from a free kick, Andy Lyons curled the ball round United's defensive wall and left Ally Maxwell flailing. That was after 19 minutes and although United took some time to recover they gained the ascendancy before half-time and refused to relinquish it as the second half developed. Maxwell's counterpart Nicky Walker was made to work overtime in the Thistle goal but for all United's pressure an equaliser proved stubbornly elusive.

Then, with just five minutes remaining, Christian Dailly came to the rescue. He lost his marker in the box and met a diagonal cross from Dave Bowman to power home a header, leaving the return at Tannadice four days later perfectly poised.

Before the match, Dailly, United's captain at 22, reflected, 'We're in a similar position to the one we found ourselves in when we played Dunfermline and had the championship in our hands. We let the prize slip that day because we hoped things would happen for us. This time, we need to make things happen for ourselves.'

For Dailly, together with Bowman, Craig Brewster, Andy McLaren and Brian Welsh, the contrast with the same week two years previously could hardly have been more stark: then they were all part of the United team that won that first Scottish Cup; now they were battling to avoid a second season in the First Division.

Live TV coverage had not diminished the determination of Arabs to be there in order to provide the vocal support to propel United back into the Premier Division. Tannadice was well-filled, but it was an occasion when both United and Thistle displayed nerves – perhaps understandably, given what was at stake.

The first half was goalless though that was certainly not due to a lack of attempts by United. Twice within a minute Walker came to Thistle's rescue, denying Gary McSwegan on both occasions. Soon after, Craig Brewster directed a free header wide.

Walker then denied McSwegan again and it was only a lack of composure in front of goal by Kirkwood's men that allowed Thistle to hang on. Shortly before the interval, after another Brewster attempt had been deflected for a corner, Welsh just failed to get a touch as the ball flashed across goal.

By midway through the second half the Glasgow side, perhaps coming to terms with being fortunate to be still alive in the tie, had stirred themselves and created several opportunities. Then, as so often happens when a dominant team fails to turn their superiority into goals, Thistle had the ball in the net with almost an hour played. Fortunately the raised flag of a linesman signalling offside brought relief to everyone in tangerine.

Thereafter, the visitors were once more penned back but they survived the onslaught, most notably when Pressley failed to find the net with a header when it seemed easier to score.

As United became frustrated at their inability to make their pressure tell, Thistle themselves began to create opportunities and the home defence began to creak. So it didn't come totally out of the blue when, with 18 minutes remaining, they grabbed the lead.

Substitute Nicky Henderson, whose effort had earlier been ruled out for offside, was pushed to the ground by Welsh as he went for a cross and referee Les Mottram awarded a penalty. With Arabs scarcely daring to look, Ian Cameron calmly slotted the ball past Maxwell.

The goal gave the Jags a big lift and initially it had the opposite effect on United. On 84 minutes Kirkwood introduced Owen Coyle in a final effort to earn extra time at least, but soon after the visitors had what seemed like a more clear-cut penalty claim turned down by Mottram when Rab Shannon brought down Henderson again.

As the minutes ticked by, United's hopes of saving the day appeared forlorn. But the mercurial talents of a player who had performed below his capabilities up to that point would dramatically turn the team's fortunes around.

Enter McLaren, who conjured up a piece of magic that took him from a seemingly impossible position, with his back to goal near the corner flag, leaving Thistle defenders floundering in his wake and somehow fashioning a cross. Coyle headed the ball back across the goal and Welsh used all of his height and strength to head in a life-saving equaliser.

Tannadice erupted in a mighty roar – largely through relief, because 40 seconds remained when the goal came, illustrating how close United came to remaining a First Division club.

With Kirkwood's team and the vast majority of the crowd now on a high, Thistle had to cope with their disappointment – and a resurgent United. In extra time there was only one side in it, Walker again proving Thistle's hero with a string of saves until even he had to admit defeat, just five minutes away from a penalty shoot-out.

Again McLaren was the architect; clever play on the left took him to the byline from where he sent the ball into the penalty area for Coyle to sweep it home from eight yards with more coolness than anyone could expect in such a cauldron of excitement.

Determined to suffocate any possible Thistle response, Kirkwood brought on midfielder Ray McKinnon in place of Brewster. But there was to be no way back for Thistle as, amid a cacophony of whistles from Arabs, the referee ended the match and with it United's absence from the Premier Division.

It was a night that could have passed as a metaphor for United's season as they again did things the hard way. There is a saying that the end justifies the means but as they flooded on to the Tannadice pitch to join the celebrations there could be no United supporter who would want to go through another 120 minutes of such torment again, even though it ultimately turned out all right on the night.

Amid the celebrations Kirkwood paid tribute to the fans, saying, 'Just listen to them, we couldn't have let them down. I thought they were magnificent tonight. They urged us on all the way and I sensed that, eventually, we were going to get something if we kept playing.'

For Coyle, the hero of the hour, there was a sense of déjà vu because a year earlier he had scored for Bolton Wanderers in their extra-time play-off defeat of Reading at Wembley to reach the Premier League, 'I said to [United coach] Gordon Wallace with about 15 minutes to go that he should get me on. Sometimes you get a feeling that you can do something and I had that feeling. After Wembley, I felt I could do it again. Even when there were only seconds left I sensed it wasn't over and after Brian's goal I was convinced we'd win it.'

Then what happened?

A year later, United finished third in the Premier, while Thistle finished sixth in the First Division. How thin the line is between success and failure.

v Aberdeen 3-1

42

Scottish League Cup Semi-Final
Tynecastle Park
15 October 1997
Attendance: 10,459

DUNDEE UNITED	ABERDEEN
Dijkstra	Leighton
Bowman	Smith (Gillies)
Malpas	Inglis (Kombouare)
Pressley	O'Neil
Perry (Skoldmark)	Tzvetanov
Pedersen	Bernard
Olofsson	Miller
Zetterlund	Rowson
Winters	Newell
Dolan (McLaren)	Windass
Easton	Glass
Manager: Tommy McLean	*Manager:* Roy Aitken

BILLY Kirkwood was not given much time to consolidate after the dramatic play-off victory which secured United's return to the Premier Division. Only four league games of the new season to be precise and, when those produced just a single point, Jim McLean was ruthless in ushering him out of the door in September. The chairman lost no time in appointing his own brother, Tommy, as Kirkwood's replacement and the change in the club's fortunes was dramatic.

Soon after his arrival the younger McLean decided to go back to the future to mine the always-rich seam of talent to be found in Scandinavia. Erik Pedersen, Kjell Olofsson, Magnus Skoldmark and Lars Zetterlund arrived three decades after Jerry Kerr's bold entry to that market.

It worked then for Kerr and it worked now for McLean because in their first season after returning United finished third in the Premier Division, their highest in 12 years. It also meant that European football was back at Tannadice after an absence of three years.

So it was understandable that, when 1997/98 began, United supporters were brimming with confidence. The manager didn't feel the need to add new faces to his squad though there was one notable departure. After almost 400 appearances in two spells, Jim McInally left to take up a player-coach role at Dens Park.

The new season got off to an unexpectedly sluggish start with the first eight league games failing to produce a win. Interest in the UEFA Cup had also ended in the second qualifying round with a 2-1 aggregate defeat to the Turkish club Trabzonspor.

Pretty much the only bright spot for Arabs had been an extra-time Coca-Cola League Cup win at Ibrox that propelled the club into the semi-final. Amazingly, that was the first time United had got the better of Rangers in the League Cup – at the 15th attempt.

A cup semi-final in Scotland's capital was not entirely an appealing prospect for United. Six months earlier the Tangerines had lost to Kilmarnock at Hibernian's ground in the last four of the Scottish Cup and, with the Ayrshire side then going on to win the trophy by beating First Division Falkirk in the final, there was a real sense of a major opportunity lost. This time, the semi-final opponents were Aberdeen and the venue was across the city at the home of Hearts.

Prior to the start of the season, anyone suggesting the New Firm would each complete the first eight Premier Division matches without recording a win between them would have been laughed at. Yet that was the position as the clubs prepared to meet in the semi-final.

After the great success enjoyed by both clubs during the 1980s, the following decade was quite different. Each had lost iconic managers in Jim McLean and Alex Ferguson but that alone didn't explain their dramatic falls from grace – United had suffered relegation while Aberdeen needed a play-off to avoid a similar fate.

That said, each did have a cup success to their name within the past three years: United with the Scottish Cup in 1994 and Aberdeen with the Scottish League Cup the following year.

But as they prepared to meet at Tynecastle, to characterise them as 'not in the best of health' was charitable. To their joint embarrassment, United were sitting one place from the bottom of the Premier Division – with the Dons below them.

While the success of McLean's first season acted as a buffer from much discontent from Arabs, Pittodrie fans were more than a little restless and were close to losing patience with their boss, Roy Aitken. Both clubs were clearly in need of the boost which achieving a place in a cup final brings.

It was a long journey for both sets of supporters, not least on a chilly midweek autumn evening, but the 10,000-plus who made the effort to be there created an atmosphere more akin to the newly all-seated stadium being full.

Arabs were surprised that Andy McLaren and Gary McSwegan – scorer of the goal that beat Rangers – were left on the bench, while Dons fans were already dismayed that their Scotland striker, Billy Dodds, was suspended.

Three of United's four Scandinavians started the match, which began at a high tempo and quickly became an exciting tie with play flowing from end to end. Aberdeen had the better of the early stages and twice came close to threatening a goal. First Mark Perry went to meet a cross into the box from Mike Newell but sliced his clearance and the ball rocketed narrowly over the bar. Then, after 17 minutes, Dean Windass back-heeled the ball into the path of Stephen Glass and Arabs breathed a collective sigh of relief as Sieb Dijkstra dived fearlessly at the winger's feet to smother the danger.

Somehow the moniker 'Sieb' didn't quite do justice to the tall, bronzed Dutchman's full name – Sybrandus Johannes Andreas Dijkstra – and that exotic collection was reflective of the personality of the man who, less than a year after being signed by McLean for £100,000 from Queens Park Rangers, was already a cult figure with the United fans.

Jamie Dolan was putting in his usual industrious shift in the middle of the park but when, after 20 minutes, he picked up a yellow card after a series of robust tackles, McLean decided it would be wise to avert the danger of a second one and replaced the combative midfielder with McLaren.

That gave his team a more attacking look and with half an hour played a Robbie Winters shot was cleared off the line by Joe Miller, with strong United claims that the Aberdeen man had used a hand. The referee was having none of it but the breakthrough by the men in tangerine was not long delayed.

Winters was proving a constant threat and with 11 minutes of the first half remaining, after McLaren had split the Aberdeen rearguard with a precise pass, the striker's first touch was calm and assured as he steered the ball beyond the reach of Jim Leighton.

That delighted McLean, though he was much less happy with Winters for overdoing his celebration; United's scorer recklessly indulged himself in front of the Dons fans and earned a yellow card.

Aberdeen struggled to re-assert themselves before the interval but they started the second half strongly and it was only three minutes old when they dragged themselves level. David Rowson squared the ball across the face of the goal where it took a deflection off Maurice Malpas, leaving Dijkstra in no-man's-land – and Windass handily placed to sweep it home.

That could have been the turning point had Aberdeen been allowed to build on their period of ascendancy, but United ensured that didn't happen. Parity would last a mere six minutes and the hero was an 18-year-old midfielder making only his fourth first-team start.

Craig Easton had already shown a maturity beyond his years as the match developed, but on 54 minutes he started and finished a move that was to prove pivotal. Receiving the ball inside his own half Easton drove at the opposition, exchanging passes with Olofsson before racing into the penalty area and leaving Leighton helpless with a clinical finish.

It was a breathtaking goal. With only slight exaggeration, it would have graced a World Cup Final and it appeared to take the wind out of Aberdeen's sails. They had worked hard to get level and having that swept away so quickly hit them hard. They never looked capable of lifting themselves to find a second equaliser and with 15 minutes remaining the tie was put beyond their reach with another slick move and flawless finish.

Olofsson steered the ball out to Winters on the right and he cut inside, running at John Inglis. As the Aberdeen defender backed off expecting a pass, Winters struck a superb shot into the top corner to spark wild celebrations among the United support. The contrasting response from the Aberdeen fans was unequivocal as a hail of red and white scarves landed on the track surrounding the pitch.

Their frustration was understandable because, like Arabs, they had been hoping a semi-final win over north-east rivals would kick-start their season. It wasn't going to happen for the men in red and the third goal caused Aitken, who had been subdued throughout, to become a picture of abject misery.

McLean moved to protect the lead by replacing a Scandinavian striker (Olofsson) with a Scandinavian defender (Skoldmark) and after 83 minutes, Mark Perry and Windass were perhaps a little fortunate to be shown only yellow cards following a scuffle. The United man became the fourth player in tangerine to be cautioned and one of those was McLaren, who had retaliated after a heavy tackle by Glass.

It wasn't until the match was over that the winger was informed he, having also picked up a booking in the previous round, would be suspended for the final.

Aberdeen had been outmanoeuvred and outplayed by United who were able to see out the remainder of the match comfortably and to anticipate another final, three and a-half years after the historic first Scottish Cup triumph.

McLean paid tribute to his men, 'I thought the players showed the kind of concentration and unity which has been missing this season. And it was encouraging that after conceding the equaliser we didn't feel sorry for ourselves – as we have been doing – but set about getting ourselves back in front.'

Midfielder Pedersen expressed the players' view, 'We didn't really start to play well until Andy came on. We were all nervous, the results recently have knocked our confidence. When they scored so quickly after the break we did well to come back and take control again.'

Then what happened?

The following Saturday United received an immediate bounce by beating Motherwell 4-0 – the first of five successive league wins. One of them was a 5-0 drubbing of Aberdeen at Tannadice, at the end of which Aitken trudged off down the tunnel and found there was no light at the end of it – he was sacked two days later.

United's fine run in the Premier Division came to a shuddering halt when they lost 4-0 at Celtic Park a week before the Scottish League Cup Final. The big day at Ibrox proved a big let-down for United supporters as Celtic almost repeated the league score, eventually settling for 3-0.

Thereafter McLean's team returned to a season of slog, winning only two of the following 19 league games. Relegation was not banished until the penultimate game of the season, although United finished seventh.

v Aberdeen 4-0

43

Scottish Premier League
Pittodrie
17 April 1999
Attendance: 11,603

DUNDEE UNITED	ABERDEEN
Dijkstra	Warner
Skoldmark	Perry
De Vos	Whyte
Jonsson (Patterson)	Smith
Malpas	Hamilton
Miller	Jess
Hannah	Mayer (Wyness)
Easton	Dow
McCulloch	Bernard (Pepper)
Dodds	Young
Olofsson	Winters
Manager: Paul Sturrock	*Manager:* Paul Hegarty

I N September 1997 the Premier Division clubs served notice of their decision to leave the Scottish Football League and form themselves into the Scottish Premier League. The driving force was the example of a similar breakaway by top clubs in England five years earlier, based on their desire to retain a greater share of the revenues generated by the game. The other SFL clubs bitterly resented the move but ultimately were powerless to prevent it.

For Dundee United, following on the heels of a narrow escape from relegation, the inaugural SPL season began against the backdrop of supporters' group United for Change campaigning for the introduction of new blood at boardroom level. Arabs didn't have long to wait for change, but it came at a different level within the club.

Part of the fans' concern related to transfer activity during the close-season. Defenders Steven Pressley and Mark Perry left on freedom of contract, joining two of United's main rivals in Hearts and Aberdeen. In addition, since striker Robbie Winters was left out of the pre-season tour of Holland after making it clear he wanted a move, it was only a matter of time before he would be on his way.

Manager Tommy McLean had brought in several new faces, though few were recognisable and those who were, former Celts Mark McNally and Joe Miller, failed to enthuse most Arabs. The remainder were overseas players and, added to the Scandinavian contingent that McLean had successfully introduced, this led to a situation where the United team for the visit of Hearts – the first SPL match at Tannadice – had just two Scots in the starting line-up.

That was a club record, though it wouldn't have bothered Arabs had it brought about a bright start to the 1998/99 season; unfortunately it achieved quite the opposite.

That the first four SPL games produced just a single point was worrying in itself, but sandwiched between them was the most disastrous result in the club's entire history. In the third round of the Scottish League Cup McLean took his squad north to face Third Division Ross County, members of the Scottish League for only four years. The clubs were then separated by three divisions and 22 league places yet part-time County won 2-0 in extra time, precipitating a crisis at Tannadice.

A listless display in a 1-0 defeat by Motherwell at Fir Park at the end of August prompted a furious reaction from the travelling fans with calls for the departure of manager and board. That match proved the final straw for McLean, who tendered his resignation two days later. Acting with an alacrity that suggested he was not exactly taken by surprise, chairman Jim McLean secured his brother's successor by bringing in St Johnstone manager Paul Sturrock and the hope must have been that Luggy's legendary United status would help steady a somewhat mutinous ship.

In that respect Sturrock's appointment was – at least initially – successful, although fortunes improved only marginally. The new manager made his first signing when Billy Dodds arrived in part-exchange for Winters. The Scotland striker, typically derided by Arabs when a Dundee player, quickly won them over in the best possible manner by scoring a hat-trick in his second match.

That came in a 3-1 win against St Johnstone, United's first of the season (in their eighth league game), and it was followed a week later by a 1-0 defeat of New Firm rivals Aberdeen. Sturrock continued re-shaping the side, paying sizeable fees for Canadian international central defender Jason de Vos (£400,000) and striker Alex Mathie (£500,000), but only three of the following 15 SPL fixtures produced wins and that left the Tangerines languishing ninth – second-bottom – in the table.

One of those victories had been a comprehensive 3-0 beating of Aberdeen at Pittodrie and the second Tannadice meeting of the clubs in February saw that result repeated, with the three points United took that day raising them above the Dons and up to the heady heights of eighth.

It appeared money was no object for chairman McLean as he gave Sturrock the green light to add to his squad. One of the 1994 Scottish Cup heroes, David Hannah, had left for Celtic in 1996 and United repaid half of the £600,000 to bring the midfielder back to Tannadice, while full-back Scott McCulloch cost a net £200,000 from Dunfermline, with Jamie Dolan going in the opposite direction.

Hopes of a first Scottish Cup Final appearance since 1994 were ended when a poor performance in the semi-final at Ibrox resulted in a 2-0 defeat by Celtic and seven days later came a match regarded by many supporters and football writers as crucial in United's fight for SPL survival.

The match saw United return to Pittodrie, scene of that three-goal win back in November. Since then Aberdeen had aped the Terrors by changing their manager, though there the similarity ended. Whereas Jim McLean had been decisive in bringing in a replacement, after dismissing Alex Miller in January Dons chairman Stewart Milne had promoted United's league-winning captain Paul Hegarty from his role as coach to interim manager for the remainder of the season.

Although Arabs travelling up the A90 would have been concerned at their club's position in the table – United had been overtaken by Aberdeen and only two points separated them from back-markers Dunfermline – they would have been encouraged by two factors. First, despite almost the length of the SPL table separating them, in their last away match United had beaten Rangers 1-0. Second, the season's three previous meetings with Aberdeen had all been won by the Tangerines with a goal difference of 7-0.

Though the two clubs' current status could hardly have been further removed, the raucous singing by both sets of supporters provided an atmosphere more akin to some of the high-value encounters that the New Firm had enjoyed during the 1980s. The rivalry remained intense and the occasion was given added piquancy with two United legends from that era in opposing dugouts, while Dodds and Winters were facing the clubs they had scored for earlier in the season. Miller and Perry were also in opposition to former clubs.

Hegarty's team made the more positive start, creating chances from which they might well have fashioned an opener had Sieb Dijkstra not shown his mettle. When the breakthrough did come it reflected the shift in the play as United had come more into the match.

After 38 minutes Scott McCulloch won the ball and set off down the left wing before firing a cross into the penalty area. Making the most of his experience, Dodds compensated for his lack of height by peeling off his marker and creating enough space to score with a well-placed header from the edge of the six-yard box.

Aberdeen responded with determined efforts to regain parity before half-time and they seemed on the brink of doing that with two minutes remaining, only for Eoin Jess to slice his shot wide from ten yards.

That would prove to be the last opportunity for the Dons to take anything from the match because United made what can only be described as a whirlwind start to the second half. Taking advantage of some inept defending, within 11 minutes of the re-start the Tangerines had quadrupled their lead. Even more remarkably, all three goals came within the space of four minutes.

On 53 minutes McCulloch split the Aberdeen defence with a superb pass to Kjell Olofsson wide on the right. The striker turned before releasing fellow Swede Magnus Skoldmark, who sent a searching low cross in to the goalmouth. Gary Smith had the opportunity to clear but instead allowed the ball to deflect off him to the unmarked Miller, who turned it into the net.

The home team had no time to reflect on the self-inflicted nature of that goal because within a minute goalkeeper Tony Warner was again retrieving the ball from his net. This time Derek Whyte slipped as he went for another inventive cross sent in by the marauding McCulloch. That left Olofsson with a clear run at Warner and he scored emphatically as the travelling Arabs again celebrated noisily.

In the 56th minute the Dons' misery was complete as they were punished for yet more disarray in defence. Olofsson was the provider on this occasion, winning the ball from Andy Dow before laying it on for Dodds to run into the box before beating the by-now-bemused Warner at his near post with a fiercely-struck angled drive.

Though in raptures – not just because of the score but the ground on which it was happening – the United supporters were barely able to contain themselves. Their taunting of the home support – 'Can we play you every week?' – probably accounted as much as the score for the Dons fans beginning to stream out of the stadium. Hegarty, who had been the epitome of sound defensive play in his Tannadice career, must have been beside himself with rage at the sheer incompetence of his team's attempts to stem the tide.

With more than half an hour to play he must have been fearing an even heavier drubbing, not least when substitute Nigel Pepper was sent off for a wild challenge on Siggi Jonsson – 19 seconds after coming on to the field.

Despite Whyte and Perry separately contributing further penalty box errors, Olofsson was unable to accept either chance to record his hat-trick and there was no further scoring.

Sturrock confessed to feeling a mixture of relief and frustration at his team's display, 'We received scathing criticism after the [Scottish Cup] semi-final but the players have responded in a professional manner.'

The win remains the most decisive recorded by United at Pittodrie and it completed four victories out of four in a league season, neither of which has been achieved since. Aberdeen have never won all four league meetings in a season.

Then what happened?

United failed to win any of their remaining six league games and ended the season second-bottom of the SPL, albeit six points ahead of Dunfermline.

The landmark clean sheet and clean sweep against Aberdeen aside, it was a season to forget. The Dons were the only club United managed to defeat in their 18 SPL home games, eight of which were lost. As two of those defeats came in derbies it meant that, to the embarrassment of all Arabs, Dundee won the same number of league games at Tannadice as United did.

Aberdeen finished one place above United, but that wasn't enough to earn Hegarty the manager's job on a permanent basis and he left at the end of the season.

v St Johnstone 3-2

44

Scottish Premier League
McDiarmid Park
12 May 2001
Attendance: 6,497

DUNDEE UNITED	ST JOHNSTONE
Gallacher	Main
Partridge (Buchan)	McCluskey
Lauchlan	Bollan
De Vos (Winters)	Dods
Griffin	McCulloch
Hannah	McClune
McCunnie	Dasovic
Miller	Forsyth (Fotheringham)
Easton	Crozier (Connolly)
Lilley	McBride
Thompson (Hamilton)	Lovenkrands
Manager: Alex Smith	*Manager:* Sandy Clark

THE 2000/01 season remains seared in the memories of many Arabs as the most traumatic they can recall. It also left them shaking their heads in disbelief at a series of events, not least the controversial resignations of manager and chairman. On top of that, United spent the entire campaign in the bottom two of the SPL table.

The omens had not been encouraging. The previous season featured a second-half collapse, easily traceable to one major event, the £1.3m transfer of Billy Dodds to Rangers. In December 1999 United lay third in the table with Dodds their leading scorer on ten goals. Five months later the season ended with United eighth – and Dodds still their leading scorer.

The only close-season signing of note by manager Paul Sturrock was Northern Ireland international Danny Griffin at £600,000 from St Johnstone and the central defender made his debut in a narrow opening-day home loss to Celtic.

That didn't set alarm bells ringing, but a week later Arabs were hit by a bombshell. Immediately after a 3-0 defeat at Hibernian, the manager informed the players in the dressing room that he was leaving the club, though it was two days before he formally tendered his resignation to the board.

Sturrock had been in the job for less than two years and apparently stress was at the root of his decision, as he later said, 'It can be extremely difficult managing a club like Dundee United. You feel you can never win. I know the pressure got to me to the extent that I made mistakes there which I thought I could never make, and will never make again.'

His successor was Alex Smith but to no immediate effect as the following eight league matches produced just one point. Then in mid-October the club's troubles spun out of control when Jim McLean was forced to resign as chairman and managing director after an altercation with a reporter.

Smith responded by discarding the McLean-driven policy of introducing overseas players and instead signed a clutch of seasoned Scots – defender Jim Lauchlan, midfielder Charlie Miller and strikers Jamie Fullarton and Derek Lilley.

A succession of unwanted records began to build up. Just two draws from the first 16 league games represented the worst start to a season in the club's 91 years, leaving United marooned at the foot of the table, eight points behind St Mirren. It was the last Saturday in November before the first win was registered, against Dunfermline at Tannadice. That ended a miserable club record run of 21 league games without a win, stretching back seven months. Almost unbelievably, it would be the solitary home league win of the calendar year 2000.

Thankfully, as the arrivals settled in form improved. At the end of February the Tangerines hauled themselves off the bottom for the first time since September and Arabs began to breathe more easily after St Mirren were beaten 4-0 at Tannadice the following week. The dogfight was far from over though, and United faced nothing less than five cup finals following the newly-introduced top six/bottom six split.

The first of these was another meeting with St Mirren, this time at Paisley. A win would almost certainly have seen United safe from relegation but, despite leading, they lost to a last-minute goal and the gap at the bottom narrowed to a single point. The players then showed great character to defeat Motherwell and Dunfermline before the season's penultimate match at St Johnstone. To describe it as 'must-win' seemed like an understatement.

St Mirren were bottom of the table with 26 points and a goal difference of -39; United had 29 points with a goal difference of -27. So, the Tangerines could effectively ensure their safety providing they at least matched the result achieved by St Mirren, who were at home to Aberdeen.

Neither the players nor the supporters were best pleased to discover that the referee was Alan Freeland. The Aberdonian had become a hate figure for Arabs five months earlier after he controversially awarded a penalty to Hibs in added time. Not only did it appear no offence had been committed, but the official had allowed play to continue for two minutes beyond the stoppage time signified.

Hibs scored from the penalty for what was the game's only goal and, adding insult to injury, goalkeeper Alan Combe was red-carded after the final whistle for protesting. Paul Gallacher replaced him and had performed so well that Combe had been unable to reclaim his place.

There was a large and raucous presence of Arabs at McDiarmid Park, filling both ends and making up more than half the crowd. Smith gave the players who had beaten Dunfermline another chance but United quickly found themselves on the back foot as St Johnstone dominated.

After just five minutes a shot by Paul Hartley was blocked by Jason de Vos but Davie McClune collected the ball and brilliantly curled a shot out of the reach of Gallacher into the top corner to give Saints the lead. That did nothing to calm United nerves but ten minutes later Arabs raised a bit of a cheer when word came through that St Mirren had gone a goal behind against Aberdeen. Midway through the half Craig Easton had a chance when he received the ball in space inside the box, but could only fire his effort straight at former United goalkeeper Alan Main.

Then, with 26 minutes played, Darren Dods brought down Charlie Miller for a penalty. Gallus as ever despite the pressure of the situation – and having missed his previous attempt from the spot – Miller took the kick. But to the dismay of everyone wearing tangerine he fluffed it again, sending his effort well wide of Main's post.

United had a let-off in the 29th minute when Dods met a corner but instead of burying the ball he sent his header straight at Gallacher from five yards. Smith's men were not playing well with too many players giving the impression that the importance of the occasion had got to them. Then, five minutes from half-time, came a body blow.

Winger Mohammed Sylla was sent through by Nick Dasovic and he brushed aside David Partridge before teeing up Hartley who, from the corner of the box, slotted the ball past the advancing Gallacher. The midfielder was booked for his provocative celebrations but everyone associated with United was more concerned by further bad news – St Mirren had turned things round at Love Street and led 2-1.

The Terrors desperately required some inspiration and, in a perverse way, they were handed it with the second half only three minutes old. Hartley, who had undoubtedly been St Johnstone's most influential figure, paid dearly for his post-goal antics when a reckless two-footed lunge on Miller brought a second yellow card.

Hartley's dismissal created some space in the middle of the park for United to exploit and they began to look more purposeful than in the first half. Further yellow cards were brandished by Freeland, first to Sylla then to United's Lilley and Miller as the match gradually came to the boil.

United were pressing the game more and more and shots came from the two Jamies, McCunnie and Buchan.

Having only turned 18 the previous month, McCunnie's performance was well beyond his years in what was only his 14th first-team game. The players certainly couldn't be faulted for effort but as the mid-point of the second half approached the score remained unchanged, leaving open the possibility of a last-day ordeal – the need to beat Aberdeen at Pittodrie to remain in the SPL.

Then came another break for the Tangerines. A poorly-directed pass from Easton was chased with typical energy by Lilley, who caught the ball just before it reached the byline and sent over a cross. It seemed certain to be claimed by Main but the goalkeeper allowed the ball to slip from his grasp and Miller was on hand to make up for his penalty blunder by sending a diving header into the net. With 65 minutes played, United were back in the game.

Smith sought to capitalise and immediately replaced Steven Thompson with Jim Hamilton to provide fresh impetus up front. Then a few minutes later, in a bold move, he replaced defender de Vos with winger David Winters. Only Lauchlan and Griffin remained at the back as United went all-out for the win they so desperately needed.

They went close twice as Lilley sent in a thundering shot that sailed narrowly past and then Main produced a top-drawer save from Miller at point-blank range. Smith's adventurism deserved reward and with only nine minutes remaining it paid off. Miller had been the creative maestro in midfield during the second half and after winning the ball he looked up and spotted an adventurous run into the box by Easton. He sent in a diagonal ball that Easton headed emphatically past Main.

The United support erupted, sending the noise level up by several more decibels. That set up a finale in which United needed either another goal or an equaliser from Aberdeen. They could only influence one of these scenarios and they certainly went for it.

In his nine years at Tannadice Main became a hugely popular figure with Arabs but they were dismayed at the fact that clearly he had lost none of his agility with the passing years and they despaired when he pulled off another acrobatic save to deny Lilley after 86 minutes.

As the clock ticked inexorably towards the end, Lilley showed how determined he was not to be denied. McCunnie swung a cross deep into the crowded penalty area which the United striker controlled before firing past Main's outstretched arm. That sent the tangerine hordes behind both goals into orbit and they descended just in time to hear the final whistle, which triggered a pitch invasion.

Though not to be condoned, it was certainly understandable. The fans had just endured the ultimate 'game of two halves' in a clash that nobody there would forget. Sensing that the invasion was driven by jubilation rather than malice, police and stewards were tolerant and allowed Arabs to remain as they celebrated along with the players, Smith and his backroom staff. The sense of relief engulfed one and all.

Although St Mirren held on to their lead, United's superb late recovery had maintained their three-point advantage and, with a goal difference better by 12, it meant SPL safety was assured – nobody would entertain suggestions it was still not mathematically certain. Joy and relief were displayed in equal measure by the supporters, though it was not an experience they would care to repeat.

Miller conveyed the relief felt by the players and revealed, 'I've not played in many like that, it was a fairytale ending. The whole team was rubbish in the first half, but we can take a lot of credit for what happened in the second. We could see what was happening at Paisley on the scoreboard so we knew we had to get the victory.'

For Smith, the dismissal of Hartley had been key, 'The sending off gave us the opportunity to push forward in the wide areas. Hartley was giving us an awful lot of trouble and then we got the chance to get right back in it.'

Then what happened?

The following week a much more relaxed United team won 2-1 at Aberdeen while St Mirren drew their final match, meaning a final five-point gap at the foot of the table.

An illustration of the extent of the turbulence at Tannadice during 2000/01 is that 41 players of 11 nationalities were used, the highest number in the history of the club, before or since. Perhaps a revolving door should have been installed at the main entrance because during the season 17 players were brought in, with the same number exiting.

v Hibernian 2-1

45

Scottish Cup Semi-Final
Hampden Park
9 April 2005
Attendance: 27,271

DUNDEE UNITED	HIBERNIAN
Bullock	Simon Brown
Archibald	Whittaker
Kenneth	Caldwell
Ritchie	Smith
Wilson	Murphy (Thomson)
Duff (Scotland)	Scott Brown
Brebner	Glass
McInnes (Kerr)	Shiels (Sproule)
Robson	Fletcher
McIntyre	O'Connor
Crawford	Riordan (Morrow)
Manager: Gordon Chisholm	*Manager:* Tony Mowbray

B Y the mid-noughties, United supporters were becoming familiar with poor starts to a league season translating into a relegation dogfight that was eventually won, though often at the last gasp. There had been three examples since United's return to the top level in 1996 and 2004/05 would be another.

Goalkeeper Paul Gallacher and midfielders Craig Easton and Charlie Miller had departed at the end of the previous campaign with the former Scotland and Hearts defender Paul Ritchie the only arrival, initially on a six-month contract.

Before the end of August, manager Ian McCall did sign midfielder Grant Brebner from Hibernian but United's SPL form was woeful: a solitary win from the first 12 matches unsurprisingly left them bottom of the table by the end of October. At least the Scottish League Cup (then sponsored by CIS) had provided some compensation for Arabs with a thrilling extra-time win over Hibernian at Tannadice securing a place in the semi-finals.

But the Edinburgh club exacted revenge when they returned the following month on league business, winning 4-1 to send McCall's men to the bottom of the table. That caused chairman Eddie Thompson to authorise the signing of Scotland striker Stevie Crawford and former Dundee defender Lee Mair, while Ritchie was given a permanent contract. Despite those additions there were no further league wins before United faced Rangers at Hampden in the League Cup semi-final in February.

The Glasgow club would end the season as champions but, despite United's uninspiring league form, both meetings in the first half of the season had ended 1-1. For much of the semi-final there was again little between them. Rangers did establish a two-goal lead inside the first 20 minutes but United battled back well and eventually reduced the deficit through Jason Scotland.

After 77 minutes they were still seeking an equaliser – then Rangers scored a third and the roof fell in. There was simply no excuse for what McCall described as 'kamikaze defending'. Incredibly, in those final 13 minutes, his team conceded five goals for a 7-1 drubbing – United's heaviest defeat since 1958.

That humiliation, added to the club's precarious position in the SPL, led to speculation over McCall's future. Despite convincing Scottish Cup wins over Queen of the South and Aberdeen to earn another semi-final place, three SPL defeats in a row convinced Thompson that McCall's two years and two months in charge should be brought to an end.

His assistant, Gordon Chisholm, was appointed on a caretaker basis, but the two further SPL matches before the Scottish Cup semi-final were also lost – the last one to the following week's Hampden opponents, Hibernian.

Hibs were enjoying a buoyant league campaign under new manager Tony Mowbray, who had blended together an attack-minded team that contained some of the most exciting young talent in Scotland. By the time of the semi-final, Hibs were nine places and 31 points ahead of United in the SPL. No dispute, then, as to the favourites.

On their return to the national stadium United initially seemed traumatised by memories of their visit ten weeks earlier. Within the first minute Hibs showed that they meant business when Stephen Glass forced Tony Bullock into a smart save.

Mowbray's team continued to dominate the opening exchanges and on 10 minutes Derek Riordan blazed over the bar when he should at least have hit the target. United started to show they were not there to make up the numbers and good interplay on the right between Mark Wilson and Stuart Duff allowed Crawford to get in a teasing cross. Barry Robson was poised to test Simon Brown in the Hibs goal but before the ball could reach him it was cleared at the back post by Steven Whittaker.

United's defence looked unsure at times and they were guilty of ball-watching as Steven Fletcher was allowed to get in a shot which missed the target. Despite the pressure from Hibernian, United were still a threat on the break and a burst from midfield by Robson was thwarted when his through ball struck Jim McIntyre's heel and the chance was lost.

Wilson then put in a deep cross from the right but as Brown dropped his attempt to gather, the ball was cleared with McIntyre threatening.

Whittaker was next to test Bullock from distance but again the big Englishman beat the ball away confidently for a corner. Riordan was proving a handful and after 28 minutes he broke free on the right. His cross evaded Bullock's grasp but central defender Garry Kenneth – who had been playing with an assurance well beyond his 17 years – cleared when it seemed inevitable the ball would end up in the net.

United were rarely able to take the play to Hibs and a curling effort by Crawford that went narrowly past after good play by Robson and Alan Archibald was an all-too-rare break in the tide. The Terrors did have a decent claim for a penalty on 33 minutes when a Robson cross hit Whittaker's hand, but the referee wasn't interested.

For all Hibernian's pressure it wasn't until five minutes before half-time that they created their first genuine opportunity. Ritchie and Bullock made a hash of dealing with a long ball into the box, allowing Fletcher the chance to score but he scooped the ball over the bar from six yards. When the interval arrived Hibernian would have been frustrated not to be ahead, having undoubtedly dominated the first period.

Chisholm must have told his players that they needed to show more inventiveness and greater confidence on the ball because United demonstrated both on the restart. The Tangerines took a grip of the opening encounters with Brebner for the first time showing the midfield drive for which he was renowned. A goalbound effort by Robson from the edge of the box was blocked by David Murphy with the Hibs defender having little idea as to what an important intervention he had made.

The game was now flowing from end to end and Stuart Duff was put through on goal by Wilson but he lacked the composure to finish, having created the opportunity for himself.

Having been unable to make the breakthrough when they were dominant, Hibs then did so at a time when United were playing their best football. It came from a penalty after Robson was judged to have impeded Dean Shiels in the box, though the contact was at best minimal. The United protests were waved aside and Riordan sent Bullock the wrong way from the spot.

Chisholm must have been aware that, were Hibernian allowed to return to their dominance of the first half they could quickly put the tie beyond his team, so he wasted no time in making changes. The manager demonstrated his tactical nous by opting to abandon the 3-5-2 formation in favour of 4-3-3, introducing Scotland, Mark Kerr and Collin Samuel, and United went from strength to strength.

By contrast, when Mowbray made his substitutions they appeared to have the opposite effect. Bringing on the inexperienced Ivan Sproule for Shiels – who had been playing well – and another youngster, Sam Morrow, for the dangerous Riordan, disrupted their rhythm and thus played into United's hands.

After getting two penalty decisions wrong in the eyes of most Arabs, the referee further enraged them when McIntyre and Brown clashed after a challenge on the goalkeeper. The Hibs man seemed to raise his hands and push McIntyre but the referee saw fit to book both players – a decision that would ultimately rob McIntyre of a place in the cup final side. If it registered, United didn't allow that setback to affect their focus and they upped the pace of their game.

Hibernian were now reduced to defending their lead but if their hope was to do so for the final 20 minutes then they were soon disabused of any such notion. After 73 minutes an incisive move saw Kerr play in Robson whose low cross-shot was side-footed into the net from five yards by McIntyre. The Hibs support had woken when their side took the lead but were quickly silenced and soon it was mainly Arab voices audible around the stadium.

United had control and they sent their supporters into raptures three minutes later. Two of the substitutes combined as Kerr picked up the ball and found Scotland 20 yards out. The Trinidadian danced inside an attempted tackle by Gary Smith before rifling the ball low past the despairing dive of Brown.

The turnaround was complete and the Hibernian players visibly sagged. From that point there was going to be only one winner.

United continued in the ascendancy, bearing no resemblance to the side that had been unable to prevent Hibs from dominating earlier. McIntyre and Samuel both went close to adding to the score, with the men in green and white reduced to long balls into the United box. Robson even struck the bar direct from a corner as United finished in style.

To the unconfined joy of everyone in tangerine the final whistle sounded, signifying United's first Scottish Cup Final appearance since winning the trophy in 1994. It was a victory borne of dogged determination to fight back from a goal down and banish the memory of the capitulation on the club's previous visit to the national stadium.

Chisholm revealed his thinking when his substitutions had not initially had the effect of levelling the score, 'At 1-0 down with 20 minutes to go I thought it was just a case of having a right go at them to see how they could handle it.'

As it transpired, Hibs couldn't handle it, though in what was just his third match in charge, the caretaker manager was unwilling to take all of the credit for guiding United to the final, paying tribute to Ian McCall, 'Ian played a big part in getting us to the semi-final and I did have a thought about him after the game.'

The manager was also aware of the task facing him before returning to Hampden the following month, 'Making the final is great, but we have to look at the bigger picture. It is important for us to stay in the SPL and we have to use this to start putting together a decent run of form.'

Then what happened?

The next day Celtic beat Hearts in the other semi-final and, with the Glasgow club already qualified for the Champions League, United were thus guaranteed a UEFA Cup place irrespective of the cup final outcome.

Chisholm didn't have long to wait for that 'decent run of form' to begin. The semi-final success immediately galvanised his players because three days later United returned to Glasgow and beat Rangers 1-0 at Ibrox, demonstrating that the 7-1 loss had been a fluke. That was one of four wins in the seven remaining SPL fixtures though the threat of relegation was not banished until the final match of the season.

After 11 weeks in a caretaker role, Chisholm's reward in the week leading up to the Scottish Cup Final was to be given the job on a three-year contract.

Buoyed by that league run-in, United put up a spirited performance in the final and 17,000 decked out in tangerine and black gave their team tremendous backing. The Glasgow club took the lead with an early deflected free kick but the Terrors were never out of contention.

Kenneth was outstanding, though he did concede a penalty after 82 minutes. But it was missed, which gave United fresh impetus and they came within inches of equalising in the dying moments when Archibald's 35-yard drive smacked against the crossbar but rebounded to safety.

Defeat was hard to stomach and many Arabs were left wondering what might have been had leading scorer McIntyre not been suspended.

v **Motherwell** 5-4

46

Scottish Premier League
Fir Park
20 August 2005
Attendance: 4,706

DUNDEE UNITED	MOTHERWELL
Stillie	Meldrum
Wilson	Quinn
McCracken	Craigen
Duff	Kinniburgh (Keogh)
Archibald	Hammell
Kerr	McCormack
Fernandez	Kerr
Brebner	O'Donnell
Robson (Samuel)	Paterson (Fitzpatrick)
Miller	McDonald
Crawford (McIntyre)	Hamilton
Manager: Gordon Chisholm	*Manager:* Terry Butcher

ORDON Chisholm's success in guiding the club to SPL safety – albeit on the final day of the league season – had seen him confirmed as the permanent successor to Ian McCall as manager and chairman Eddie Thompson provided the new boss with an undertaking that he would be given resources to strengthen the squad, with the intention of avoiding yet another backs-to-the-wall fight to preserve Dundee United's place at the top level.

Chisholm hadn't anticipated losing any of his players but the close-season of 2005 was dominated by attempts to retain Jason Scotland. The Trinidad & Tobago international was ultimately unable to secure a renewal of his visa but Chisholm replaced him with Lee Miller, who cost £225,000 from Bristol City.

Thompson's willingness to invest in improving the squad was evidenced by United beating off competition from Aberdeen and Hearts to land the Scotland under-21 cap who, in 2014, remained the last player to cost United a six-figure fee. The Dons later signed United's Stevie Crawford, but by that time Chisholm had added Spanish striker David Fernandez from Celtic to his squad.

Miller made a scoring debut on the opening day of the season, a closely-fought draw with Aberdeen at Tannadice. But the following two games – at Celtic and Hearts – were both lost, although in between them United travelled to Finland to play their first game in European competition since 1997.

If anyone had suggested, during the 14 consecutive seasons of European football between 1977 and 1990, that within the foreseeable future seven seasons would pass without Tannadice hosting a single European tie, they would not have been taken seriously. Yet that is what occurred and at the root of the malaise was United's often dismal league form which prevented them from earning European qualification.

In 2005, reaching the Scottish Cup Final had been sufficient as Celtic – despite finishing as SPL runners-up – qualified for the Champions League, allowing United to take the UEFA Cup slot.

The long-anticipated return to Europe took place in the semi-rural setting of a small Finnish town named Anjalankoski, home to MyPa. Around 300 Arabs made the arduous journey but the crowd still totalled only 1,820. In what was not a great performance, Chisholm's team defended confidently to emerge with a goalless draw.

Fernandez had not been signed in time to play in the UEFA Cup so he made his debut the following Sunday against Hearts at Tannadice. He was a second-half substitute, which absolved him of any responsibility for the team's dreadful start, conceding twice in the first 13 minutes. They did at least steady the ship and were unfortunate not to reduce the deficit before a third Hearts goal in added time put an unduly harsh complexion on the scoreline.

The team – in particular the defence – was missing the experience and leadership of Paul Ritchie who had suffered an injury in the first game of the season but, with just one point from the opening three SPL matches, the next one, at Motherwell, assumed considerable importance.

Chisholm gave Fernandez his first start, playing just behind the front two of Miller and Crawford. The manager must surely have counselled his players to make sure there was no repeat of the disastrous opening against Hearts and on this occasion they certainly did not allow themselves to fall two behind by the 13th minute – because it only took 12.

Terry Butcher's team had made a slightly better start to the season and had four points from their first three matches – though they had conceded eight goals in the process. Against United they began in confident fashion, attacking from the kick-off and early warning signs were there when Scott McDonald glanced a header wide inside the first minute.

United were not so fortunate five minutes later when McDonald outpaced David McCracken and his cross from the byline was met by Alan McCormick, who headed decisively past Derek Stillie from ten yards.

Almost immediately, former United midfielder Jim Paterson fired a dangerous ball into the box and again one of his colleagues reached it ahead of a player in tangerine. This time it was another ex-Terror, striker Jim Hamilton, but his header drifted wide.

Paterson was involved again as the home side doubled their lead in the 12th minute. He was allowed enough time to drill in a shot that was cleared off the line by Grant Brebner but the danger wasn't over because McDonald pounced on the rebound and squeezed the ball under the dive of Stillie.

Worryingly, it was a start that almost mirrored United's last match and they were on the rack. Only a large slice of good fortune prevented them going three behind when McDonald again wriggled his way to the byline before squaring the ball into the path of Hamilton, who missed the ball completely from only a yard out.

Chisholm was visibly agitated on the touchline and he decided it was time to opt for Plan B. The game was only 20 minutes old when he made the switch from three to four in the back line, the 4-4-2 formation involving Fernandez now pushed up front and Crawford moved out to the right. The changes were an admission that United were embroiled in a fight merely to stay in touch.

Motherwell's domination continued and Stillie had to produce a quite magnificent save to tip a 20-yard volley from McCormick over the crossbar after a Hamilton knock-down. That was after 29 minutes and would be a key moment because, had the home side secured the third goal their play clearly merited, there would surely have been no way back for United.

Motherwell then seemed to take their foot off the gas as the Terrors edged their way into the match for the first time. They were still unable to threaten Colin Meldrum in the Motherwell goal, though that just made it all the more surprising when United pulled one back in the 41st minute. Fernandez released Crawford on the right and his pinpoint cross was headed low into the corner from ten yards by the diving Miller.

If the home side had indeed eased off as half-time approached they had been punished for it. Until then United had been unable to fashion even one attempt on target and might well have been dead and buried; instead, they had been thrown a lifeline with the half-time score at 2-1.

Motherwell made two midfield changes at the break, bringing on David Keogh and Marc Fitzpatrick, and they had an immediate impact. The second half was just four minutes old when Keogh's cross was nodded into the path of Fitzpatrick, who stabbed home from close range with the United defence posted AWOL: 49 minutes, 3-1.

The Motherwell supporters' joy was short-lived as United countered three minutes later. Fernandez and Crawford were again involved, on this occasion the Spaniard accepting a pass from the Scotland international and allowing the ball to run across him before hammering a superb left-footed shot low into the net from 20 yards for his first goal in tangerine: 52 minutes, 3-2.

Chisholm's men required a period of consolidation before building some momentum towards a possible equaliser but they were not permitted that luxury. After 57 minutes Motherwell established a two-goal lead for the third time as Hamilton outjumped the United defence to head home a Steven Hammell free kick. Those three goals in eight minutes took the score to 4-2.

It is probable that even the most optimistic of Arabs would then have concluded that goal was likely to end United's resistance. If so, they were out of sync with their manager because, underlining his determination to find a way back into the contest, Chisholm brought on strikers Collin Samuel and Jim McIntyre.

That commendably positive approach was soon rewarded, when fine play from Samuel afforded Mark Wilson the room to cross from the right and Miller bravely threw himself in front of Motherwell defender Stephen Craigan to claim his second goal with another excellent diving header: 67 minutes, 4-3.

Butcher must have been intensely frustrated at his team's inability to kill off United but before he could develop a response the scores were levelled with the goal of the game. The Tangerines moved the ball slickly from left to right before Samuel took possession and outpaced Hammell to reach the byline; his low driven cross was met by captain Brebner, who darted in front of the Motherwell defenders to send the ball past Meldrum: 70 minutes, 4-4.

Motherwell didn't know what had hit them and they were dealt a further blow before they could muster a recovery. The game had become a mirror-image of its earlier stages with Motherwell in disarray and United rampant. Their fifth quickly followed with Brebner again leading by example. Another cross from one of Wilson's surging runs was met by Miller and his clever back-flick was pounced on by the stand-in skipper who stabbed the ball home from close range for what was the Tangerines' third goal in just seven minutes: 74 minutes, 4-5.

Motherwell did raise themselves in search of an equaliser as Butcher brought on striker Andy Smith and changed the shape of his team to 4-3-3. They came close when Stillie again came to United's rescue, diving full-length to turn away a drive from Hamilton. Then, with just two minutes remaining, McDonald appeared to have a strong claim for a penalty when he was brought down by Samuel, but the referee waved away strident protests as the Tangerines breathed a sigh of relief.

Even that wasn't the last action of a frenetic match because United almost added a sixth in injury time after a scintillating break. Stillie threw the ball to Mark Kerr who hit a superb crossfield ball to Fernandez. His pass picked out the run of McIntyre, whose chip beat the onrushing Meldrum but skimmed the wrong side of the post.

Only when the final whistle sounded could supporters finally draw breath. It was an astonishing match which, for United, comprised a hapless first half to forget and a stunning second half to remember. A suitable summary, at least from their point of view, would be all's well that ends 'Well.

Then what happened?

The following week United returned to the UEFA Cup. Having secured that draw in Finland the tie was theirs to lose – and lose it they duly did. An apparently secure 2-0 lead was thrown away with the loss of two late goals and a near-10,000 Tannadice crowd demonstrated the extent of the damage in financial terms, to say nothing of the club's reputation.

That exit was followed by another first-round defeat in the Scottish League Cup the next month and when the same happened at the same stage of the Scottish Cup in January chairman Thompson announced that Chisholm had been relieved of his duties after just ten months.

Since the epic Fir Park encounter United's league form had not been convincing: they then lay ninth out of 12 in the SPL. Scottish Cup-winning hero Craig Brewster was Chisholm's replacement but he was unable to bring about a change in fortune and ninth was where the Tangerines ended the season.

v Aberdeen 4-1

Scottish League Cup Semi-Final
Tynecastle Park
5 February 2008
Attendance: 12,046

DUNDEE UNITED	ABERDEEN
Załuska	Langfield
Flood (Dillon)	McNamara (Bus)
Kalvenes	Considine (Aluko)
Wilkie	Nicholson
Dods	Diamond
Kerr	Severin
Gomis (Buaben)	Young
Robertson	Walker
De Vries	Foster
Hunt	Miller
Conway	Mackie
Manager: Craig Levein	*Manager:* Jimmy Calderwood

D URING the summer of 2007 much of the focus at Tannadice was, unusually, on a pre-season friendly. Not just any pre-season friendly, though, because the visitors were Barcelona, returning for the first time since the UEFA Cup quarter-final of 1987, and the tickets quickly sold out. The game had an attendance of 14,223, still an all-seated record for Tannadice, which was appropriate as the all-time record was also set for a visit by the Catalan club when 28,000 watched the Fairs Cup tie in 1966.

Having been appointed the previous October, 2007/08 was Craig Levein's first full season in charge. As United had been bottom of the SPL when he arrived, a final placing of ninth was regarded by most Arabs as satisfactory in the circumstances.

But Levein was ambitious and prior to the start of the new season he predicted that his team would secure a top-six finish. That may have appeared a modest aim, though it should be said it was something that United had proved incapable of achieving in all but one of the previous ten seasons.

Levein had begun to re-shape the playing squad, bringing in Polish goalkeeper Łukasz Załuska, central defender Darren Dods and Republic of Ireland under-21 midfielder Willo Flood.

It was immediately apparent that this was not going to be another season to add to the recent litany of uphill struggles. After four of the first six SPL matches were won United occupied third place, their highest position for almost eight years. That form continued into the new year and, along the way, progress had been made in the CIS Scottish League Cup. Three victories (only one, against Falkirk, involved an SPL opponent) had opened the door to the semi-final where New Firm rivals Aberdeen awaited.

The season's three SPL meetings between the clubs, two at Tannadice, had all gone with home advantage and as they prepared for their clash at Tynecastle the Terrors again lay third in the table, two places above the Dons.

Jimmy Calderwood's men were enjoying a successful season in cup competitions and had exceeded all expectations by reaching the knockout stage of the Europa League where their opponents the following week would be Bayern Munich. The Tynecastle tie was scheduled for Tuesday 29 January but severe weather left the pitch waterlogged and, unusually for a semi-final, it was postponed. It was re-scheduled for seven days later but by that time United had lost arguably their most influential player when Celtic paid £1.5m for midfielder Barry Robson.

Although Levein had added to his squad in the January transfer window, bringing in wing-back Danny Grainger and Dutch striker Mark De Vries, there was no disguising the fact that the departure of Robson was a serious blow.

De Vries added to what was a cosmopolitan group of players at Tannadice and for the semi-final Levein fielded a minority of Scots, five of them being supplemented by the Dutchman plus two Irishmen, a Frenchman, a Norwegian and a Pole. During the match another Irishman and a Ghanaian would further boost the foreign contingent.

The week's delay in the tie also meant the teams were aware that Rangers awaited the winners in the final.

The match began at breakneck speed with each side apparently determined to gain the upper hand and deny the other the chance to settle. No one could have been surprised that United were employing De Vries in a target-man role and after six minutes a cross from Christian Kalvenes on the left found the big man, who guided his knock-down into the path of the onrushing David Robertson. But Barry Nicholson produced a superb tackle to prevent the midfielder getting his shot on target.

Levein's team were looking the more dangerous and they had the first real attempt on goal after 12 minutes when Noel Hunt latched on to a clever De Vries flick, but the Irishman's shot flew narrowly wide.

United had made much of the early running but Aberdeen began to force their way into the game, although an effort from 25 yards by Josh Walker was the only one to cause Załuska even to adjust his feet. Then, as so often happens, against the run of play Aberdeen opened the scoring in the 18th minute.

A corner from the right by Nicholson was won rather too easily in the air by Zander Diamond and his downward header was blocked by Załuska's legs. The United defence failed to react quickly enough to clear the danger and Andrew Considine slammed the ball into the net from close range.

The United players didn't fret and hit back almost immediately. After 22 minutes it was Aberdeen's turn to pay the price for a poorly-defended set piece when Kalvenes whipped in a free kick from the right and Dods rose highest to head home from six yards.

The central defensive partnership of Dods and Lee Wilkie was now looking comfortable while Flood was proving effective down the right, sending some teasing crosses into the penalty area. De Vries was causing the Aberdeen defenders all sorts of problems as he tried to get on the end of them and five minutes before half-time Diamond had to perform heroics to prevent the Dutchman from getting his shot away after he had burst into the penalty area.

There was no shortage of action, though no further clear-cut chances as the first half of what was already a crackling tie drew to a close.

When the teams emerged for the second half Aberdeen were defending the end where the 6,000 Arabs were congregated. As a former Dundee goalkeeper Jamie Langfield was always likely to attract a hostile reception, though the extent of it seemed to unsettle him. At one stage the referee found it necessary to halt the game in order to have the large number of objects that had landed in the goalmouth – mainly pies and polystyrene cups – removed. It was not behaviour that reflected well on the fans wearing tangerine and black but it may have been a contributory factor in the events that led to United forging into the lead after an hour.

Langfield scuffed his attempt to clear a simple pass and the ball went out for a very cheap corner. The United players were in no mood to dwell on that and when Craig Conway sent over the kick it was met powerfully by Kalvenes, whose header from 12 yards hurtled in.

With Arabs in full voice, United seized the initiative – and thereby the game. Five minutes after gaining the lead they went 3-1 ahead when Conway latched on to a through ball from De Vries and as he approached the advancing Langfield the goalkeeper lost his footing, allowing the winger to slot the ball into the empty net from a tight angle.

Two minutes later, just as Aberdeen must have been thinking that things couldn't get any worse, the Dons were reduced to ten men. It was a moment of madness because former United striker Lee Miller launched himself at Kalvenes when he had no need to and was rightly shown a yellow card. Having been booked in the first half, his departure was inevitable.

With a quarter of the match remaining, it would now have required a spectacular collapse by United to deflect them from their path to the final but that didn't mean that they attempted simply to wind down the clock.

They went looking for a fourth goal and it came after 77 minutes – again as the result of inept defending by Aberdeen. A pass back from Scott Severin to Langfield was woefully short and was chased down by Morgaro Gomis, who rolled the ball over the line to the unconfined joy of his team-mates and the wildly-celebrating Arabs.

As much as United reaching their first Scottish League Cup Final in 11 years meant to the players and supporters, they all had an extra dimension to their exultation. Since assuming control of Dundee United in 2003 it had been chairman Eddie Thompson's greatest ambition to see his club win a major trophy. Having come close in the 2005 Scottish Cup Final, he now had another opportunity – one he, and everyone in the United family, knew would almost certainly be his last, having battled prostate cancer for four years.

The chairman was emotional as he gave his reaction to the victory, 'It was absolutely fantastic. I was in tears up there in the directors' box but that's just me, I can't help it. Everybody out there contributed for us and I'm looking forward to the final.'

Levein was himself close to tears as he paid tribute to Thompson, 'It's a great night for the players and the fans but the person I'm most pleased for is the chairman. He has shown more courage than anybody with his current health situation and has shown great bravery and fortitude. That victory was for him.'

Then what happened?

The lead-up to the Scottish League Cup Final at Hampden was turned into a special tribute to United's chairman and benefactor, whose health was clearly deteriorating. Many of the 17,500 United supporters at the national stadium wore tangerine T-shirts bearing the words 'One Eddie Thompson' – an undoubted truism. The sad fact that the players were ultimately unable to deliver the trophy their chairman so coveted doubled the pain of defeat for all associated with the club.

That defeat did not occur in open play. Leading through Noel Hunt's first-half goal United were, agonisingly, just five minutes away from triumph when a calamitous backpass presented Rangers with an equaliser. De Vries restored the Tangerines' lead in extra time but Rangers again levelled, leaving the outcome to the lottery of penalties.

Only half of the ten spot-kicks found the net but Rangers scored three to United's two to take the trophy and deny Thompson the day of glory he so richly deserved.

Inevitably, following the crushing disappointment at Hampden, the remainder of the season was an anti-climax, though the chase for third place in the SPL was not relinquished until early May.

United eventually finished fifth, meaning Levein had delivered on his promise of a top-six place and, in addition to equalling the club's best SPL position, the campaign saw the most points won, the most goals scored and the fewest goals conceded since the competition began in 1998.

Eddie Thompson, MBE, died in October 2008 at the age of 68. The East Stand at Tannadice was re-named in his honour, a mark of deep respect for all that he had done for his beloved Dundee United.

v Rangers 3-3

48

Scottish Cup Quarter-Final
Ibrox
14 March 2010
Attendance: 24,096

DUNDEE UNITED	RANGERS
Pernis	McGregor
Kovacevic	Whittaker
Dillon	Weir
Dods	Wilson
Kenneth	Papac
Gomis (Sandaza)	Thomson (Edu)
Buaben	McCulloch
Conway	Davis
Swanson (D Robertson)	Novo (Beasley)
Daly	Boyd (Lafferty)
Casalinuovo (Shala)	Miller
Manager: Peter Houston	*Manager:* Walter Smith

I N May 2009 the club formed as Dundee Hibernian celebrated its centenary. Those 100 years – all but the first 13 as Dundee United – had seen some exceptional highs and some dreadful lows with the one constant being the club's home, Tannadice Park.

Many an Arab mused to friends, 'Wouldn't it be brilliant to win a trophy in our centenary year?' Given that United had won just four major trophies throughout their history, that could easily have been dismissed as wishful thinking.

When Craig Levein was appointed manager in October 2006 the club sat bottom of the SPL. The new man steered them to safety in his first six months and the following season guided the club to fifth place, also taking them to the Scottish League Cup Final.

That ended in heart-breaking defeat by the cruellest of methods, a penalty shoot out, but Levein re-energised his squad for the new campaign and they again ended fifth – the first time United had managed consecutive top-six finishes since 1994.

So impressed had Eddie Thompson been with Levein as a man as well as a manager that, shortly before the chairman's untimely death in 2008, he had appointed Levein to the board with the title of director of football.

Arabs assessed the progress their club had made under Levein and the crop of young players pushing for places in the squad and many felt that, although the huge disparity in wealth between Celtic and Rangers and the rest made a league championship extremely unlikely, success in one of the cup competitions was within United's capabilities.

Such thinking was based on Levein's influence continuing to be brought to bear on the club and its players. Four months into 2009/10, that ceased to be the case.

The manager's third full season had begun well and by mid-December, with 15 SPL games played, United sat fourth in the table, had lost just twice and were undefeated on the road.

Having come through the ranks, David Goodwillie, David Robertson and Danny Swanson were now first-team regulars and Levein had blended them into what was a settled side, one that seemed set to continue improving.

The decision by Levein to leave his post as manager and his position as director of football was not one he took lightly. By all accounts he was as happy with United as the club hierarchy and its supporters were with him and the job offer that he received was almost certainly the only one that would have prised him from Tannadice.

Loath as they were to lose him, everyone associated with United understood and accepted that the opportunity to take charge of your country's national team is not one that any ambitious manager could refuse. And who would want a manager lacking in ambition?

So off he went and on 26 December his assistant, Peter Houston, stepped in as caretaker. After his second match in charge ended in the humiliation of a 7-1 drubbing at Ibrox, Houston said he wouldn't be applying for the job on a permanent basis. Fortunately he re-considered and a month later was appointed for the remainder of the season.

That sparked a United revival, including away victories in their first two Scottish Cup ties at Partick Thistle and St Johnstone. But Houston was faced with a sterner test of his and his players' resolve in the next round when the cup draw didn't just produce a third away tie, it sent United back to Ibrox just ten weeks after that horror show.

Nor was the challenge made any more manageable by the absence of two key defenders. After joining United on a season-long loan from Rangers, Andy Webster had become a rock but he was unavailable for the tie as the terms of his loan agreement rendered him unable to play against his parent club. Wing-back Paul Dixon had also been enjoying an excellent season, his surging runs and cultured left foot being used to deliver many a penetrating ball into the goalmouth. But injury ruled him out and United suffered a further blow on the morning of the match when Goodwillie, always a potent goal threat, called off because of a stomach bug.

Rabbie Burns told us that 'the best laid plans o' mice and men gang aft agley', but Houston's plans went twice agley because Goodwillie's replacement, Damian Casalinuovo, pulled up with a hamstring strain just two minutes into the match. In a move that didn't change the shape of the team his replacement was Andis Shala, who had made just four starts in his two seasons at Tannadice. The Kosovan immediately rose to the occasion, playing confidently and showing clever movement that he used to give United the lead after 24 minutes.

Jon Daly intercepted a loose pass from Steven Whittaker and sent Shala in on goal. One-on-one situations are always much more demanding than they appear but the 21-year-old kept his cool and fired the ball past Allan McGregor.

United's possession game was preventing Rangers from building any kind of momentum and they looked comfortable. But ten minutes after the goal they were undone by an error that was almost a carbon copy of Whittaker's. Under no pressure in midfield, Morgaro Gomis was short with a pass and the ball was picked up by Steven Davis. He quickly delivered a precise pass that sent Kenny Miller clean through with only Dusan Pernis to beat and as he attempted to round the goalkeeper the Rangers and Scotland striker went to ground, although Pernis clearly got a touch to the ball first.

But referee Dougie McDonald controversially awarded a penalty and although the United players protested – TV evidence subsequently supported their case – he was unmoved and Kris Boyd fired the ball into the bottom corner to level the score. United were fortunate that Miller was heading away from goal at the time, which meant the card showed to Pernis by McDonald was yellow and not red.

The 1,000 Arabs, who had been giving their team tremendous backing, left McDonald in no doubt as to their take on the incident but two minutes before half-time their anger would turn to outright fury as Rangers were awarded another penalty, this one even more dubious.

Sasa Papac floated the ball into the area and as Sean Dillon and Boyd both rose to challenge for it there was no more than a meeting of bodies. Yet the Rangers striker collapsed to the ground and McDonald was sufficiently taken in to point to the spot once more. As before, United protested. As before, McDonald stood his ground. As before, Boyd put the ball into the net.

That gave the home side a half-time advantage even they would have admitted they didn't merit and Houston's team talk no doubt made that point. He might also have reminded his players of their last visit and the need to avoid losing another goal. Unfortunately, that's precisely what happened.

United re-emerged in determined mood, exemplified by an opportunist half-volley from 20 yards by Craig Conway that bounced off the crossbar on its way over. But any optimism that engendered among the travelling Arabs was crushed almost immediately when Rangers claimed a third goal three minutes after the re-start.

The Tangerines were on the attack when Swanson tried to beat one player too many and lost possession. Rangers broke forward, with the ball played through to Nacho Novo on the right and the Spaniard strode into the penalty box before sending a shot across Pernis. The ball entered the net despite the long leg of Garry Kenneth coming desperately close to clearing it.

Being only human, with almost all of the second half remaining the United players might have thought, 'Oh, no, here we go again.'

But Houston later revealed he knew different, 'I saw how much the 7-1 defeat hurt them. Character is something that you have in-built, it's in your heart. When the going gets tough you need people to stand up and that's something I think we have in abundance. This time, when we went 3-1 behind, under no circumstances did I think we were going to fold.'

The urgent need was to steady the ship and this United did, perhaps benefiting from a less than fully-focussed state of mind among the Rangers players, born because it's rare for them to score three times at Ibrox and fail to win.

Houston's assessment of his players proved accurate and he brought new energy to his midfield by bringing on David Robertson in place of the tiring Swanson. United gradually worked their way back into the match, eventually getting their reward in the 63rd minute. A Conway corner was headed clear but only as far as Gomis, some 25 yards from goal.

The midfielder fired in a volley that seemed to be going wide but Whittaker was unable to react quickly enough and the ball deflected off his head and into his own net. Fortunate? Undoubtedly, but luck is an essential ingredient in cup ties and, after the events of the first half, who could deny that United had earned a slice?

Rangers suddenly realised they had a fight on their hands but they were now on the back foot and United were in control. Houston brought on Fran Sandaza to add fresh firepower up front as the Tangerines chased an equaliser and it had been on the cards for some time when it finally arrived in the 79th minute.

Again a corner by the impressive Conway was at the root of it. The ball was met by the unmarked Shala, whose header hit the crossbar, but Mihael Kovacevic was quickest to react, heading home the rebound and sending Arabs – those in the stadium as well as the thousands watching on TV – into raptures.

The comeback was complete and if the remaining minutes had produced another goal it would more likely have come from United. Ultimately the players were happy to settle for a replay – and a result that buried the demons of that December night, while restoring some wounded pride.

Kovacevic revealed the extent to which he and his team-mates were determined to atone for their previous visit to Govan, 'That game was on the players' minds. But it was because we were angry and wanted to show that we're better than that. We were more like the real Dundee United today.'

Then what happened?

Ten days later the clubs met in the replay at Tannadice, with Goodwillie fit but Dixon not yet recovered. The match was every bit as close as the first with one crucial exception – David Robertson scored a last-minute winner to send United into the semi-final and a meeting with Raith Rovers at Hampden Park. A trophy in the club's centenary year remained a possibility.

v Ross County 3-0

49

Scottish Cup Final
Hampden Park
15 May 2010
Attendance: 47,122

DUNDEE UNITED	ROSS COUNTY
Pernis	McGovern
Kovacevic (Watson)	Miller
Dillon	Morrison
Webster	Scott (Wood)
Kenneth	Boyd
Buaben	Keddie
Swanson (S. Robertson)	Gardyne (Di Giacomo)
Gomis	Barrowman
Goodwillie (D. Robertson)	Craig (Lawson)
Daly	Brittain
Conway	Vigurs
Manager: Peter Houston	*Manager:* Derek Adams

T HE dramatic defeat of Rangers in the Scottish Cup quarter-final replay at Tannadice provided evidence that Peter Houston had begun to establish himself as a manager in his own right for the first time.

Following a career as a striker in the lower divisions, principally with Albion Rovers and Falkirk, Houston moved into coaching, initially at youth level under Jim Jefferies at Falkirk. When Jefferies was appointed manager of Hearts in 1995 he took Houston with him as his assistant, a position Houston retained when Craig Levein took over at Tynecastle in 2000. They left for Leicester City in 2004 and when, in December 2006, Levein was given the manager's job at Tannadice, Houston again joined him as his assistant.

By the time of Levein's departure, United had enjoyed a relatively successful first half to 2009/10. Having ended the previous campaign in fifth place the Tangerines had improved upon that, occupying fourth continuously since the end of September.

That the 7-1 drubbing at Ibrox in Houston's second match as caretaker was simply a one-off can be gauged by the fact that in the 16 SPL games preceding it United had conceded just 15 goals. There was no need for panic and, showing a cool head, Houston steadied the ship and soon had the team making progress in both the league and the Scottish Cup. By the time United returned to Ibrox for the cup tie they were secure in third, a position they would maintain for the remainder of the season.

Meanwhile, what had initially seemed like an improbable triumph had removed the Glasgow club from the Scottish Cup and opened the door to United's first semi-final in five years. Their opponents were Raith Rovers, one of two First Division clubs to reach the last four. Celtic and Ross County were to meet in the other tie, which would be played at Hampden Park 24 hours before United's at the same venue.

When the semi-final draw was made it was not difficult to arrive at the conclusion that the 2010 Scottish Cup Final would likely see a repeat of the 2005 showpiece, involving United and Celtic. That may have been what logic dictated but the day logic decides every Scottish Cup tie is the day the competition dies.

Those making such assumptions had short memories: two years previously two First Division clubs had also contested the semi-finals. While St Johnstone took Rangers to extra time before bowing out on penalties, Queen of the South went one better, beating Aberdeen to reach their first final.

Further warnings to Celtic and United – were any still required – had been posted during the 2010 competition when Ross County eliminated Hibernian and Raith Rovers knocked out Aberdeen, both following replays.

For his part, there was no chance Houston would allow complacency among his players. Three consecutive league wins had maintained the momentum following the defeat of Rangers and when the time came for the semi-final United could hardly have been better prepared. The players' confidence also received a considerable boost as they gathered in their hotel to watch the other semi-final – and saw Ross County cause one of the all-time Scottish Cup sensations by convincingly beating Celtic to claim their place in the final.

The following day it was Raith who took the early initiative and forced several corners as United took some time to get into their stride. The Terrors suffered a setback after just 15 minutes when wing-back Paul Dixon sustained an injury and couldn't continue but gradually Houston's men settled and a fine piece of individual skill by David Goodwillie gave them the lead on 27 minutes. Raith continued to pressurise but the game was fairly balanced up until half-time, with no further scoring.

Almost an hour had been played when United doubled their lead and allowed Arabs to breathe a little easier. Leading by example, captain Andy Webster got his head to a Craig Conway corner to send the ball into the net – and United into the final.

With that match four weeks away and four SPL games still to play, Houston was already able to point to tangible success from his first four months in charge. United's victory at rivals Motherwell guaranteed a Europa League place, with third place in the league also secured barring an unlikely sequence of results. To return to the European scene after a gap of five years was welcome, but even more so was that it had been achieved on the basis of league form – the first time that had happened since 1997.

As the final approached it was natural that, given the difference in status between the clubs, United were clear favourites. Understandable that may have been but it added pressure to Houston and his players, for whom the weight of expectation was not something that could be shaken off.

The strong sense of anticipation among Arabs was shown by United selling an unprecedented 27,000 tickets. A further factor was the absence of both of Glasgow's big two clubs and the baggage they inevitably bring with them, which made the occasion much more inclusive and family-friendly.

That was reflected not just in those who coloured most of Hampden tangerine but in the 18,000 who had effected a modern-day Highland clearance to be there. They waved their dark blue flags in support of Ross County, who were aiming to become the first club from outside the top flight to win the trophy since East Fife in 1938.

Houston set out his team in a 4-4-2 formation with Goodwillie and Jon Daly up front and Danny Swanson and Conway to be used as fleet-footed wide attackers. County manager Derek Adams appeared to have anticipated such a plan because he opted for a more defensive 4-5-1, designed to contain the threat down the flanks.

It has to be said that the national stadium presented a wonderful spectacle around the pitch, though rather less so on it. Perhaps that was inevitable as United took the play to Ross County from the start and the early crunching tackle by Richard Brittain on

Swanson indicated the uncompromising nature of the resistance the First Division club intended to offer.

Soon after, Gary Miller brought Goodwillie to a shuddering halt and it was wise of referee Dougie McDonald to issue a yellow card at that point as thereafter the County defenders were constrained to remain within the laws of the game.

United had a strong claim for a penalty after 11 minutes when Swanson was blocked by Alex Keddie, though the ref indicated that the County man was unable to avoid the collision. Keddie was already emerging as the rock on which many attacks foundered and that was the pattern for the remainder of the first half, with goalkeeper Michael McGovern rarely called into action.

United continually probed in search of an opening but on the two occasions when it seemed they might have found one, Keddie was again the man who denied Conway and Goodwillie.

Initially the second half saw a continuation of that pattern, with Ross County unable to find the form that had got them to the final. Being kept on the back foot prevented the men who had been most instrumental in subduing and then dissecting Celtic a month earlier from making a meaningful impression this time. Essentially, whereas the Glasgow club stood off County, United did the opposite.

It always seemed likely that United's dominance would tell, yet the players – to say nothing of the massed ranks of Arabs – were becoming just a little concerned as the hour-mark approached with the scoreline still blank. That was a tribute to County's doggedness but, suddenly, that all changed.

Sixty-one minutes had passed when Morgaro Gomis hoisted a ball towards his front men. It was characterised more by hope than precision but, as it drifted beyond Daly, McGovern advanced far from his goal to collect the ball before realising he had strayed outside the penalty area.

He then opted to head it clear but in doing so committed his second error, sending the ball straight to Goodwillie. The striker controlled it with his chest and quickly sized up the situation before lofting an exquisite chip from 25 yards that landed on the goal line before entering the net, just beyond the despairing lunge of Keddie.

The huge United support erupted, a mighty roar signifying that at last the deadlock had been broken. It was a stunning finish and one of the highest quality. Had that been the only goal it would have been worthy of winning any cup, but soon there was more.

The attitude of Houston's men had been superb from the start, an object lesson in how to turn the mantle of favourites to advantage, never slackening in their determination to force the pace and turn their pressure into goals. Now they had one that attitude remained as they went in search of what they knew would be a decisive second.

It came after 75 minutes and began with a throw-in from Sean Dillon. Daly and Goodwillie nodded the ball on, the latter sending it to Conway. The winger's pace took him beyond Miller and Keddie and he raced into the box with just McGovern to beat, which he did with confidence to double United's lead.

Houston's joy was unconfined as he, together with his players and the celebrating supporters giving full voice to 'Beautiful Sunday', knew then the cup was won. Not that Houston or his men considered slackening off. The team retained the high tempo that had been a feature since the start and, with County now a dispirited lot, a third goal was very much on the cards.

Had it not materialised, no one in tangerine would have been the slightest bit concerned but with four minutes remaining Daly collected the ball on the edge of the penalty area and laid it off to Gomis. The midfielder sent a deft flick towards Conway who made only partial contact with the ball, though enough to direct it past the dive of McGovern.

The celebrations began in earnest at that point, reaching a crescendo as the final whistle signalled the return of the Scottish Cup to Tannadice after a gap of 16 years. In every sense, on and off the pitch, the United family had embraced the occasion and were now entitled to enjoy the rewards.

The presentation of the trophy was a poignant occasion for two reasons. Andy Webster wore the captain's armband, a unique honour for a player who was on a season-long loan from Rangers. But, in a fitting tribute to the man who, but for a career-ending injury, would have been collecting the cup himself, Webster ushered forward retired club captain Lee Wilkie. The two men climbed the stairs together to receive and raise the trophy which, for so many years, had seemed determined to resist having tangerine and black ribbons attached to it.

And many a United supporter's thoughts turned at that point to the memory of the late Eddie Thompson. The man who took control of the club in 2003 had longed for the opportunity of seeing a trophy come to Tannadice during his time as chairman. Sadly, his death in 2008 meant that was not to be, though it was not difficult to imagine him enjoying the occasion hugely from on high, not least because his son Stephen was his successor as chairman.

For Houston it had been an incredible five months in charge. Although he was the first to acknowledge the fact that he had simply picked up where Levein had left off, that's not what the history books will show.

United had marked their centenary year by winning the Scottish Cup and finishing third in the league, arguably their best season since 1986/87. When the bicentenary history of Dundee United is published in 2109 it will record that Houston was manager when they won their fifth major trophy.

Then what happened?

Dundee is a sea of tangerine
The colour dark blue is nowhere to be seen
For United have won a second Scottish Cup
Leaving Dundee fans disgruntled and a little fed up

William Topaz McGonagall
(attributed)

v Motherwell 4-0

50

Scottish Premiership
Fir Park
9 November 2013
Attendance: 5,103

DUNDEE UNITED	MOTHERWELL
Cierzniak	Neilsen
Wilson	Cummins (McFadden)
Souttar	Kerr
Gunning	McManus
Robertson	Francis-Angol
Paton	Carswell (Murray)
Rankin	Lasley
Mackay-Steven	Vigurs
Gauld (Graham)	Ainsworth
Armstrong (Goodwillie)	Sutton
Ciftci (Gomis)	Anier (Moore)
Manager: Jackie McNamara	*Manager:* Stuart McCall

N Scottish football, 2012 will long be remembered as the year when Rangers' massive debt caught up with them and they were liquidated as a consequence. For United there was a benefit in that the vacant place in the SPL went to Dundee, bringing the return of derby matches after a seven-year gap.

Big crowds at all three were welcome, as were the seven points United claimed. But as the season developed the Tangerines – having finished fourth in the SPL the previous two seasons – became stuck in the lower half of the table in what was the least successful period of Peter Houston's three years as manager.

The man who had led the club to Scottish Cup success in 2010 departed by mutual agreement in January 2013 and was replaced by former Celtic and Scotland defensive midfielder Jackie McNamara.

His first task was to ensure that the club secured a place in the top six by the time the league split in two in mid-April and he succeeded, though only in the final minute of the final pre-split match. Arabs were naturally pleased with that and even more so because that last-gasp win was against Aberdeen which denied the Dons sixth place.

The following week United were unfortunate to lose 4-3 in extra time to Celtic in the semi-final of the Scottish Cup, with a team containing several youth products. McNamara had signalled his intention to promote any young player he deemed sufficiently talented, irrespective of their age, and for John Souttar (16) and Ryan Gauld (17) to feature in his starting line-up at Hampden provided powerful testimony of that pledge.

The summer of 2013 was lively as, not without some acrimony, the SPL and the Scottish League merged to form the SPFL, with the top division named the Scottish Premiership. The close-season was also lively at Tannadice as Johnny Russell left for Derby County in a £750,000 deal while Jackie McNamara brought in a clutch of new players. Nadir Ciftci, Chris Erskine, Brian Graham, Paul Paton and Andy Robertson all arrived but the name that most excited the supporters was David Goodwillie, who returned on a six-month loan.

Right from the start, McNamara went with the young players, Gauld and Robertson featuring in the season's opener at Partick Thistle. They became regulars and were soon joined by Souttar, although the player who made the biggest impact early in the season was Stuart Armstrong.

At 21, the central midfielder was not seen as a youngster because he had already made 50 appearances and at the end of the previous season had been called up to the Scotland squad. He still awaited his debut at that level but was captain of the Scotland under-21 side.

McNamara was encouraging the use of wide players but United didn't get off to the best of starts in 2013/14, scoring just once in their first three matches. But before long, as the new players became accustomed to one another, the goals began to mount up. By the end of October, United had scored four goals on three occasions in the Premiership and once in the Scottish League Cup. Ciftci was already emerging as a real threat, his strength and shooting power already making him a favourite with Arabs.

The Turkish-born striker was at the centre of a controversial incident at Inverness in the Scottish League Cup quarter-final in October. After an altercation involving several players and staff members from both sides, Ciftci was sent off shortly before half-time, leaving United to play almost 80 minutes with ten men after the tie went to extra time.

They appeared to have earned the right to decide the match on penalties until being cruelly denied by a last-minute goal. There can be no doubt that the dismissal of their main striker contributed to the exit and the anger felt by many at the club as well as by supporters was compounded when Ciftci's red card was later rescinded. By then, of course, the damage had been done.

Three days later United faced the daunting journey to Celtic Park but their response to the cup defeat was disciplined and it marked a clear sign that the new-look United were developing into a team who could challenge at the upper end of the Premiership.

A goal of real quality from Armstrong wrong-footed the home side and United were good value for their lead, also spurning two good chances to increase it. As so often happens in such situations, they were made to pay when Celtic grabbed an equaliser in added time, but the overall performance of the team drew many plaudits in the media.

Despite that display, United sat sixth when McNamara took his players to Motherwell the following week for an encounter with a team who had begun the season particularly strongly. The Lanarkshire club were second and had an enviable home record; they were seeking a sixth consecutive win at Fir Park, a feat they had not achieved since the mid-1970s.

United started strongly and rarely let up throughout what was an exhilarating performance, one Motherwell simply could not live with.

With Gauld, Armstrong and Gary Mackay-Steven in full flow playing behind the sole front man in Ciftci, the home midfield were left chasing shadows. The trio's quick passing and movement, to say nothing of their ability to ghost past two or three opponents apparently at will, left the Motherwell rearguard so confused that it contributed to both of the goals United crafted in the opening 18 minutes.

With 16 minutes played Gauld won a free kick when he was brought down by Adam Cummins. The defender received a yellow card but his team received harsher punishment when Stephen McManus got caught under the kick which Souttar floated into the penalty area. McManus's header succeeded only in helping the ball on its way, which put goalkeeper Gunnar Neilsen under pressure. His weak punch sent the ball only as far as Gauld who scored on the half-volley from just inside the area.

That was the catalyst for the Tangerines really turning the screw and two minutes later they doubled their advantage. Again Gauld was involved as he and Mackay-Steven pressurised Zaine Francis-Angol and the defender was caught in possession by Gauld. He pushed the ball to Mackay-Steven who in turn moved it on to Ciftci. The striker's shot was blocked but the ball came back to him and he lifted it over Neilsen to Paul Paton, who was waiting to nod into the net.

That was his first goal for United and with the home team in disarray, it was very much one-way traffic as some tremendous flowing football followed. They had the ball in the net again after 34 minutes when a defence-splitting pass from Gauld found Andy Robertson galloping into the area where he finished confidently. Unfortunately an assistant referee's flag cut short the celebrations, though it was a tight call.

Just before half-time Ciftci worked his way into the area but pulled his shot across the face of goal with the goalkeeper scrambling to prevent further damage. He went even closer from 30 yards, the ball shaving the post with Neilsen beaten. Motherwell did have one effort of note when, in a rare foray towards Radoslaw Cierzniak's goal, John Sutton sent in an angled shot that the Pole pushed wide of the post.

Stuart McCall introduced former Scotland international James McFadden after the break, though it made no difference to United's dominance. Within the first 15 minutes they hit the bar twice, first from Robertson's deflected shot then when Mackay-Steven's cross bounced on top of it.

With 63 minutes on the clock United created a brilliant third goal. Armstrong found Ciftci who sent a clever reverse pass to Gauld who dispatched a low, angled shot under the diving Neilsen and into the corner.

Motherwell then suffered the indignity of seeing Gauld, Armstrong and Ciftci being withdrawn, though even that didn't interrupt the flow of the game. Mackay-Steven teed up substitute David Goodwillie, who was only denied by yet another full-length save by Neilsen.

But with four minutes remaining, Robertson got the goal his excellent all-round display merited. Again it was beautifully crafted, Brian Graham and John Rankin each requiring just one touch on the edge of the penalty area before the ball was laid into the path of the onrushing Robertson who drove it high into the net for another goal of real quality.

It was the most complete performance of the season by McNamara's team and underlined their much-vaunted potential. Commendably, given how he must have been feeling, McCall was unstinting in his praise for his opponents, 'I have been in this job for three years and that is by far and away the best away performance I have seen here. I include European teams and Celtic and Rangers. Today you've got to hold your hands up…to an outstanding young side who were playing at the top of their game.'

If anything, McNamara was more restrained, 'We were excellent from start to finish and looked a real threat with the chances we created. We had to be on our game and we certainly were. If we can maintain that standard we should do well.'

Then what happened?

That was the start of an astonishing burst of scoring by United. The following four matches produced 4-1 wins in the Premiership against Partick Thistle, Hearts and Kilmarnock, with a 5-2 Scottish Cup defeat of the Ayrshire side thrown in for good measure. It meant United had scored four or more goals in five consecutive competitive matches for the first time since 1936.

The manager's use of the term 'if we can maintain that standard' was relevant and, as you suspect he foresaw, his team could not do so on a regular basis. That said, he would not have anticipated that such a blistering run would have been followed by seven league games without a win.

With a young team inconsistency is inevitable, though the peaks and troughs that United experienced during 2013/14 were exceptional. Goodwillie had been a disappointment and his loan arrangement was not extended, but the team did re-discover their form and it coincided with their run to the final of the Scottish Cup.

The Tangerines dealt confidently with the challenges of three Premiership clubs before brushing aside Rangers of League 1 in the semi-final, despite the integrity of the competition being called into question when the tie was played at the Glasgow club's home ground.

League form had returned, though not to the level of that early winter spell and McNamara was optimistic the post-split matches could be used to re-discover that early winter success. Perhaps it was just coincidence, but the only time United came close to finding that level of performance was when Motherwell came to Tannadice at the end of April and were again comprehensively beaten, this time 5-1.

A fourth-place finish represented improvement over the previous season and some outstanding performances by the younger players were recognised with Mackay-Steven and Robertson earning full Scotland caps, while Robertson completed an astonishing first season by being named Scotland's Young Player of the Year by his fellow professionals.

Yet the feeling was that the club deserved something more tangible from the season and the Scottish Cup Final against St Johnstone offered the opportunity.

Unfortunately it proved a real anti-climax for the players and the 28,000 Arabs at Celtic Park, whose noisy and colourful presence made up the biggest support in the club's history. Despite twice hitting the woodwork, over the piece United simply didn't do themselves justice. If only the performance from that day at Motherwell could have been reproduced in the final.

Bibliography

Primary sources:
Courier and Advertiser
Daily Record
Herald/Glasgow Herald
People's Journal
Scotland on Sunday
Scotsman
Sporting Post
Sunday Herald
Sunday Mail
Sunday Post
Dundee United official programme (selected issues from 1947–2013)
www.dundeeunitedfc.co.uk

Secondary sources:
Steve Gracie
A Passion for Survival (Arabest Publishing, 2008)
The Rise of the Terrors (Arabest Publishing, 2009)
The Shed Go Marching On (Arabest Publishing, 2010)
Paul Hegarty
Heading for Glory (John Donald, 1987)
Gwen McIlroy
Kissing Strangers (David Winter, 1994)
A Kind of Madness (David Winter, 1998)
Jim McLean with Ken Gallacher
Jousting with Giants (Mainstream Publishing, 1987)
David Ross
The Roar of the Crowd (Argyll Publishing, 2005)
Peter Rundo
Dundee United: Champions of Scotland 1982-83 (Desert Island Books, 2003)
Peter Rundo and Mike Watson
Dundee United: The Official Centenary History (Birlinn, 2009)
Paul Sturrock with Charlie Duddy and Peter Rundo
Forward Thinking (Mainstream Publishing, 1989)
www.glenrothesarabs.com
www.arabarchive.co.uk
www.wikipedia.org